A Left that Dares to Speak Its Name

To Alain Badiou, my absolute friend.

A Left that Dares to Speak Its Name

Untimely Interventions

Slavoj Žižek

polity

First published in 2020 by Polity Press

Reprinted 2020 (twice), 2021

Polity Press
65 Bridge Street
Cambridge CB2 1UR, UK

Polity Press
101 Station Landing
Suite 300
Medford, MA 02155, USA

ISBN-13: 978-1-5095-4117-1
ISBN-13: 978-1-5095-4118-8(pb)

A catalogue record for this book is available from the British Library.

Library of Congress Cataloging-in-Publication Data

Names: Žižek, Slavoj, author.
Title: A left that dares to speak its name : 34 untimely interventions / Slavoj Žižek.
Description: Cambridge, UK ; Medford, MA : Polity, 2020. | Includes bibliographical references. | Summary: "With irrepressible humour Slavoj Žižek dissects our current political and social climate, discussing everything from Jordan Peterson and sex 'unicorns' to Greta Thunberg and Chairman Mao. This is Žižek's attempt to elucidate the major political issues of the day from a truly radical left position"-- Provided by publisher.
Identifiers: LCCN 2019027646 (print) | LCCN 2019027647 (ebook) | ISBN 9781509541171 (hardback) | ISBN 9781509541188 (paperback) | ISBN 9781509541195 (epub)
Subjects: LCSH: Right and left (Political science) | Communism. | Social history--21st century. | World politics--21st century.
Classification: LCC JA83 .Z59 2020 (print) | LCC JA83 (ebook) | DDC 320.53/2--dc23
LC record available at https://lccn.loc.gov/2019027646
LC ebook record available at https://lccn.loc.gov/2019027647

Typeset in 10 on 16.5 Utopia Std by
Servis Filmsetting Ltd, Stockport, Cheshire
Printed and bound in the United States by LSC Communications

The publisher has used its best endeavours to ensure that the URLs for external websites referred to in this book are correct and active at the time of going to press. However, the publisher has no responsibility for the websites and can make no guarantee that a site will remain live or that the content is or will remain appropriate.

Every effort has been made to trace all copyright holders, but if any have been overlooked the publisher will be pleased to include any necessary credits in any subsequent reprint or edition.

For further information on Polity, visit our website: politybooks.com

Contents

CONTENTS

Introduction: From the Communist Standpoint

This book brings together my (substantially rewritten) most recent interventions in the public media. They cover the entire panoply of topics that aroused public attention, from economic turmoil to the struggle for sexual emancipation, from populism to political correctness, from the vicissitudes of Trump's presidency to the ongoing tensions in and with China, from ethical problems raised by sexbots to the Middle East crisis. The concluding supplement contains fragments from two polemics I was engaged in. The collected interventions are untimely because their premise is that only a communist standpoint provides the appropriate way to grasp these topics. So why communism?

Signs abound that our global situation calls increasingly for such a standpoint. Apologists of the existing order like to point out that the dream of socialism is over, that every attempt to realize it turned out to be a nightmare (just look at what goes on in Venezuela!). However, at the same time, signs of panic grow everywhere: how are we to deal with global warming, with the threat of total digital control over our lives, with the influx of refugees? In short, with the effects and consequences of this same triumph of global capitalism? There is no surprise here: when capitalism wins, its antagonisms explode.

On the one hand, signs of anti-Enlightenment madness multiply everywhere. In Koszalin, a city in northern Poland, three Catholic priests have burned books they say promote sorcery, including one of the Harry Potter novels, in a ceremony they photographed and posted on Facebook: they carried the books in a large basket from inside a church to a stone area outside, where the books were set alight as prayers were said and a small group of people looked on.[1] An isolated incident, yes – but if we put it together with other similar incidents, a clear anti-Enlightenment pattern emerges. For example, at the 106th Indian Science Congress in Punjab (in January 2019), local scientists made a series of claims, among them: Kauravas were born with the help of stem cell and test tube technologies; Lord Rama used "astras" and "shastras," while Lord Vishnu sent a Sudarshan Chakra to chase targets. This shows that the science of guided missiles was present in India thousands of years ago; that Ravana didn't just have the Pushpaka Vimana, but had 24 types of aircraft and airports in Lanka; that theoretical physics (including the contributions of Newton and Einstein) is totally wrong, gravitational waves will be renamed "Narendra Modi Waves," and the gravitational lensing effect will be renamed the "Hashvardhan Effect"; that Lord Brahma discovered the existence of dinosaurs on earth and mentioned it in the Vedas.[2] This is also a way to fight the remnants of Western colonialism, and the book burning in Poland can be viewed as a way to fight Western commercialized consumerism. The conjunction of these two examples, one from Hindu India and the other from Christian Europe, demonstrates that we are dealing with a global phenomenon.

While we are sinking deeper and deeper into this madness (which coexists easily with a thriving global market), the real crisis is approaching. In January 2019, an international team of scientists proposed "a diet it says can improve health while ensuring sustainable food production to reduce further damage to the planet. The 'planetary health diet' is based on cutting red meat and sugar consumption in half and upping intake of fruits, vegetables and nuts."[3] We are talking about a radical reorganization of our entire food production and distribution – so how to do it? "The report suggests five strategies to ensure people can change their diets and not harm the planet in doing so: incentivizing people to eat healthier, shifting global production toward varied crops, intensifying agriculture sustainably, stricter rules around the governing of oceans and lands, and reducing food waste." OK, but, again, how can this be achieved? Is it not clear that a strong global agency is needed with the power to coordinate such measures? And is not such an agency pointing in the direction of what we once called "communism"? And does the same not hold for other threats to our survival as humans? Is the same global agency not needed also to deal with the problem of exploding numbers of refugees and immigrants, with the problem of digital control over our lives?[4]

Communist interventions are needed because our fate is not yet decided – not in the simple sense that we have a choice, but in a more radical sense of choosing one's own fate. According to the standard view, the past is fixed, what happened happened, it cannot be undone, and the future is open, it depends on unpredictable contingencies. What we should propose here is a reversal of this standard view: the past is open to retroactive reinterpretations, while the future is closed since we live in a determinist universe. This doesn't mean that we cannot change the future; it just means that, in order to change our future we should first (not "understand" but) change our past, reinterpret it in such a way that opens up toward a different future from the one implied by the predominant vision of the past.

Will there be a new world war? The answer can only be a paradoxical one. *If* there is to be a new war, it will be a necessary one. This is how history works – through weird reversals as described by Jean-Pierre Dupuy: "If an outstanding event takes place, a catastrophe, for example, it could not not have taken place; nonetheless, insofar as it did not take place, it is not inevitable. It is thus the event's actualization – the fact that it takes place – which retroactively creates its necessity."[5] And exactly the same holds for a new global war: once the conflict explodes (between the US and Iran, between China and Taiwan), it will appear inevitable, that is to say, we will automatically read the past that led to it as a series of causes that necessarily caused the explosion. If it does not happen, we will read it in the same way that today we read the Cold War – as a series of dangerous moments where the catastrophe was avoided because both sides were aware of the deadly consequences of a global conflict. (So we have today many interpreters who claim that there never was an actual danger of World War III during the Cold War years, that both sides were just playing with fire.) It is at this deeper level that communist interventions are needed.

Jürgen Habermas is often described as the state philosopher of the German (European even) liberal Left – no wonder, then, that about two decades ago, the conservative Spanish Prime Minister, José Mariá Aznar, even formally proposed that Habermas be declared the Spanish (and European) state philosopher (on account of Habermas's idea of constitutional patriotism, a patriotism grounded in emancipatory values embedded in a constitution rather than in one's own ethnic roots). While disagreeing with Habermas on many points, I always found the role he was not afraid to play – that of a critical supporter of, participant in even, power – honorable and necessary, a more-than-welcome retreat from basically irresponsible "politics at a distance."

The majority of Leftist thought in recent decades got caught in the trap of oppositionalism: it adopts as self-evident the claim that true politics is only possible at a distance from the state and its apparatuses

- the moment an agent immerses itself fully into state apparatuses and procedures (like parliamentary party politics), the authentic political dimension is lost. (From this standpoint, the Bolshevik triumph - taking power in Russia in October 1917 - appears also as their self-betrayal.) But is there not in such a stance an indelible aspect of avoiding responsibility? Withdrawal into non-participation in power is also a positive act, since one is aware that somebody else will have to do it, and the dirtiest thing is to leave to another the dirty job and then, after the job is done, accuse this other of unprincipled opportunism. (Among others, Eamon de Valera did this when he let Michael Collins do the "dirty" negotiations with the British, which led to the Free Irish State, and then, after profiting himself from it, accusing him of treason.) An authentic political agent is never afraid to take power and assume responsibility for what is going on, without resorting to excuses ("unfortunate circumstances," "enemy plots," or whatever). Therein resides Lenin's greatness: after taking power, he knew the Bolsheviks found themselves in an impossible situation (with no conditions for an actual "construction of socialism"), but he persisted in it, trying to make the best out of a total deadlock.

The true dimension of a revolution is not to be found in the ecstatic moments of its climax (one million people chanting in the main square . . .); one should rather focus on how the change is felt in everyday life when things return to normal. This is why Trotsky lost against Stalin: after Lenin's death, the population of the Soviet Union was slowly emerging from 10 years of hell (World War I, civil war) with untold suffering, and people longed for a return to some kind of normalcy. This is what Stalin offered them, while Trotsky, with his permanent revolution, promised them just more social upheaval and suffering.

Perhaps, then, instead of the increasingly boring variations on the topic of "distance from the state," what we need today are honest state philosophers, philosophers who are not afraid to dirty their hands in fighting for a different state. Apropos homosexuality, Oscar Wilde cited "the love that dare not speak its name" – what we need today is a Left that dares to speak its name, not a Left that shamefully covers up its core with some cultural fig leaf. And this name is communism.

The Global Mess

1

200 Years After: Is Marx Alive, Dead, or a Living Dead?

The question of the continuing relevance of Marx's work in our era of global capitalism has to be answered in a properly dialectical way: not only is Marx's critique of political economy, his outline of the capitalist dynamics, still fully actual; one should even take a step further and claim that it is only today, with global capitalism, that, to put it in Hegelese, reality arrived at its notion. However, a properly dialectical reversal intervenes here: at this very moment of full actuality, the limitation has to appear, the moment of triumph is that of defeat; after overcoming external obstacles, the new threat comes from within, signaling immanent inconsistency. When reality fully reaches up to its notion, this notion itself has to be transformed. Therein resides the properly dialectical paradox: Marx was not simply wrong, he was often right, but more literally than he himself expected to be.

For example, Marx couldn't have imagined that the capitalist dynamics of dissolving all particular identities would, in addition, affect ethnic and sexual identities: sexual "one-sidedness and narrow-mindedness become more and more impossible," and, concerning sexual practices, "all that is solid melts into air, all that is holy is pro-faned," so that capitalism tends to replace the standard normative heterosexuality with a proliferation of unstable shifting identities and/ or orientations. Today's celebration of "minorities" and "marginals" *is* the predominant majority position – even alt-Rightists who complain about the terror of liberal political correctness present themselves as protectors of an endangered minority. Or take those critics of patriarchy who attack it as if it were still a hegemonic position, ignoring what Marx and Engels wrote more than 150 years ago, in the first chapter of *The Communist Manifesto*: "The bourgeoisie, wherever it has got the upper hand, has put an end to all feudal, patriarchal, idyllic relations." What becomes of patriarchal family values when a child can sue his parents for neglect and abuse, i.e., when family and parenthood itself are *de jure* reduced to a temporary and dissolvable contract between independent individuals?

How does ideology function in such conditions? Recall the classic joke about a man who believes himself to be a grain of seed and is taken to the mental institution where the doctors do their best to finally convince him that he is not a grain but a man. When he is cured (convinced that he is not a grain of seed but a man) and allowed to leave the hospital, he immediately returns, trembling; there is a chicken outside the door and he is afraid that it will eat him. "Dear fellow," says his doctor, "you know very well that you are not a grain of seed but a man." "Of course I know that," replies the patient, "but does the chicken know it?" Exactly the same holds true for Marx's theory of commodity fetishism, which is today even more actual than in Marx's time. "Commodity fetishism" is an illusion that is operative in the very heart of the actual production process. Note the very beginning of the subchapter on commodity fetishism in *Capital*: "A commodity appears at first sight an extremely obvious, trivial thing. But its analysis brings out that it is a very strange thing, abounding in metaphysical subtleties and theological niceties."[1]

Marx does not claim, in the usual "Marxist" way, that critical analysis should demonstrate how a commodity – what appears to be a mysterious theological entity – emerged out of the "ordinary" real-life process. He claims, on the contrary, that the task of critical analysis is to unearth the "metaphysical subtleties and theological niceties" in what appears, at first sight, to be just an ordinary object. Commodity fetishism (our belief that commodities are magic objects, endowed with an inherent metaphysical power) is not located in our mind, in the way we (mis) perceive reality, but in our social reality itself. We may know the truth, but we act as if we don't know it – in our real life, we act like the chicken from the joke.

Niels Bohr, who already gave the right answer to Einstein's "God doesn't play dice" ("Don't tell God what to do!"), also provided the perfect example of how a fetishist disavowal of belief works in ideology: seeing a horse-shoe on his door, the surprised visitor said that he doesn't believe in the superstition that it brings luck, to which Bohr snapped back: "I also do not believe in it; I have it there because I was told that it works also if one does not believe in it!" This is how ideology works in our cynical era: we don't have to believe in it. This is how ideology functions today: nobody takes seriously democracy or justice, we are all aware of their corruption, but we practice them – i.e., display our belief in them – because we assume they work even if we do not believe in them.

Perhaps this is why "culture" is emerging as the central life-world category. With regard to religion, we no longer "really believe," we just follow (some of the) religious rituals and mores as part of the respect for the "lifestyle" of the community to which we belong (nonbelieving Jews obeying kosher rules "out of respect for tradition"). "I do not really believe in it, it is just part of my culture" seems to be the predominant mode of the displaced belief, characteristic of our times. "Culture" is the name for all those things we practice without really believing in them, without taking them very seriously. This is why we dismiss fundamentalist believers as "barbarians," as anticultural, as a threat to culture – they dare to take seriously their beliefs. The cynical era in which we live would have no surprises for Marx.

Marx's theories are thus not simply alive: Marx is a living dead whose ghost continues to haunt us – and the only way to keep him alive is to focus on those of his insights that are today more true than in his own time, especially his call for universality of the emancipatory struggle. The universality to be asserted today is not a form of humanism, but the universality of the (class) struggle: more than ever, global capital has to be countered by global resistance. One should therefore insist on the difference between class struggle and other struggles (anti-racist, feminist, etc.) which aim at a peaceful coexistence of different groups and whose ultimate expression is identity politics. With class struggle, there is no identity politics: the opposing class has to be destroyed, and we ourselves should, in this same move, disappear as a class. The best concise definition of fascism is: the extension of identity politics onto the domain of class struggle. The basic fascist idea is that of the class piece: each class should be recognized in its specific identity and, in this way, its dignity will be safeguarded and antagonism between classes avoided. Class antagonism is here treated in the same way as the tension between different races: classes are accepted as a quasi-natural fact of life, not as something to be left behind.

The status of Marx as a living dead demands that we are also critical of the Marxist legacy – there should be no sacred cows here. Just two interconnected examples should suffice here. According to the standard Marxist dogma, the passage from capitalism to communism will proceed in two phases, the "lower" and the "higher." In the lower phase (sometimes called "socialism"), the law of value will still hold:

[T]he individual producer receives back from society – after the deductions have been made – exactly what he gives to it. What he has given to it is his individual quantum of labor. For example, the social working day consists of the sum of the individual hours of work; the individual labor time of the individual producer is the part of the social working day contributed by him, his share in it. He receives a certificate from society that he has furnished such-and-such an amount of labor (after deducting his labor for the common funds); and with this certificate, he draws from the social stock of means of consumption as much as the same amount of labor cost. The same amount of labor which he has given to society in one form, he receives back in another. . . . In a higher phase of communist society, after the enslaving subordination of the individual to the division of labor, and therewith also the antithesis between mental and physical labor, has vanished; after labor has become not only a means of life but life's prime want; after the productive forces have also increased with the all-around development of the individual, and all the springs of co-operative wealth flow more abundantly – only then can the narrow horizon of bourgeois right be crossed in its entirety and society inscribe on its banners: From each according to his ability, to each according to his needs![2]

The standard critique of this distinction is that, while the "lower stage" can somehow be imagined and managed, the "higher stage" (full communism) is a dangerous utopia. This critique seems justified by the fact that the really-existing socialist regimes were caught in endless debates about what stage they are in, introducing subdivisions; for example, at some point, in the late Soviet Union, the opinion prevailed that they were already above mere "socialism," although not yet in full "communism" – they were in the "lower stage of the higher stage." But a surprise awaits us here: the temptation in many socialist countries was to jump over the "lower stage" and proclaim that, in spite of the material poverty (or, at a deeper level, precisely on account of it), we can directly enter communism. During the Great Leap Forward in the late 1950s, Chinese communists decided that China should bypass socialism and directly enter communism. They referred to Marx's famous formula of communism: "From everyone according to his abilities, to everyone according to his needs!" The catch was the reading given to it in order to legitimize the total militarization of life in agricultural communes: the Party cadre who commands a commune knows what every farmer is able to do, so he sets the plan and specifies the individuals' obligations according to their abilities; he also knows what farmers really need for survival and organizes accordingly the distribution of food and other life provisions. The condition of militarized extreme poverty thus becomes the actualization of communism, and, of course, it is not sufficient to claim that such a reading falsifies a noble idea – one should rather notice how it lies dormant in it as a possibility. The paradox is thus that we begin with the shared poverty of "war communism," then, when things get better, we progress/regress to "socialism" in which ideally, of course, everybody is paid according to his/her contribution, and . . . and, at the end, we return to capitalism (as in China today), confirming the old saying that communism is a detour from capitalism to capitalism. What these complications attest to is that the true utopia is that of the "lower stage" in which the law of value still holds, but in a "just" way, so that every worker gets his/her due – an impossible dream of "just" social exchange where money-fetish is replaced by non-fetishized simple certificates. And we are at a similar point today: the threat of looming apocalypses (ecological, digital, social) compels us to abandon the socialist dream of "just" capitalism and to envisage more radical "communist" measures.

So how should we imagine communism? In *Capital III*, Marx renounced his earlier utopian vision of communism as a state in which the opposition between necessity and freedom, between necessity and work, will disappear, and insisted that, in every society, the distinction between the realm of necessity (*Reich der Notwendigkeit*) and the realm of freedom (*Reich der Freiheit*) will persist; the realm of our free playful activities will always have to be sustained by the realm of work necessary for society's continuous reproduction:

> The realm of freedom actually begins only where labour which is determined by necessity and mundane considerations ceases; thus in the very nature of things it lies beyond the sphere of actual material production. Just as the savage must wrestle with Nature to satisfy his wants, to maintain and reproduce life, so must civilised man, and he must do so in all social formations and under all possible modes of production. With his development this realm of physical necessity expands as a result of his wants; but, at the same time, the forces of production which satisfy these wants also increase. Freedom in this field can only consist in socialised man, the associated producers, rationally regulating their interchange with Nature, bringing it under their common control, instead of being ruled by it as by the blind forces of Nature; and achieving this with the least expenditure of energy and under conditions most favourable to, and worthy of, their human nature. But it nonetheless still remains a realm of necessity. Beyond it begins that development of human energy which is an end in itself, the true realm of freedom, which, however, can blossom forth only with this

realm of necessity as its basis. The shortening of the working-day is its basic prerequisite.[3]

This line of thought has to be rejected; what makes it suspicious is precisely its self-evident commonsense character. We should take the risk of reversing the relationship between the two realms: it is only through the discipline of work that we can regain our true freedom, while as spontaneous consumers we are caught in the necessity of our natural propensities. The infamous words at the entrance to Auschwitz, "*Arbeit macht frei,*" are thus true – which doesn't mean that we are coming close to Nazism but simply that the Nazis took over this motto with cruel irony.

To be a communist today means that one is not afraid to draw such radical conclusions, also with regard to one of the most sensitive claims of the Marxist theory, the idea of the "withering away" of the state power. Do we need governments? This question is deeply ambiguous. It can be read as an offshoot of the radical leftwing idea that government (state power) is in itself a form of alienation or oppression, and that we should work toward abolishing it and building a society of some kind of direct democracy. Or it can be read in a less radical liberal way: in our complex societies we need some regulating agency, but we should keep it under tight control, making it serve the interests of those who invest their votes (if not money) into it. Both views are dangerously wrong.

As for the idea of a self-transparent organization of society that would preclude political "alienation" (state apparatuses, institutionalized rules of political life, legal order, police, etc.), is the basic experience of the end of really-existing socialism not precisely the resigned acceptance of the fact that society is a complex network of "subsystems," which is why a certain level of "alienation" is constitutive of social life, so that a totally self-transparent society is a utopia with totalitarian potentials. It is no wonder that today's practices of "direct democracy," from favelas to the "postindustrial" digital culture (do the descriptions of the new "tribal" communities of computer hackers not often evoke the logic of council democracy?) all have to rely on a state apparatus – i.e., their survival relies on a thick texture of "alienated" institutional mechanisms: where do electricity and water come from? Who guarantees the rule of law? To whom do we turn for healthcare? Etc., etc. The more a community is self-ruling, the more this network has to function smoothly and invisibly. Maybe we should change the goal of emancipatory struggles from overcoming alienation to enforcing the right kind of alienation: how to achieve a smooth functioning of "alienated" (invisible) social mechanisms that sustain the space of "non-alienated" communities?

Should we then adopt the more modest traditional liberal notion of representative power? Citizens transfer (part of) their power onto the state, but under precise conditions: power is constrained by law, limited to very precise conditions of its exercise, since the people remain the ultimate source of sovereignty and can repeal power if they decide so to do. In short, the state with its power is the minor partner in a contract that the major partner (the people) can at any point repeal or change, basically in the same way each of us can change the contractor who takes care of our waste or our health. However, the moment one takes a close look at an actual state power edifice, one can easily detect an implicit but unmistakable signal: "Forget about our limitations – ultimately, we can do whatever we want with you!" This excess is not a contingent supplement spoiling the purity of power but its necessary constituent – without it, without the threat of arbitrary omnipotence, state power is not a true power, it loses its authority.

So it's not that we need the state to regulate our affairs and, unfortunately, have to buy its authoritarian underside as a necessary price – we need precisely and maybe even primarily this authoritarian underside. As Kierkegaard put it, to claim that I believe in Christ because I was convinced by the good reasons for Christianity is a blasphemy – in order to understand reasons for Christianity I should already believe. It's the same with love: I cannot say that I love a woman because of her features – to see her features as beautiful, I should already be in love. And it's the same with every authority, from paternal to that of the state.

The basic problem is thus: how to invent a different mode of passivity of the majority, how to cope with the unavoidable alienation of political life. This alienation has to be taken at its strongest, as the excess constitutive of the functioning of an actual power, overlooked by liberalism as well as by Leftist proponents of direct democracy.

2

Why Secondary Contradictions Matter: A Maoist View

A quick glance at our imbroglio already makes it clear that we are caught up in multiple social struggles: the tension between the liberal establishment and the new populism, ecological struggle, the struggle for feminism and sexual liberation, ethnic and religious struggles, the struggle for universal human rights, the struggle against the digital control of our lives. How to bring all these struggles together without simply privileging one of them (economic struggle, feminist struggle, anti-racist struggle . . .) as the "true" struggle provides the key to all other struggles. Half a century ago, when the Maoist wave was at its strongest, Mao Zedong's distinction between "principal" and "secondary" contradictions (from his treatise "On Contradiction" written in 1937) was common currency in political debates. Perhaps this distinction deserves to be brought back to life.

When Mao talks about "contradictions," he uses the term in the simple sense of the struggle of opposites, of social and natural antagonisms, not in the strict dialectical sense articulated by Hegel. Mao's theory of contradictions can be summed up in four points. First, a specific contradiction is what primarily defines a thing, making it what it is: it is not a mistake, a failure, a malfunctioning of a thing, but, in some sense, the very feature that holds a thing together – if this contradiction disappears, a thing loses its identity. A classic Marxist example: hitherto, throughout history, the primary "contradiction" that defined every society was class struggle. Second, a contradiction is never single, it depends on other contradiction(s). Mao's own example: in a capitalist society, the contradiction between the proletariat and the bourgeoisie is accompanied by other "secondary" contradictions, such as the one between imperialists and their colonies. Third, while this secondary contradiction depends on the first one (colonies exist only in capitalism), the principal contradiction is not always the dominant one: contradictions can trade places of importance. For example, when a country is occupied, it is the ruling class that is usually bribed to collaborate with the occupiers to maintain its privileged position, so that the struggle against the occupiers becomes a priority. The same can go for the struggle against racism: in a state of racial tension and exploitation, the only way to effectively struggle for the working class is to focus on fighting racism (this is why any appeal to the white working class, as in today's alt-Right populism, betrays class struggle). Fourth, a principal contradiction can also change: one can argue that today, maybe, the ecological struggle designates the "principal contradiction" of our societies, since it deals with a threat to the collective survival of humanity itself. One can, of course, argue that our "principal contradiction" remains the antagonism of the global capitalist system, since ecological problems are the result of the excessive exploitation of natural resources driven by capitalist thirst for profit. However, it is doubtful if our ecological mess can be so easily reduced to an effect of capitalist expansion – there were man-related ecological catastrophes before capitalism, and there is no reason why a thriving postcapitalist society would not also confront the same deadlock.

To resume, while there is always one principal contradiction, contradictions can trade places of importance. Consequently, when we are dealing with a complex series of contradictions, we should locate the superior one, but we should also remember that no contradiction remains static – over time, they transform into one another. This multiplicity of contradictions is not just a contingent empirical fact; it defines the very notion of a (single) contradiction: every contradiction is dependent on the existence of "at least one" (other contradiction), its "life" resides in how it interacts with other contradictions. If a contradiction were to stand alone, it wouldn't be a "contradiction" (struggle of opposites) but a stable opposition. "Class struggle" resides in how it overdetermines relations between sexes, the struggle with nature in production process, tensions between different cultures and races . . .

Old-fashioned and hopelessly dated as these ruminations may appear, they acquire a new actuality today. My first "Maoist" point is that, in order to take a correct stance in each of today's struggles, one should locate each of them into the complex interaction with other struggles. An important principle here is that, contrary to today's fashion, we should stick to "binary" forms of opposition and translate every appearance of multiple positions to a combination of "binary" opposites. Today, we don't have three main positions (liberal-centrist hegemony, Rightist populism, and the new Left) but two antagonisms – Rightist populism versus a liberal-centrist establishment – and both of them together (the two sides of the existing capitalist order) face the Leftist challenge.

Let's begin with a simple example: Macedonia – what's in a name? Not long ago, the governments of Macedonia and Greece concluded an agreement on how to resolve the problem of the name "Macedonia": it should be changed to "Northern Macedonia." This solution was instantly attacked by radicals in both countries. Greek opponents insisted that "Macedonia" is an old Greek name, and Macedonian opponents felt humiliated by being reduced to a "Northern" province, since they are the only people who call themselves "Macedonians." Imperfect as it was, this solution offered a glimpse of hope toward ending a long and meaningless struggle by a reasonable compromise. But it was caught in another "contradiction": the struggle between big powers (the US and EU on the one side, Russia on the other). The West put pressure on both sides to accept the compromise so that Macedonia could quickly join the EU and NATO, while, for exactly the same reason (seeing in it the danger of its loss of influence in the Balkans), Russia opposed it, supporting rabid conservative nationalist forces in both countries. So which side should we take here? I think we should decidedly take the side of the compromise, for the simple reason that it is the only realist solution to the problem – Russia opposed it simply because of its geopolitical interests, without offering another solution, so supporting Russia here would have meant sacrificing the reasonable solution of the singular problem of Macedonian and Greek relations to international geopolitical interests.

Now let's take the arrest of Meng Wanzhou, Huawei's chief financial officer and daughter of the firm's founder, in Vancouver. She is accused of breaking US sanctions on Iran and faces extradition to the US, where she could be jailed for up to 30 years if found guilty. What is true here? In all probability, one way or another, all big corporations discreetly break the laws. But it's more than evident that this is just a "secondary contradiction" and that another battle is actually being fought here: it's not about trade with Iran, it's about the big struggle for domination in the production of digital hardware and software. What Huawei symbolizes is a China that is no longer the Foxconn China, the place of half-slave labor assembling machines developed elsewhere, but a place where software and hardware are also conceived. China has the potential to become a much stronger agent in the digital market than Japan with Sony or South Korea with Samsung. Reports abound now in our media on grueling work conditions in Huawei factories in China, and there are even suggestions that the sanctions against Huawei will really help these workers – but no one called for a boycott when the same (or even worse) appalling conditions were discovered in Foxconn factories.

But enough of particular examples – things get more complex with the "contradiction" between the alt-Right descent into racist/sexist vulgarity and the politically correct stiff regulatory moralism. It is crucial, from the standpoint of progressive struggle for emancipation, *not* to accept this "contradiction" as primary, but to unravel in it the displaced and distorted echoes of class struggle. As in fascist ideology, the Rightist populist figure of the Enemy (the combination of financial elites and invading immigrants) combines both extremes of the social hierarchy, thereby blurring the class struggle; on the opposite end, and in an almost symmetrical way, politically correct antiracism and antisexism barely conceal the fact that their ultimate target is white working-class racism and sexism, thereby also neutralizing class struggle. That's why the designation of political correctness as "cultural Marxism" is false: political correctness, in all its pseudo-radicality, is, on the contrary, the last defense of "bourgeois" liberalism against the Marxism concept, obfuscating/displacing class struggle as the "principal contradiction."

Things get more complex with the struggle for universal human rights. Here, there is a "contradiction" between proponents of these rights and those who warn that, in their standard version, universal human rights are not truly universal but implicitly privilege Western values (individuals have primacy over collectives, etc.) and are thereby a form of ideological neocolonialism – it is no wonder that the reference to human rights served as a justification for many military interventions, from Iraq to Libya. Partisans of universal human rights counter that their rejection often serves to justify local forms of author-itarian rule and repression as elements of a particular way of life. How to decide here? A middle-of-the-road compromise is not enough; one should give preference to universal human rights for a very precise reason: a dimension of universality has to serve as a medium in which multiple ways of life can coexist, and the Western notion of universality of human rights contains the self-critical dimension that makes visible its own limitations. When the standard Western notion of universal human rights is criticized for its particular bias, this critique itself has to refer to some notion of more authentic universality, which makes us see the distortion of a false universality. But some form of universality is always here, even a modest vision of the coexistence of different and ultimately incompatible ways of life has to rely on it. In short, what this means is that the "principal contradiction" is not that of the tension(s) between different ways of life, but the "contradiction" within each way of life ("culture," organization of its *jouissance*) between its particular-ity and its universal claim – to use a technical term, each particular way of life is by definition caught in "pragmatic contradiction," its claim to validity is undermined not by the presence of other ways of life but by its own inconsistency.

The ultimate example of the importance of secondary contradic-tions were the European elections of 2019 – are there any lessons to be learned from them? The sometimes spectacular details (like the crush-ing defeat of both main parties in the UK) should not blind us to the basic fact that nothing really big and surprising happened. Yes, the populist new Right did make progress, but it remains far from pre-vailing. The phrase, repeated like a mantra, that people demanded change, is deeply deceptive – yes, but what kind of change? It was basi-cally the variation on the old motto "some things have to change so that all remains the same."

The self-perception of Europeans *in toto* is that they have too much to lose to risk a revolution (a radical upheaval), and that's why the majority tend to vote for the parties that promise them peace and a calm life (against financial elites, against the "immigrant threat," . . .). That's also why one of the losers of the 2019 European elections was the populist Left, especially in France and Germany: the majority doesn't want political mobilization. Rightist populists understood this message much better: what they really offer is not active democracy but a strong authoritarian power which would work for (what they present as) the people's interests. Therein resides also the fatal limitation of former Greek finance minister Yanis Varoufakis's DIEM (Democracy in Europe Movement): the core of its ideology is the hope of mobilizing the bulk of ordinary people, to give them a voice by way of breaking the hegemony of the ruling elites.

Some years ago, I heard an anecdote from a friend of Willy Brandt. After the fall of the Berlin Wall, Mikhail Gorbachev – at this time already a private citizen – wanted to visit Brandt, and he appeared unannounced at the door of his house in Berlin, but Brandt (or his servant) ignored the ringing of the bell and refused even to open the door. Brandt later explained to his friend his reaction as being an expression of his rage at Gorbachev: by allowing the disintegration of the Soviet bloc, Gorbachev had ruined the foundations of Western social democracy. It was the constant comparison with the East European communist countries that maintained the pressure on the West to tolerate the social democratic welfare state, and once the communist threat disappeared, exploitation in the West became more open and ruthless and the welfare state also began to disintegrate.

Simplified as this idea is, there is a moment of truth in it: the final result of the fall of communist regimes is the fall (or, rather, the prolonged disintegration) of social democracy itself. The naive expectation that the fall of the bad "totalitarian" Left will open up space for the good "democratic" Left sadly proved wrong. A new division of the political space in Europe is gradually replacing the old opposition between a center-Left party and a center-Right party replacing each other in power: the opposition between a liberal-center party (pro-capitalist and culturally liberal: pro-choice and gay rights, etc.) and a populist Right movement. The paradox is that the new populists, while culturally conservative, often advocate and even enforce, when they are in power, measures that are usually associated with social democracy but which no actual social democratic party dares to impose.

Even the success of Green parties in the 2019 European elections fits this formula: it is not to be taken as the sign of an authentic ecological awakening; it was more an ersatz vote, the preferred vote of all those who clearly perceive the insufficiency of the hegemonic politics of the European establishment and reject the nationalist-populist reaction to it, but are not ready to vote for the social democratic or even more radical Left. It was a vote of those who want to keep their conscience clean without really acting. That is to say, what immediately strikes the eye in today's European Green parties is the predominant tone of moderation: they largely remain embedded in the "politics as usual" approach; their aim is just capitalism with a green face. We are still far from the much-needed radicalization that can only emerge through the coalition of Greens and the hard-core Left.

But what is really at stake in today's mess is not primarily the destiny of the social democratic parties as political agents, but the destiny of what Peter Sloterdijk called "objective" social democracy: the true triumph of social democracy occurred when its basic demands (free education and healthcare, etc.) became part of the program accepted by all main parties and inscribed into the functioning of the state institutions themselves. Today's trend goes rather in the opposite direction: when Margaret Thatcher was asked what she considered to be her greatest success, she snapped back "New Labour," hinting at the fact that even her Labour Party opponents had adopted her economic politics.

The remaining radical Leftists have a quick answer to this: social democracy is disappearing precisely because it adopted neoliberal economic politics, so the solution is . . . what? This is where the problems begin. Radical Leftists don't have a feasible alternative program, and the disappearance of European social democracy is a more complex process. First, one should note its recent electoral successes in Finland, Slovakia, Denmark, and Spain. Second, one should note that, measured by European standards, American "democratic socialists" like Bernie Sanders are not extremists but modest social democrats. In previous decades, the standard radical Leftist stance toward social democracy was one of patronizing distrust: when social democracy is the only Leftist option, we should support it, knowing that it will ultimately fail – this failure will be an important learning experience for the people. Today, however, old-style social democracy is more and more perceived by the establishment as a threat: its traditional demands are no longer acceptable. This new situation demands a new strategy. The lesson for the Left from all this is: abandon the dream of a big popular mobilization and focus on changes in daily life. The real success of a "revolution" can only be measured the day after, when things return to normal. How is the change perceived in the daily lives of ordinary people?

Back in the UK, the Brexit mess is not an exception but just the aggravated explosion of a tension that runs across all of Europe. What the situation in the UK demonstrates is that, as Mao would have put it, secondary contradictions matter. Corbyn's mistake was to act as if the choice of "Brexit or not" is of no great importance, so (although his heart was with Brexit) he opportunistically navigated between the two sides; trying not to lose votes from either side, he lost them from both. But secondary contradictions do matter: it was crucial to take a clear stance. This is, more generally, the tough question that the European Left is carefully avoiding: how, instead of succumbing to the nationalist populist temptation, to elaborate a new Leftist vision of Europe.

3

Nomadic Proletarians

In his "Political Considerations About Lacan's Later Work," Jean-Claude Milner quotes Lacan's "Joyce le symptôme": "*Ne participent à l'histoire que les déportés: puisque l'homme a un corps, c'est par le corps qu'on l'a* [The only ones to participate in history are the deported: since man has a body, it is by means of the body that others have him]." . . . "*Il* [= Joyce] *a raison, l'histoire n'étant rien de plus qu'une fuite dont ne se racontent que des exodes* [Joyce is right, history being nothing more than a flight, about which only exodus is told]." Lacan refers here to the opposition between "flight" (wandering around without goal) and "exodus" (when we wander with a final destination in mind, like the Jews in search of a promised land): "flight" is the real of history, lawless wandering, and this flight becomes part of narrated history only when it changes into exodus. Milner then applies this opposition to today's immigrants: they wander around and the place where they eventually land is not their chosen destination. This impossibility to organize their experience into the narrative of an exodus is what makes the immigrant refugees real and, as such, unbearable. Their bodies (often the only thing they possess) are an embarrassment, disturbing our peace – we perceive these bodies as a potential threat, as something that demands food and care, that pollutes our land. Hence, the hate they [the immigrants] are subjected to as well as the necessity of humanitarian pity in order to avoid the only logical consequence that western political systems should draw explicitly, if they were to accept their own real structure: the physical elimination of immigrants. As a middle term between verbal pity and factual cruelty, the honorable souls have discovered the virtues of segregation. Since the beginning of 1970s, Lacan considered segregation as the social fact par excellence, racism being but a subcase of that general process.[4]

How do these wandering intruders relate to proletarians? In some Leftist circles, the exploding growth of homeless refugees gave rise to the notion of the "nomadic proletarian." The basic idea is that, in today's global world, the main antagonism (the "primary contradiction") is no longer between the capitalist ruling class and the proletariat, but between those who are safe beneath the cupola of a "civilized" world (with public order, basic rights, etc.) and those who are excluded, reduced to a bare life. "Nomadic proletarians" are not simply outside the cupola but somewhere in between: their premodern substantial life-form is already in ruins, devastated by the impact of global capitalism, but they are not integrated into the cupola of the global order, so they roam in an in-between netherworld. They are not proletarians in the strict Marxian sense; paradoxically, when they enter the cupola of developed countries, the ideal of most of them is precisely to become "normal" exploited proletarians. Recently, a refugee from Salvador who tried to enter the US on the Mexico–US border said to the TV cameras: "Please, Mr. Trump, let us in, we just want to be good hard workers in your country."

Can the distinction between proletarians proper (exploited workers) and the nomadic (less than) proletarians be somehow blurred in a new more encompassing category of today's proletarians? From the strict Marxian standpoint, the answer is a resounding NO: for Marx, proletarians are not only "the poor" but those who are, by way of their role in the production process, reduced to subjectivity deprived of all substantial content; as such, they are also disciplined by the production process to become bearers of their future power (the "dictatorship of the proletariat"). Those who are outside the production process – and thereby outside a place in social totality – are treated by Marx as "lumpenproletarians," and he doesn't see in them any emancipatory potential; rather, he treats them with great suspicion, as the force that is, as a rule, mobilized and corrupted by reactionary forces (like Napoleon III.).

Things got complicated with the victory of the October Revolution, when Bolsheviks exerted power in a country where not only the large majority of the population were small farmers (and Bolsheviks gained power precisely by promising them land), but where, as the result of violent upheavals during the civil war, millions of people found themselves in the position not of classic lumpenproletarians, but of homeless nomads who were not yet proletarians (reduced to the "nothing" of their working force) but literally less-than-proletarians (less-than-nothing). Their massive presence is the central topic of the work of Andrei Platonov, who described in detail their way of life, elaborating a unique "materialist ontology of poor life."[5] From the standpoint of the "ontology of poor life," the parallel between Samuel Beckett and Platonov is fully relevant: is the experience of a "poor life" also not the core of Beckett's great trilogy of novels *Molloy, Malone Dies, The Unnamable*? The entire topic, as well as the details of *Malone Dies*, clearly relate to the French *péripéties* during the German occupation and its aftermath: Nazi and collaborationist control, terror and oppression, the revenge against collaborationists, and the way refugees were treated when returning home and recuperating. What gives such power to the novel is precisely that these three domains are condensed into a single suffocating experience of a displaced homeless individual, an individual lost in the web of police, psychiatric, and administrative measures.

The difference between Platonov and Beckett is that, while Beckett renders the experience of homeless refugees as individuals at the mercy of state institutions, Platonov focuses on displaced nomadic groups in a post-revolutionary situation when the new communist power tries to mobilize them for the communist struggle. Each of his works "departs from the same political problem of how to build communism: of what communism means and how the communist idea meets the concrete conditions and reality of the post-revolutionary society." Platonov's answer to this problem is paradoxical, far from the usual dissident rejection of communism. His result is a negative one; all his stories are stories of a failure; the "synthesis" between the communist project and the displaced nomadic groups end in a void; there is no unity between proletarians and less-than-proletarians:

In Chevengur (1926–28), the orphan Sasha Dvanov becomes a communist in the year of the revolution, joins the Bolsheviks and goes on a party errand to support the revolution in a village. During his long journey, Dvanov discovers "communism in one village," established by poor peasants. The communism of the Chevengur village is accompanied by various absurd experiments with urban planning and farming, permanent terror and hunger. The wandering organic intellectuals are a supplement to the wandering masses, classes and communities, and they are all accompanied in their migration by animals, plants and natural landscape. The protagonist of Dzhan [1936; in English, "Soul"],

Nazar Chagataev, returns to his native town in Turkestan on a party errand to find the lost nomadic nation Dzhan, from which he had come, in order to establish a socialist order. *Dzhan* was written after Platonov's two journeys in Turkestan as a member of writers' delegations. This was during the period when the civil war in Turkestan had just ended and a campaign against traditional nomadic forms of life had been initiated. The task of the delegation was to write an orthodox socialist realist story about a successful "civilizing" process in the local communities. The central problem of Platonov's *Dzhan* may seem to conform to this brief, narrating as it does the story of a "Red Moses" leading the nomadic inhabitants of the Asian desert to socialism. However, Chagataev goes back to Moscow when his mission has ended and one is left with doubts about the future of communism in the desert. . . . The most famous work of Platonov, *The Foundation Pit* (1930), was also created in the context of the first five-year plan. It unfolds by way of a series of meetings between the protagonist Voshchev and the residents of a small provincial town, who are involved in the construction of an enormous proletarian house. While Voshchev challenges the representatives of different class groups, engaging in a Socratic inquiry into truth, the project acquires a more and more grandiose plan, before finally coming to an end with no result.

But we are at the same time as far as possible from the old conservative liberal critique of revolution as a violent attempt to impose on actual life models that are foreign to it. First, Platonov articulates his despair from the position of an engaged fighter for communism (he was actively engaged with nomadic groups in the 1920s, also at a very practical technical level, planning and organizing irrigation projects, etc.). Second, Platonov is not depicting a conflict between the traditional texture of social life and the radical revolutionary attempt to change it (in the style of Edmund Burke's critique of the French Revolution): his focus is not on the traditional forms of life but on the dispossessed nomads whose lives were already irretrievably ruined by the process of modernization. In short, the radical cut Platonov depicts is not between the "spontaneous" proletarian crowd and the organized communist forces, but between the two aspects of the proletarian crowd itself, between the two social "nothings": the strictly proletarian "nothing" of the modern workers generated by capitalism, and the "less-than-nothing" of those not integrated into the system, not even as its immanent negativity, as is made clear in this short exchange from Chevengur: "'Who did you bring us?' Chepurny asked Prokofy . . . 'That's proletarians and others,' Prokofy said. Chepurny was disturbed 'What others? Again the layer of residual swine?' . . . 'The others are the others. Nobody. They're even worse than the proletariat.'" Here are some passages that describe these social "less-than nothings":

Platonov's heroes have different national and cultural backgrounds, but nonetheless they represent the same category: the proletariat. The idea behind "the international" and "non-Russian" faces is the idea of an average multinational proletariat that makes up one class. There is a significant explanation of the "non-Russianness" of the nomadic declassed people in Chevengur: "This is the true international proletariat: look – they're not Russians, they're not Armenians, they're not Tartars – they're not anything! I bring you live international." It is precisely this multinational, and one can even say anticolonial, perspective that leads Platonov to the deconstruction of the dominant image of the white industrial working class that was so typical among the hard-

34

liners in Proletkult. . . . He saw comrades the likes of whom he had never encountered before, people without any understanding or appearance of class and without revolutionary worth. These were instead some sort of nameless others who lived utterly without significance, without pride, and off to one side of the impending world-wide triumph. Even the age of these others was impossible to grasp, for all that could be made out was that they were poor, had bodies that grew unwillingly, and were foreign to all. . . . Platonov names his marginal declassed wanderers as "handmade people with an unknown designation," "uncounted," "mistakable," or "*prochie*" – "others," in the English translation of Robert Chandler. The Russian word *prochie* also refers to the "rest," the "remainder." Thus others is the rest of the people; they don't belong to any class category existing in Marxist theory, because they are too poor and detached from normal social life. . . . The other, therefore, refers to someone who remains unaccounted for due to their amorphous and marginal status, but who is also part of a multiplicity which is not countable – part of a scattered and nomadic people, an anomaly of humanity, trapped between life and death, social and biological.

As the last quoted sentence makes clear, one has to avoid absolutely the elevation of *prochie* into an original site of productivity, its living presence oppressed by state representation. *Prochie* are not the Deleuzian multitude, they are, on the contrary, "living dead" caught in a non-productive passivity, basically deprived of the very will to be active. This is why we should take the risk of offering yet another translation of *prochie*: neighbors, with all the biblical weight of this term, those who are "others" and precisely as such always too close to us, no matter how far away they are. What makes them too close is that we lack a proper distance toward them because they don't possess a clear identity, a place in society. The Christian motto "love your neighbor as yourself" acquires here its full weight: true social love is the love for the unaccountable less-than-nothings. However, this love can take different forms, and while Bolsheviks certainly loved them, wanted to help and redeem them, they followed the model of what Lacan called "university discourse": *prochie* were their *objet petit a*, and they put all their effort into enlightening them, into changing them in modern subjects. The conflict that lies at the heart of Platonov's work is thus not a conflict between enemies but a kind of lovers' quarrel: Bolsheviks wanted to help the homeless others, to civilize them, and the others (depicted by Platonov) sincerely endorsed the communist ideals and fought for them, but everything went wrong: "Others in Platonov's novels are always manipulated by 'more conscious' comrades, party leaders and intellectuals, but always unsuccessfully – it is almost impossible to integrate others into the collective body of the workers and to establish a normalized sociality based on the collectivization of labor and industrial production."

However, Platonov subtly noted that this gap is not just the gap between self-conscious revolutionary force and the inertia of the crowds: while Bolsheviks focused on the operational aspect of social transformation, the core of the communist utopia was directly present in the dreams of Others who expected something radically new to arise. Communism was nowhere closer than in the immobility of the Others, in their resistance to get caught in concrete operative measures: "the special status of the poor and declassed elements, which unlike the organized workers, the party representatives and the intellectuals, are ready to stay where they are in order to do something radically new. In a way theirs is a life that remains in a state of waiting, and the question is what kind of politics will be established here."

Platonov's famous inflections of language also located in this context of the tension between official Party language and the "primitive" speech of the others:

> Platonov reflected the historical development of a new Soviet language made of revolutionary slogans, the vocabulary of Marxian political economy, the jargon of the Bolsheviks and party bureaucrats and its absorption by the illiterate peasants and workers. Historical research shows that for most of the post-revolutionary population, especially in the provinces, the language of the party was foreign and unintelligible, so that "they themselves perforce began to absorb the new vocabulary . . . often garbled its unfamiliar, bookish terms or reconfigured them as something more comprehensible, however absurd." Thus, "deistvyushchaya armia" – "acting army" – became "devstvyushchaya armia" – "virginal army" – because "acting" and "virginity" sound identical in Russian; "militsioner" ("militiaman") became "litsimer" ("hypocrite").

Is this unique bastard mixture, with all its "senseless" mobilization of sound resemblances that can engender sparks of unexpected truth (in an oppressive regime, policemen *are* hypocrites; revolutionaries *are* supposed to act virginally, in a kind of innocence, freed of all egotist motives), not an exemplary case of what Lacan called *lalangue*, language traversed by all social and sexual antagonisms which distort it beyond its linguistic structure? This *lalangue* emerges through Platonov's use of two (almost) symmetrically opposed devices:

> [First,] he interprets an abstract ideological definition through the use of the common man, the person from the people, and

secondly, he makes an inverse operation, when he overloads the simplest and clearest everyday words and expressions . . . with a set of ideological associations, to such an extent that these words become "so terribly improbable and confusing that, finally, they lose their initial meaning."

What is the political implication of this loss of meaning? Although interpenetrating, the two levels – official Bolshevik speech and the everyday speech of the Others – remain forever antagonistic: the more the revolutionary activity tried to combine them, the more their antagonism becomes palpable. This failure is not empirical and contingent; the two levels simply belong to radically heterogeneous spaces. For this reason, one should also avoid the trap of celebrating the "undercurrent" of Soviet Marxism, the other line suppressed by official Soviet Marxism-Leninism, the line that rejected the controlling role "from above" of the Party and counted on the workers' direct self-organization "from below" (as was the case with Bogdanov), indicating a hope for a different, less oppressive, development of the Soviet Union, in contrast to Lenin's approach, which laid the foundations for Stalinism. True, this other line was a kind of "symptom" of official Leninist Marxism; it registered what was "repressed" from official Soviet ideology, but precisely as such it remained parasitical on official Marxism – i.e., it didn't stand on its own. In short, the trap to be avoided here is to elevate the "poor life" of the Others into some kind of authentic communal life out of which an alternative to our ill-fated capitalist modernity can emerge. There is nothing "authentic" in the poor life of the Others; its function is purely negative, it registers (and even gives body to) the failure of social projects, including the communist one.

And, sadly, the same failure, which is necessary for structural reasons, also characterizes a homologous project of fusion of today's working class and today's "less-than-proletarians" (refugees, immigrants) – i.e., the idea that the "nomadic proletarian" is the potential source of revolutionary change. Here also, one has to fully assume Platonov's lesson: the tension is not only between the local conservative racist lower classes and the immigrants; the difference in the entire "way of life" is so strong that one cannot count on an easy solidarity of all the exploited. Perhaps the antagonism between proletarians and less-than-proletarian "others" is an antagonism that is in some sense even more unsurpassable than the class antagonism within the same ethnic community. Precisely at this point when the "subsumption" (of Others into "our" proletarians) seems the most obvious, and the universality of all oppressed seems at hand, it slips out of our grasp. In other words, the "less-than-proletarian" Others cannot be subsumed, integrated, not because they are too different, too heterogeneous with regard to our life world, but because they are absolutely inherent in it, the result of its own tensions.

This, of course, in no way implies that the Marxian proletarian position is only possible in the developed West. During a visit to India, I met representatives of the movement of the lowest part of the lowest cast (the "untouchables"), the dry-toilets cleaners, and they gave me a wonderfully concise answer to what they want to achieve: "We don't want to be what we are." So there is no identity politics, no search for recognition and respect for the unique job they are doing, just the demand for social change that will render their identity superfluous and impossible.

One is thus tempted to propose a radical reformulation here: in today's global capitalism the problematic elements are not the nomadic "less-than-nothings" who resist being subsumed into the proletarian "nothing" as the eventual site of a possible radical social change; the problematic elements are, more and more, (local) proletarians themselves who, when confronted with the nomadic "less-than-noth-ings," all of a sudden realize that their "nothing" (the zero-level, the "place of no-place" in the existing social order) is nonetheless a deter-minate nothing, a position within the existing social order with all the privileges (education, healthcare, etc.) that this implies. No wonder, then, that when "local" proletarians encounter the nomadic "less-than-nothings," their reaction is the rediscovery of their own cultural identity. To put it in speculative Hegelian terms, the "local" proletari-ans discover that their "nothing" is nonetheless sustained by a series of particular privileges, and this discovery, of course, makes them much less prone to engage in radical emancipatory acts – they discover that they have much more to lose than their chains.

There is a well-known joke about Jews gathered in a synagogue to publicly declare their failures. First, a mighty rabbi says: "Forgive me, god, I am nothing, not worthy of your attention!" After him, a rich mer-chant says: "Forgive me, god, I am a worthless nothing!" Then a poor ordinary Jew steps forward and says: "Forgive me, god, I am also noth-ing." The rich merchant whispers to the rabbi: "Who does he think he is, this miserable guy, that he can also say he is nothing?" There is a deep insight in this joke: to "become nothing" requires the supreme effort of negativity, of tearing oneself away from immersion in a cobweb of particular determinations. Such a Sartrean elevation of the subject into a void, a nothingness, is not a true Lacanian (or Hegelian) position: Lacan demonstrates how, to do this, one has to find support in a par-ticular element that functions as a "less than nothing" – Lacan's name for it is *objet a*, object-cause of desire. Let's take a political example. The politically correct prohibition of asserting the particular identity of White Men (as the model of oppression of others), although it presents itself as the admission of their guilt, confers on them a central posi-tion: this very prohibition to assert their particular identity turns them into the universal-neutral medium, the place from which the truth about the others' oppression is accessible. And this is why white liberals indulge so readily in self-flagellation: the true aim of their activity is not really to help the others but to achieve the *Lustgewinn* brought about by their self-accusations, the feeling of their own moral superiority over others. The problem with the self-denial of white identity is not that it goes too far, but that it does not go far enough: while its enunciated content seems radical, its position of enunciation remains that of a privileged universality. So yes, they declare themselves to be "nothing," but this very renunciation to a (particular) something is sustained by the surplus enjoyment of their moral superiority, and we can easily imagine the scene from the quoted Jewish joke repeated here: when, say, a black guy says "I am also nothing!" a white guy whispers to his (white) neighbor: "Who does this guy think he is to be able to claim that he is also nothing?" But we can easily move from imagination to reality here. A decade or so ago, at a round table in New York where the politically correct Leftists predominated, I remember a couple of big names among the "critical thinkers" engaging, one after the other, in self-flagellation, blaming the Judeo-Christian tradition for our evils, pronouncing scathing verdicts on "Eurocentrism," etc. Then, unexpectedly, a black activist joined the debate and also made some critical remarks about the limitations of the black Muslim movement. Hearing this, the white "critical thinkers" exchanged annoyed glances whose message was something like "Who does this guy think he is that he can also claim he is a worthless nothing?" And does something similar not hold for the way "our" proletarians tend to react to the nomadic proletarians? "We are the true nothing – who are they to also claim that they are nothing?"

Back to Platonov: at an abstract level, he thus raises the question of subsumption (of Others into the proletariat), and today we are facing the same problem not just with regard to refugees and other migrants (can they be subsumed into the global capitalist order?), but also at a more formal level of what Balibar calls "total subsumption" as the basic tendency of today's capitalism.[6] This term does not cover only the phenomenon of so-called "cultural capitalism" (the growing commodification of the cultural sphere), but, above all, full subsumption under the logic of the capital of the workers themselves and the process of their reproduction:

> Whereas Marx explained that "capital" ultimately could be reduced to (productive) labour or was nothing other than labour in a different form, appropriated by a different class, the theory of human capital explains that labour – more precisely "labouring capacity" [*Arbeits vermögen*] – can be reduced to capital or become analysed in terms of capitalist operations of credit, investment and profitability. This is, of course, what underlies the ideology of the individual as a "self-entrepreneur," or an "entrepreneur of oneself."[7]

The issue here is "not so much to describe a growth of markets for existing products; it is much more to push the range of the market beyond the limits of the 'production sphere' in the traditional sense, therefore to add new sources of permanent 'extra surplus-value' that can become integrated into valorization, overcoming its limitations, because capital is valorized both on the 'objective' side of labour and production, and on the 'subjective' side of consumption and use."[8]

So it's not just about making the workforce more productive, it is to conceive of the workforce itself directly as another field of capitalist investment: all aspects of its "subjective" life (health, education, sexual life, psychic state, . . .) are considered not only as important for the productivity of the workers, but as fields of investment that can generate additional surplus-value. Health services do not only serve the interests of capital by way of making workers more productive; they are themselves an incredibly powerful field of investment, not only for capital (health services comprise the single strongest branch of the US economy, much stronger than defense) but for the workers themselves (who view paying health insurance as an investment for their future). The same goes for education: it does not only get you ready for productive work; it is in itself the field of a profitable investment for institutions as well as for individuals who invest in their future. It is as if, in this way, commodification not only becomes total, but also gets caught up in a kind of self-referential loop: working power as the ultimate "source of (capitalist) wealth," the origin of surplus-value, becomes itself a moment of capitalist investment. Nowhere is this loop more clearly expressed than in the idea of the worker as a "self-entrepreneur," a capitalist who decides freely where to invest his (meager) surplus resources (or, mostly, resources acquired through loans): into education, health, housing property . . . Does this process have a limit? When, in the very last paragraph of his essay, Balibar approaches this question, he strangely resorts to a Lacanian reference, to Lacan's logic of non-All (from his "formulas of sexuation"):

This is what I call a total subsumption (after "formal" and "real" subsumption) because it leaves nothing outside (no reservation for "natural" life). Or, anything that is left outside must appear as a residue, and a field for further incorporation. Or must it? That is of course the whole question, ethical as much as political: are there limits to commodification? Are there internal and external obstacles? A Lacanian might want to say: every such totalization includes an element of impossibility which belongs to the "real"; it must be *pas tout,* or not whole. If that were the case, the heterogeneous elements, the intrinsic remainders of the total subsumption, could appear in many different forms, some apparently individualistic, such as pathologies or anarchist resistances, others common or even public. Or they may become manifest in certain difficulties in implementing the neoliberal agenda, such as the difficulty of dismantling a Medicare system once it has been legalized.[9]

What Balibar says here is, for a Lacanian, very strange. He condenses (or, rather, just confuses) the two sides of Lacan's formulas of sexuation, and simply reads exception as non-All: the totality of subsumption is non-All since there are exceptions that resist being subsumed to capital. But Lacan precisely opposes non-All and exception: every universality is based on an exception, and when there are no exceptions, the set is non-All, it cannot be totalized. (An interesting example of exception to the politically correct control of public speech are rap lyrics: there you can say it all, celebrate rape, murder, etc., etc. Why this exception? The reason is easy to guess: blacks are considered the privileged image of victimhood, and rap the expression of the misery of black youth, so the brutality of rap lyrics is absolved in advance as the authentic expression of black suffering and frustration.) This opposition should also be applied to the topic of subsumption: one should pass from the search for exception, for those who resist (universal) subsumption and are as such the "site of resistance," to endorsing subsumption without exception and count on its non-All. The subsumption of individual lives to which Balibar refers cannot be reduced to a particular case of universal capitalist subsumption; they remain a particular case which, on account of its self-relating nature (the workforce itself becomes capital), redoubles the production of surplus-value.

In Marx's critique of political economy there are two main cases of universality through exception: money, workforce. The field of commodities can only be totalized through a special commodity which functions as a general equivalent of all commodities but is, as such, deprived of use-value; the field of the exchange of commodities only gets totalized when individual producers not only sell their products on the market, but when the workforce (as a commodity whose use-value is to generate surplus-value) is also sold on the market as a commodity. So maybe there is a third case here: when this commodity, which produces surplus-value, itself becomes an object of capital investment bringing surplus-value, so that we get two types of surplus-value: the "normal" surplus-value generated by the products of the workforce, and the surplus generated by the production of the workforce itself. A nice example of Hegel's insight into how the Absolute always involves self-splitting and is, in this sense, non-All: with the production of workforce itself as a field of capital investment, the subsumption under capital becomes total – but, precisely as such, it becomes non-All, it cannot be totalized, the self-referential element of the workforce itself as a capital investment introduces a gap that introduces imbalance into the entire field. For example, what do the enormous investments in education actually amount to? Many empirical studies demonstrate that most of higher education is not really of use for the reproduction of capital – even business schools actually do very little to train individuals to become effective managers. Consequently, although the media bombard us with the message that education is crucial for a successful economy, most college studies are irrelevant for business purposes. This is why state and business institutions complain all the time about how the humanities serve no purpose, and how universities should be made to serve the needs of actual life (i.e., of capital). But what if this, precisely, is what makes our enormous educational system so precious? It serves no clearly defined goal, it just multiplies "useless" culture, refined thinking, sensitivity for art, etc. Consequently, we find ourselves in a paradoxical situation: at the very moment when, formally, even education gets more and more subsumed under capital as a field of investment, the actual result of this subsumption is that enormous amounts of money are spent on the cultivation of knowledge and art as its own aim. We thus get hundreds of thousands of highly educated individuals who are of no use to capital (who cannot find jobs). But instead of protesting against this meaningless spending of financial resources, should we not celebrate this result as an unexpected sign of the expansion of the "realm of freedom"?

Maybe this gap can function as a source of hope, maybe it opens up the possibility of radical change: the logic of capital gets threatened not from some external nonintegrated rest, but from its own inner inconsistency, which explodes when subsumption gets total.

4

Should the Left's Answer to Rightist Populism Really Be a "Me Too"?

We all know Magritte's famous painting of a pipe, with the words beneath the drawing of a pipe: "Ceci n'est pas une pipe." We find a surprising new version of this paradox in the recent twists and turns of Israeli politics.

On Tuesday, March 19, 2019, a campaign ad was released in Israel in which Ayelet Shaked, the rightwing justice minister, moving in slow motion, appears to be modeling for a luxury perfume. The perfume bottle label reads "Fascism," and while Shaked sprays herself with it, the narrator's voice is heard: "Judiciary revolution. Reduction of activism. Appointment of judges. Governance. Separation of powers. Restraining the Supreme Court." Finally the minister breaks the fourth wall and addresses the camera (i.e., us, the viewers) directly: "Smells like democracy to me."[10] The (rather clumsy) irony of the ad is clear: Shaked's Left-liberal critics attack her for (what they perceive as) the fascist elements in her program (and in the measures enforced by her ministry); in her reply to her critics, she ironically assumes the term ("fascist"), while the voice enumerates her actual measures, which are democratic.

Although, in the ongoing electoral campaign in Israel, Shaked is trying to overcome Netanyahu from the right, Netanyahu took the same path in his recent statements on Instagram where, after asserting that all citizens of Israel, including Arabs, had equal rights, he added: "Israel is not a state of all its citizens." (A reference to the controversial law passed in 2018 declaring Israel the nation-state of the Jewish people.)[11] So we come closer to the truth if we simply turn Shaked's publicity spot around: she sprays herself with a perfume called "Democracy" while a narrator enumerates her achievements – apartheid system with second-class citizens, more than a million Palestinians in a legal limbo, bombings of civilians. A passer-by (not Shaked herself) then comments: "Smells like fascism to me."

However, it is all too easy to insist that Shaked and Netanyahu are in truth nonetheless fascists – the truth is a little bit more complex. While they continue to respect the democratic parliamentary rules, they play a populist game, and the logic of today's populism can also be characterized as democratic fascism, with democracy limited to "our side," our ethnic group – others are (as Trump likes to say, resuscitating the old Stalinist term that he maybe learned from one of his four great friends – not from Kim Yong Un, Mohammad bin Salman, or Jair Bolsonaro, but from Putin) enemies of the people.

This is what makes today's racist populism so dangerous: not only its claim to represent ordinary people's real worries, but its democratic legitimization. This is how "fascism that smells like democracy" operates today. Shaked is right: what makes today's racist populism so traumatic is not that it is fascist but that it *is* in some sense genuinely democratic, that it stands for a new mode of functioning of democracy – to criticize it, one should criticize dangerous potentials that inhere to democracy itself. So should the Left copy it to achieve the same success? The latest trend in the vagaries of Leftist politics is effectively a weird version of MeToo: the Left should learn from the rise of Rightist populism – WeToo can play the populist game. We are repeatedly told that Leftist populism is de facto winning and it works – but where and how does it work? Everywhere it became a serious force, from Latin America to Spain's Podemos party, it stumbled upon a fatal limit. As for Corbyn's Labour Party, its politics cannot be called populist in any meaningful way (furthermore, it hasn't yet gained power where the real test will come). Against Rightist populist passions (from Nigel Farage to Boris Johnson), today's Labour Party politics are precisely a triumph of rational pragmatic argumentation – one can disagree with some proposed measures, but the line of argumentation is always clear. Can one imagine a politician less prone to outbursts of passion than Corbyn (which, to avoid a misunderstanding, is for me what makes Corbyn great)?

This fact alone renders problematic the Left populists' reliance on the opposition between cold pragmatic rational argumentation and passionate confrontation – although Left populists insist that there are limits to this confrontation: they remain within the democratic frame; antagonisms should be transposed into agonistic competition in which all sides obey basic democratic rules. But what if these rules are no longer accepted by all agents? When, a few years ago, I was answering questions from the readers of *Süddeutsche Zeitung* about the refugee crisis, the question that attracted by far the most attention concerned precisely democracy, but with a Right populist twist: when Angela Merkel made her famous public appeal inviting hundreds of thousands of immigrants into Germany, what was her democratic legitimization? What gave her the right to bring such a radical change to German life without democratic consultation? My point here, of course, is not to support anti-immigrant populists, but to clearly show the limits of democratic legitimization. The same goes for those who advocate the radical opening of borders to refugees. Are they aware that, since our democracies are nation-state democracies, their demand amounts to a suspension of democracy? Should such a gigantic change be allowed to affect a country without democratic consultation of its population? (Their answer would have been, of course, that refugees should also be given the right to vote – but this is clearly not enough, since this is a measure that can only happen after refugees are already integrated into the political system of a country.) I remember some time ago watching George Soros on TV, where he advocated the idea that Europe should accept a further one million refugees. In spite of his best humanitarian motifs, one aspect did trouble me: what right does he, a billionaire, have to promote such a large displacement of people without even raising the question of what the local population in Europe may think of it? Yuval Harari points out how the ongoing troubles with immigrants in Germany already confront us with the limits of democracy. How are we to counter anti-immigrant populists who demand a referendum on immigrants, assured that the majority of Germans will vote against them? Is then the solution to give voting rights also to immigrants? To whom among them? To those who are already in Germany, to those who want to go there?

At the end of this line, we get the idea of worldwide elections, which is self-defeating for a simple and precise reason: *since there is no* "agreement on the basics" *at a world-wide level*, the only procedure at our disposal (outside outright war, of course) is to negotiate. (That's why the Middle East conflict cannot be solved by elections but only by war or negotiations.) And negotiations by definition imply the overcoming of the antagonistic logic of Us against Them. According to Left populists, the main reason for the defeat of the Left is the noncombative stance of rational argumentation and lifeless universalism in theory epitomized by the names of Anthony Giddens, Ulrich Beck, and Jürgen

Habermas. This post-political Third Way cannot combat in an efficient way the agonistic logic of Us against Them successfully mobilized by anti-immigrant Right populists. Consequently, the way to combat this Rightist populism is to have a recourse to Leftist populism, which, while retaining the basic populist coordinates (agonistic logic of Us against Them, of the "people" against a corrupted elite), fills them in with a Leftist content: "Them" do not consist of poor refugees or immigrants but refer to financial capital, technocratic state bureaucracy, etc. This populism moves beyond the old working-class anti-capitalism; it tries to bring together a multiplicity of struggles from ecology to feminism, from the right to employment to free education and healthcare, etc., as the Podemos party is doing in Spain.

With regard to pragmatic dispassionate politics of rational compromise, one should first note that the ideology of neoliberalism (also in its liberal-Left version) is anything but "rational": it is *extremely* confrontational, it brutally excludes those who do not accept it as dangerous anti-democratic utopians, its expert knowledge is ideology at its purest, etc. The problems with the Third Way Left (which endorsed neoliberal economics) was not that it was too pragmatic-rational, but that it was just not truly rational – it was permeated by unprincipled pragmatism which in advance endorses the opponent's premises. Leftist politics today does not need (just) confrontational passion; it needs much more true cold rationality. Cold analysis and passionate struggle not only do not exclude each other, they need each other.

The formula of agonistic politicization, of passionate confrontation, directed against lifeless universalism, is just all too formal – it ignores the big question that lurks in the background: why did the Left abandon the agonistic logic of Us against Them decades ago? Was it not because of the deep structural changes in capitalism, changes that cannot be confronted by means of simple populist mobilization?

The Left abandoned antagonistic confrontation because it failed in its struggle with capitalism, because it accepted the global triumph of capitalism. As Peter Mandelson said, in terms of the economy, we are all Thatcherites, so all that remains to the Left is the multiplicity of particular struggles: human rights, feminism, anti-racism, and, especially, multiculturalism. (It is interesting to note that Ernesto Laclau, the theoretical father of Leftist populism, first enthusiastically greeted Blair's Third Way politics – as a liberation from class essentialism, etc. – and only later targeted it as the mode of non-antagonist politics.)

Podemos undoubtedly stands for populism at its best: against the arrogant politically correct intellectual elites who despise the "narrowness" of ordinary people who are considered "stupid" for "voting against their interests," the party's organizing principle is to listen to and organize those "from below" against those "from above," beyond all traditional Left and Right models. The idea is that the starting point of emancipatory politics should be the concrete experience of the suffering and injustices of ordinary people in their local life-world (home quarter, workplace, etc.), not abstract visions of a future communist or whatsoever society. Although the new digital media seem to open up the space for new communities, the difference between these new communities and the old life-world communities is crucial: these old communities are not chosen, I am born into them, they form the very space of my socialization; while the new (digital) communities include me into a specific domain defined by my interests and thus depending on my choice. Far from making the old "spontaneous" communities deficient, the fact that they do not rely on my free choice makes them superior with regard to the new digital communities, since they compel me to find my way into a pre-existing not-chosen life-world in which I encounter (and have to learn to deal with) real differences, while the new digital communities, depending on my choice, sustain the ideological myth of the individual who somehow pre-exists in a communal life and is free to choose it. While this approach undoubtedly contains a (very big) grain of truth, its problem is that, to put it bluntly, not only, as Laclau liked to emphasize, does society not exist, but "people" also don't exist.

This thesis is not to be taken as an abstract theoretical statement about the inconsistency that traverses the social body: it refers to a quite concrete, even experiential, fact. "People" is a false name for the social totality – in our global capitalism, totality is "abstract," invisible, there is no way to ground it in concrete life-worlds. In other words, in today's global capitalist universe, a "concrete experience" of being a member of a particular life-world, with its customs, living links, forms of solidarity, etc., is already something "abstract" in the strict sense of a particular experience that obliterates the thick network of financial, social, etc., processes that rule and regulate this concrete particular world. Here Podemos will encounter problems if at some point it takes power: what specific economic measures (beyond the standard Keynesian bag of tricks) will it enact to limit the power of capital?

Therein resided the difference between Syriza and Podemos: Syriza touched the Real of our global order; it threatened the reign of capital, which is why it had to be humiliated without mercy. The heroism of Syriza was that, after winning the democratic political battle, the party risked a step further into disturbing the smooth flow of the reproduction of capital. The lesson of the Greek crisis is that capital, although ultimately a symbolic fiction, is our Real. That is to say, today's protests and revolts are sustained by the combination (overlapping) of different levels, and this combination accounts for their strength: they fight for ("normal" parliamentary) democracy against authoritarian regimes; against racism and sexism, especially the hatred directed at immigrants and refugees; for the welfare state against neoliberalism;

against corruption in politics and the economy (companies polluting the environment, etc.); for new forms of democracy that reach beyond multi-party rituals (participation, etc.); and, finally, questioning the global capitalist system as such and trying to keep alive the idea of a non-capitalist society.

Both traps are to be avoided here: false radicalism ("what really matters is the abolition of liberal parliamentary capitalism, all other fights are secondary"), as well as false gradualism ("now we fight against military dictatorship and for simple democracy, forget your Socialist dreams, this comes later – maybe . . ."). When we have to deal with a specific struggle, the key question is: how will our engagement in it or disengagement from it affect other struggles? The general rule is that, when a revolt begins against an oppressive half-democratic regime, as was the case in the Middle East in 2011, it is easy to mobilize large crowds with slogans that one cannot but characterize as crowd pleasers – for democracy, against corruption, etc. But then we gradually approach more difficult choices: when our revolt succeeds in its direct goal, we come to realize that what really bothered us (our un-freedom, humiliation, social corruption, lack of prospect of a decent life) goes on under a new guise. In Egypt, protesters succeeded to get rid of the oppressive Mubarak regime, but corruption remained, and the prospect of a decent life moved even further away. After the overthrow of an authoritarian regime, the last vestiges of patriarchal care for the poor can fall away, so that the newly gained freedom is de facto reduced to the freedom to choose the preferred form of one's misery – the majority not only remains poor, but, to add insult to injury, it is being told that, since they are now free, poverty is their own responsibility. In such a predicament, we have to admit that there was a flaw in our goal itself, that this goal was not specific enough – say, that standard political democracy can also serve as the very form of un-freedom: political freedom can easily provide the legal frame for economic slavery, with the underprivileged "freely" selling themselves into servitude. We are thus brought to demand more than just political democracy; we have to admit that what we first took as the failure to fully realize a noble principle (of democratic freedom) is a failure inherent to this principle itself – understanding this is the big step of political pedagogy.

The double U-turn that the Greek crisis took in July 2015 cannot but appear as a step not just from tragedy to comedy but, as Stathis Kouvelakis noted, from tragedy full of comic reversals directly into a theater of the absurd – is there any other way to characterize the extraordinary reversal of one extreme into its opposite that would bedazzle even the most speculative Hegelian philosopher? Tired of the endless negotiations with the EU executives, in which one humiliation followed another, Syriza called for a referendum to take place on Sunday July 5, 2015, asking the Greek people whether they supported or rejected the EU proposal of new austerity measures. Although the government itself clearly stated that it supported the "NO" vote, the result was a surprise for the government itself: the surprisingly overwhelming majority of over 61 percent voted "NO" to European blackmail. Rumors began to circulate that the result – a victory for the government – was a bad surprise for Prime Minister Alexis Tsipras himself, who secretly hoped that the government would lose, and that a defeat would allow him to save face by surrendering to the EU demands ("we have to respect the voters' voice"). However, literally the morning after, Tsipras announced that Greece was ready to resume negotiations, and days later Greece negotiated an EU proposal that was basically the same as what the voters rejected (in some details even harsher) – in short, he acted as if the government had lost, not won, the referendum. Here we encounter the truth of populism: its failure to confront the real of the capital. The supreme populist moment (referendum victory) immediately reverted into capitulation, into a confession of impotence with regard to the capitalist order – there is no simple betrayal in this reversal, but the expression of a deep necessity.

The sad fate of Syriza is emblematic of the European Left's new situation. In capitalism as we knew it, when a severe economic crisis made impossible the system's normal reproduction, some kind of authoritarian rule (usually a military dictatorship) was imposed for a decade or so until the economic situation was renormalized enough so that a return to democracy could be tolerated again – recall the cases of Chile, Argentina, South Korea . . . The unique role of Syriza is that it was allowed to play this role that is usually the reserve of rightwing dictatorships: it took power at a time of deep upheaval and crisis, it fulfilled its task of enacting tough austerity measures, and then it left the stage, replaced by a party called New Democracy, the same party that landed Greece in a crisis in the first place.

The achievements of the Syriza government are mixed: it did some good things (which could also have been done by a rational centrist government, like the agreement with Macedonia on the change of its name), but overall the result is a double catastrophe. First, it undertook the job of imposing austerity measures – the very task its entire program was opposed to. The perverse genius of EU bureaucrats was to allow Syriza to do this – it was much better to have a radical Leftist party do it because in this way protests against austerity were minimalized; one can only imagine what public protests would have been organized by Syriza if a Rightist government had introduced austerity. Even worse, by enacting the austerity measures, Syriza de facto destroyed its own social base, the rich texture of civil society groups out of which it had emerged as a political party – Syriza now is just a political party like all the others.

When Syriza took over and engaged in negotiations with the EU, it was clear that, when the only choice was austerity or Grexit, the battle was lost. Accepting the need to impose austerity measures meant betraying the basic tenet of its program, and Grexit would have caused a further 30 percent drop in living standards and a collapse of social life (lack of medicines, of food, . . .) leading to a state of emergency. Now we know that Grexit was in fact quite acceptable to the European financial elite. Varoufakis reports that when he mentioned Grexit as a threat to Wolfgang Schäuble (at that time the German finance minister), Schauble immediately offered billions of euros to help Greece to do it. What was intolerable for the EU elite was not Grexit but Greece remaining *in* the EU and mounting a counter-offensive there. The idea was clear: the collapse caused by Grexit would have served as a good lesson to all Leftists not to play with any radical economic measures. The establishment likes a more radical Left to take power every two to three decades, just to warn people what dangers lie ahead along this path.

So everything hinged on avoiding this choice and finding a third way. Naively, we who supported Syriza thought they had a plan for this third way, and in all the debates I had with them I was assured they knew what they were doing and not to worry: Syriza has a dream team and they would win. Even I fell for it for some time, because, in spite of all the Leftist critique of the brutality of EU pressure on Greece, the EU did nothing unexpected, the administrators in Brussels acted precisely as expected – there were no surprises here.

I remember how, in the 2015 debates, I warned against the fascination with great public events – all the fuss about "one million of us at Syntagma Square, we were all clapping and singing together." What really matters is what happens the morning after, when the drunkenness of the collective trance is over and the enthusiasm has to be translated into concrete measures. I often mockingly evoked a group of participants who, once a year, meet in a cafeteria at the anniversary of past demonstrations and sentimentally remember the bygone moments of ecstatic unity – but then a cellphone rings and they have to run back to their boring jobs. We can easily imagine such a scene today: members of Syriza meet in a cafeteria fondly remembering the unique spirit of their 2015 mass protests, and then a phone rings and they have to run back to their offices to pursue the job of austerity.

The failure of Syriza brings us back to the fateful limits of populism. Laclau insisted on the necessity to construct some Enemy figure as immanent to populism – this is not its weakness, but the resource of its strength. Left populism should construct a different figure of the Enemy, not the threatening racial Other (immigrant, Jew, Muslim . . .) but the financial elites, fundamentalists, and other "usual suspects" of the progressives. This urge to construct the Enemy is another fatal limitation of populism: today, the ultimate "enemy" is not a concrete social agent but in some sense the system itself, a certain functioning of the system that cannot be easily located as agents. Years ago, Alain Badiou wrote that one doesn't fight capitalism, but its concrete agents – but therein resides the problem, since the true target *is* capitalism. Today, it seems easy to say that the Enemy is neo-fascist, anti-immigrant nationalism or, in the US, Trump. But the fact remains that the rise of Trump is ultimately the effect of the failure of a liberal democratic consensus, so although one should, of course, not exclude new forms of "anti-fascist" alliances with the latter, this consensus remains *the* thing to be changed. So was I wrong when, in two interviews undertaken before the US presidential elections, I preferred Trump to Clinton? No. Events that followed proved me right: the victory of Trump threw the establishment into a crisis and opened up the way for the rise of the left wing of the Democratic Party. If the Trumpian excesses do not mobilize the US Left, then the battle is really lost.

It is because of their focus on concrete enemies that Left populists seem to privilege national sovereignty, the strong nation-state, as a defense against global capital (even Auferstehen in Germany basically follows this path). In this way, most of them (by definition) endorse not only populism but even nationalism, presenting their struggle as a defense against international financial capital. Some Left populists in the US already used the term "national socialism";[12] while, of course, it would be stupid and unfair to claim that they are closet Nazis, one should nonetheless insist that internationalism is a key component of any project of radical emancipation. Whatever critical remarks one sustains against Varoufakis's DIEM, at least DIEM sees clearly that resistance against global capital has itself to be global, a new form of universalism. There definitely are enemies, and the topic of conspiracies is not to be simply dismissed. Years ago, Fredric Jameson perspicuously noted that in today's global capitalism, things happen that cannot be explained by reference to some anonymous "logic of capitalism" – for example, we know now that the financial meltdown of 2008 was the result of a well-planned "conspiracy" of some financial circles. However, the true task of social analysis still remains to explain how contemporary capitalism opened up a space for such "conspiratorial" interventions. This is also why reference to "greed" and the appeal to capitalists to show social solidarity and responsibility are misplaced: "greed" (search for profit) *is* what motivates capitalist expansion, the wager of capitalism *is* that acting out of individual greed will contribute to the common good. So, again, instead of focusing on individual greed and approaching the problem of growing inequality in moralist terms, the task is to change the system so that it will no longer allow or even solicit "greedy" acting.

One has to accept that some kind of extra-strong economy of jouissance is at work in the identification with one's own "way of life," some core of the Real that is very difficult to rearticulate symbolically. Recall Lenin's shock at the patriotic reaction of social democrats to the outburst of World War I – people are ready to suffer for their way of life, including today's refugees, who are not ready to "integrate." In short, there are two Reals (the real of capital, the real of ethnic identification), which cannot be dissolved into fluid elements of symbolic hegemony.

Let's take an (artificially) clear-cut case: imagine a democracy in which a large majority of voters succumb to the anti-immigrant populist propaganda and decide in a referendum to close the borders to refugees and make life more difficult to those who already are within a country; imagine then a country in which, despite such propaganda, voters assert in a referendum their commitment to solidarity and their will to help the refugees. The difference is not just objective – i.e., it is not just that, in one case, voters made a reactionary racist decision and, in the other case, they made the right choice of solidarity; the difference was also "subjective" in the precise sense that a different type of political passion was at work in each of the two cases. However, one should not be afraid to posit that, in the first case, no matter how sincerely convinced they appeared to be, they somehow, "deep in themselves," knew that what they did was a shameful act – all their agitated reasoning just covers up their bad feeling. And, in the second act, people are always somehow aware of the liberating effect of their act: even if what they did was risky and crazy, they did achieve a true breakthrough. Both acts in a sense achieve the impossible, but in an entirely different way. In the first case, the public space is spoiled, the ethical standards are lowered; what was up to that moment a matter of private dirty rumors, unacceptable in the public space, becomes something one can talk about publicly – one can be openly racist, sexist, preach hatred, and spread paranoia. Today's model of such "liberation" is, of course, Donald Trump, who, as they say, "says publicly what others are only thinking about." In the second case, most of us are ashamed that we didn't trust people more: before the referendum, we were silently expecting a defeat, and the ethical composure of the voters surprises us. Such "miracles" are worth living for.

But how are we to prepare the ground for such "miracles"? How are we to mobilize "our" people to fight for the rights of the refugees and immigrants? In principle, the answer is easy: we should strive to artic-ulate a new ideological space in which the struggle for refugees will be combined with the feminist struggle, the ecological struggle, etc. However, such an easy way out is purely rhetorical and runs against the (ideologically determined, of course) "experience," which is very difficult to undo. More profoundly, the catch is that today's constella-tion doesn't allow for a direct link between the program and the direct experience of "real people." The basic premise of classic Marxism is that, with the central role of the proletariat, humanity found itself in a unique situation in which the deepest theoretical insight found an echo in the most concrete experience of exploitation and alienation – it is, however, deeply questionable whether, in today's complex situa-tion, a similar strategy is feasible. Left populists would, of course, insist that this is precisely why we should abandon the Marxist reliance on the proletariat as the privileged emancipatory subject and engage in a long and difficult work of constructing new hegemonic "chains of equivalences" without any guarantee of success (there is no assur-ance that feminist struggle, struggle for freedom, and struggle for the rights of immigrants will coalesce in one big Struggle). My point is, however, that even this solution is too abstract and formal. Left popu-lists remind me of a doctor who, when asked by the worried patient what to do, tells him: "Go and see a doctor!" The true problem is not one of formal procedure – a pragmatic search for unity versus antago-nist confrontation – but a substantial one: how to strike back at global capital? Do we have an alternative to the global capitalist system? Can we even imagine today an authentic communist power? What we get is disaster (Venezuela), capitulation (Greece), or a controlled full return to capitalism (China, Vietnam).

So what happens with populist passion here? It disappears, and it has to disappear. When populism takes power, the choice is, to designate it with names, Nicolás Maduro (passage from genuine populism into its authoritarian version with social decay) or Deng Hsiao-Ping (authoritarian-capitalist normalization, ideological return to Confucius). Populism that thrives in a state of emergency cannot, by definition, last. It needs the figure of an external enemy – let us take Laclau's own precise analysis of why one should count Chartism as populism:

> Its dominant leitmotiv is to situate the evils of society not in something that is inherent in the economic system, but quite the opposite: in the abuse of power by parasitic and speculative groups which have control of political power – "old corruption," in Cobbett's words. ... It was for this reason that the feature most strongly picked out in the ruling class was its idleness and parasitism.[13]

In other words, for a populist, the cause of the troubles is ultimately never the system as such, but the intruder who corrupted it (financial manipulators, not capitalists as such, etc.); not a fatal flaw inscribed into the structure as such, but an element that doesn't play its role within the structure properly. For a Marxist, on the contrary (like for a Freudian), the pathological (deviating misbehavior of some elements) is the symptom of the normal, an indicator of what is wrong in the very structure that is threatened with "pathological" outbursts: for Marx, economic crises are the key to understanding the "normal" function-ing of capitalism; for Freud, pathological phenomena like hysterical outbursts provide the key to the constitution (and hidden antago-nisms that sustain the functioning) of a "normal" subject. That's why populism tends to be nationalist; it calls for people's unity against the (external) enemy, while Marxism focuses on the inner split that cuts across each community and calls for international solidarity because we are all affected by this split.

The hard fact to accept is that "ordinary people" do *not* "know": they possess no authentic insight or experience, they are no less con-fused and disoriented than everyone else. I remember, in the debate after a talk of mine, a brief exchange with a supporter of Podemos, who reacted to my claim that the demands of Podemos (getting rid of corrupted power structures; authentic democracy rooted in peo-ple's actual interests and worries) do not include any precise ideas about how to reorganize society. He replied: "But this is not a reproach since Podemos wants just this: not another system but a democratic system that would actually be what it claims to be!" In short, Podemos wanted the existing system without its symptoms, to which one should retort that it's OK to begin with this, but then sooner or later comes the moment when we are forced to realize that symptoms (corruption, failure, etc.) are part of the system, so that, in order to get rid of the symptoms, we have to change the system itself.

One of the versions of radical politics today is waiting for a catas-trophe: many of my radical friends are telling me privately that only a big ecological catastrophe, economic meltdown, or war can mobilize people to work for radical change. But is this very stance of waiting for a catastrophe not already a catastrophe, an admission of utter defeat? In order to find a proper orientation in this conundrum, one should become aware of the fateful limitation of the politics of interests.

Parties like die Linke in Germany effectively represent the interests of their working-class constituency - better healthcare and retirement conditions, higher wages, etc.; this puts them automatically within the confines of the existing system, and is therefore not enough for authentic emancipation. Interests are not to be just followed; they have to be redefined with regard to ideas that cannot be reduced to interests. This is why we witness again and again the paradox of how the Rightist populists, when they get in power, sometimes impose measures that are effectively in workers' interests - as is the case in Poland, where PiS (Law and Justice, the ruling Rightist populist party) has managed to enact the largest social transfers in Poland's contemporary history. PiS did what Marine le Pen also promises to do in France: a combination of anti-austerity measures (social transfers no Leftist party dares to consider) plus the promise of order and security that asserts national identity and deals with the immigrant threat - who can beat this combination, which directly addresses the two main worries of ordinary people? We can discern on the horizon a weirdly perverted situation in which the official "Left" is enforcing austerity politics (while advocating multicultural etc. rights), while the populist Right is pursuing anti-austerity measures to help the poor (while pursuing the xenophobic nationalist agenda) - the latest figure of what Hegel described as *die verkehrte Welt*, the topsy-turvy world. The obvious (not only) populist reaction to this is: should we not reestablish the "normal" state? In other words, should the Left not enact the anti-austerity measures that the populist Right is enacting, just without the accompanying racist-nationalist baggage? "Logical" as it may sound, this, precisely, is what cannot be done: the Right can do it precisely *because* its anti-austerity measures are accompanied by racist-nationalist ideology; this ideological coating is what makes anti-austerity acceptable.

This logic is vaguely similar to the fact that, as a rule, it is only a great Rightist leader who can make a historical agreement with a Leftist force: only Nixon could establish links with China or conclude peace in Vietnam; only de Gaulle could recognize the independence of Algeria. For a Leftist leader, such a step would have been self-destructive. Today, we also have the opposite example: only the Leftist Syriza was able to implement austerity measures in Greece – if a Rightist government were to do it, it would have triggered an explosion of protests. What this means at a more general level is that, in a hegemonic chain of equivalences, the position of elements is overdetermined by the composition of other elements: recognition of a radical anticolonialist struggle by the colonial power is more readily compatible with a general conservative orientation than it is an element of a much more "natural" chain, where it is coupled with Leftist politics.

Populism ultimately *never* works. In its Rightist version, it cheats by definition: it constructs a false figure of the enemy – false in the sense that it obfuscates the basic social antagonism ("Jew" instead of "capital," etc.) and, in this way, its populist rhetoric serves the very financial elites it pretends to oppose. In its Left version, it's false in a more complex Kantian sense. In a vague but pertinent homology, we can say that the construction of the Enemy in an antagonistic relation plays the role of Kant's schematism: it allows us to translate theoretical insight (awareness of abstract social contradictions) into practico-political engagement. This is how we should read Badiou's statement that "one cannot fight capitalism": one should "schematize" our fight into activity against concrete actors who work like the exposed agents of capitalism. However, the basic wager of Marxism is precisely that such a personalization into an actual enemy is wrong – if it is necessary, it is a kind of necessary structural illusion. So does this mean that Marxist politics should permanently manipulate its followers (and itself), acting in a way it knows it is misleading? Marxist engagement is condemned to this immanent tension, which cannot be resolved by claiming that now we fight the Enemy and later we will move to a more fundamental overhaul of the system itself. Left populism stumbles upon the limit of fighting the Enemy the moment it takes power.

In a situation like today's, Left populism's fatal flaw is clearly visible: its weakness is precisely what appears to its partisans as its strength, namely the construction of the figure of the Enemy and the focus on the struggle against it. What is needed today are, above all, positive visions of how to confront our problems – the threat of ecological catastrophes, the destabilizing implications of global capitalism, the traps of the digitalization of our minds. In other words, what is needed is not just to fight big financial institutions, but to envisage new modes of financial politics, to provide feasible answers to the question, "OK, so how would you organize finances if you gain power?" It's not just to fight against walls and for open borders, but to envisage new social and economic models that would no longer generate refugees. Today, more than ever, our system is approaching such a deep crisis that we can no longer just bombard it with our demands, expecting that it will somehow manage to meet them while continuing to function smoothly.

Instead of just focusing on antagonism, it is therefore crucial for a Leftist government today to define a role for the private sector, to offer the private sector precise conditions under which it can operate. As long as (at least a good part of) the private sector is needed for the smooth functioning of our societies, one should not just antagonize it, but instead propose a positive vision of its role. Social democracy at its best was doing exactly this.

The obvious Left populist counterargument is here, of course: but is not the fact that Left populism does not provide a detailed vision of the alternative society precisely its advantage? Such an openness is what characterizes a radical democratic struggle: there are no prescriptions decided in advance, rearrangements are going on all the time, with short-term goals shifting. Again, this smooth reply is all too easy, it obfuscates the fact that the "openness" of the Left populist struggle is based on a retreat, on avoiding the key problem of capitalism.

So why persist in a radical struggle, if radical change is today unimaginable? Because our global predicament demands it: only a radical change can enable us to cope with the prospect of ecological catastrophe, with the threats of biogenetics and digital control over our lives, etc. The task is impossible, but no less necessary. Decades ago, in a debate in the Irish parliament, Gerald Fitzgerald, Prime Minister at that time, rejected a proposal with a nice Hegelian reversal of the commonplace wisdom "This may be good for theory, but it is not good for practice." His counter-argument was: "This may be good for practice, but it is not good enough for theory." This is how things stand with Left populism: without fully endorsing it, we should treat it as part of a short-term pragmatic compromise. We should support it (when it is at its best, at least, as is the case of Podemos), but without any illusions, knowing it will ultimately fail and hoping that through this failure something new may emerge.

5

When Unfreedom Itself Is
Experienced as Freedom

Our media recently reported that Steve Bannon established in Brussels a rightwing populist body destined to coordinate nationalist populists all around Europe. "The Movement," as the body is called, will research and write policy proposals, commission polling, and share expertise on messaging and data targeting. It already employs 80 people and its ultimate goal is nothing less than to radically change the political landscape of Europe, to sideline the liberal consensus and replace it with "my-country-first" anti-immigrant nationalism. American public opinion is obsessed by the Russian meddling in the US electoral process – but just imagine Putin sending someone to Washington to act like Bannon in Brussels. We encounter here the old paradox: separatist forces of disunity are better at establishing transnational unity than the forces of international solidarity. No wonder liberal Europe is in a panic.

We are bombarded by the idea that today, in the early twenty-first century, our precious liberal legacy of human rights, democracy, and individual freedoms is threatened by the explosive rise of "fascist" populism, and that we should gather all our strength to keep this threat at bay. This idea should be resolutely rejected at two levels. First, populism didn't hit the earth like a comet (as Joschka Fischer wrote about

Donald Trump): its rise is more like a crack in the earth, a flow of lava streaming out – it is the result of the disintegration of the liberal consensus and the inability of the Left to offer a viable alternative. The first step in fighting populism is therefore to cast a critical glance at the weaknesses of the liberal project itself – populism is a symptom of this weakness.

Second, and more important, the real danger resides elsewhere. The most dangerous threat to freedom does not come from an openly authoritarian power; it takes place when our unfreedom itself is experienced as freedom. Since permissiveness and free choice have been elevated to a supreme value, social control and domination can no longer appear as infringing on a subject's freedom: it has to appear as (and be sustained by) the very self-experience of individuals as free. There is a multitude of forms of this apparent un-freedom in the guise of its opposite: when we are deprived of universal healthcare, we are told that we are given a new freedom of choice (to choose our healthcare provider); when we can no longer rely on long-term employment and are compelled to search for new, precarious, work every couple of years, we are told that we are being given the opportunity to reinvent ourselves and discover unexpected creative potentials that lurk in our personality; when we have to pay for the education of our children, we are told that we become "entrepreneurs of the self," acting like a capitalist who has to choose freely how he will invest the resources he possesses (or borrowed) – in education, health, travel. Constantly bombarded by imposed "free choices," forced to make decisions for which we are mostly not properly qualified (or possess enough information about), we more and more experience our freedom as a burden that causes unbearable anxiety.

Furthermore, most of our activities (and passivities) are now registered in some digital cloud which also permanently evaluates us, tracing not only our acts but also our emotional states; when we experience ourselves as free to the utmost (surfing on the web where everything is available), we are totally "externalized" and subtly manipulated. The digital network gives new meaning to the old slogan "the personal is political." And it's not only control of our intimate lives that is at stake: everything today is regulated by some digital network, from transport to health, from electricity to water. That's why the web is our most important commons today, and the struggle for its control is *the* struggle today. The enemy is the combination of privatized and state-controlled commons, corporations (Google, Facebook), and state security agencies (the NSA). This fact alone renders insufficient the traditional liberal notion of representative power: citizens transfer part of their power to the state, but on precise terms (this power is constrained by law, limited to very precise conditions in the way it is exercised, since the people remain the ultimate source of sovereignty and can repeal power if they decide to do so). In short, the state with its power is the minor partner in a contract that the major partner (the people) can at any point repeal or change, basically in the same way each of us can change the supermarket where we buy our provisions.

Media bombard us with news about the threats to our security: will China invade Taiwan as a punishment for the US trade war? Will the US attack Iran? Will the EU descend into chaos after the Brexit mess? But I think there is one topic that – in the long view, at least – dwarfs all others: the effort of the US to contain the expansion of Huawei. Why?

The digital network that regulates the functioning of our societies as well as their control mechanisms is the ultimate figure of the technical grid that sustains power today. Shoshana Zuboff baptized this new phase of capitalism "surveillance capitalism": "Knowledge, authority and power rest with surveillance capital, for which we are merely 'human natural resources.' We are the native peoples now whose claims to self-determination have vanished from the maps of our own experience."[14] We are not just material, we are also exploited, involved in an unequal exchange, which is why the term "behavioral surplus" (playing the role of surplus-value) is fully justified here: when we are surfing, buying, watching TV, etc., we get what we want, but we give more – we lay ourselves bare, we make the details of our life and its habits transparent to the digital big Other. The paradox is, of course, that we experience this unequal exchange, the activity that effectively enslaves us, as our highest exercise of freedom – what is more free than freely surfing on the web? Just by exerting this freedom of ours, we generate the "surplus" appropriated by the digital big Other which collects data . . .

And this brings us back to Huawei: the battle around Huawei is the battle for who will control the mechanism that controls our lives. It's maybe *the* crucial power struggle that is going on. Huawei is not just a private corporation, it is totally blended with Chinese state security, and we should bear in mind that its rise was largely financed and directed by the state. We already see how digitalized state control works in today's China:

Would-be air travellers were blocked from buying tickets 17.5 million times last year for "social credit" offenses including unpaid taxes and fines under a controversial system the ruling Communist Party says will improve public behaviour. Others were barred 5.5 million times from buying train tickets, according to the National Public Credit Information Centre. In an annual report, it said 128 people were blocked from leaving China due to unpaid taxes. The ruling party says "social credit" penalties and rewards will improve order in a fast-changing society after three decades of economic reform have shaken up social structures.

The system is part of efforts by President Xi Jinping's government to use technology ranging from data processing to genetic sequencing and facial recognition to tighten control.[15]

This is the political reality of Huawei's expansion. So yes, accusations that Huawei poses a security threat to all of us are true – however, what we should bear in mind is that the Chinese authorities are just doing more openly what our "democratic" authorities do in a more subtle way, hidden from the public view. From the new law in Russia that limits access to the internet to the latest EU regulations of the web, we witness the same effort to limit and control our access to the digital commons. The digital network is arguably today's main figure of what Marx called "commons," the shared social space that constitutes the base of our interaction. The battle for freedom is ultimately the battle for the control of the commons, and today this means the battle for who will control the digital space that regulates our lives. So it's not "the West against China" – the ongoing struggle between Huawei and the West is secondary, the struggle between different factions of those who want to dominate us. The true struggle is between all of them together and us, ordinary people controlled by them. There is one name that symbolizes this struggle for the commons: Julian Assange. We should thus avoid all easy China bashing and those who don't want to defend Assange should also keep silent about the Chinese abuses of digital control.

Liberalism and its great opponent, classical Marxism, both tend to reduce the state to a secondary mechanism that obeys the needs of the reproduction of capital; they both thereby underestimate the active role played by state apparatuses in economic processes. Today (perhaps more than ever) one should not fetishize capitalism as the big bad wolf controlling states: state apparatuses are active in the very heart of economic processes, doing much more than just guaranteeing legal and other (educational, ecological . . .) conditions of the reproduction of capital. In many different forms, the state is active as a direct economic agent (it helps failing banks, it supports selected industries, it orders defense and other equipment) – in the US today, around 50 percent of production is mediated by the state (a century ago, this figure was between 5 and 10 percent).

As we have already seen, the digital network that sustains the functioning of our societies as well as their control mechanisms is the ultimate figure of the technical grid that sustains power today – and does this not confer a new actuality to Trotsky's old idea that the key to the state lies not in its political and secretarial organizations, but in its technical services? Consequently, in the same way that, for Trotsky, taking control of the postal service, of electricity, the railways, etc., was the key moment in the revolutionary seizure of power, is it not the case that, today, the "occupation" of the digital grid is absolutely crucial if we are to break the power of the state and capital? And, in the same way that Trotsky required the mobilization of a narrow well-trained "storming party, technical experts and gangs of armed men led by engineers" to resolve this "question of technique," so the lesson of the last decades is that neither massive grassroots protests (as we have seen them in Spain and Greece) nor well-organized political movements (parties with elaborated political visions) are enough – we also need a narrow striking force of dedicated "engineers" (hackers, whistle-blowers . . .) organized as a disciplined conspiratorial group. Its task will be to "take over" the digital grid, to rip it from the hands of corporations and state agencies that now, de facto, control it.

Or, to put it in the well-known terms from 1968, in order for its key legacy to survive, liberalism needs the brotherly help of the radical Left.

6

Only Autistic Children Can Save Us!

Sometimes, an event takes place that, although totally explainable as part of the natural run of things, acquires an unexpected dimension of a sign of our global predicament. This is what happened in April 2019 in the suburbs of Seattle, where, every day, bald eagles began to drop trash, including a blood-filled biohazard container, into upper-middle-class suburbanite people's yards. The trash comes from a nearby landfill that takes in two tons of fresh trash each day: the bald eagles pick out the juicy morsels of food found in the landfill, and then discard the junk that they don't want in the nearby neighborhoods.[16] "There's something almost poetic about the American national bird reminding people that the trash they throw in a landfill doesn't simply disappear. In a way, these birds are a visceral demonstration of the usually hidden consequences of extreme consumption."[17] We live in one world, so no wonder that the shit we thought we safely flushed away is thrown back into our face.

Is not something similar going on with temperature rises to over 50 degrees Celsius? This is no longer big news; it happens regularly in the crescent from Emirates to southern Iran, in parts of India, in Death Valley, and now we have learned that the prospects are much darker, threatening not only desert areas. In Vietnam, many farmers decided to sleep during the day and work at night because of the unbearable heat. The most populous region in the world – China's northern plain from Beijing to Shanghai, densely populated and food-producing – will become uninhabitable if global warming goes on. The cause will be the deadly combination of heat and humidity measured as the "wet bulb" temperature (WBT). Once the WBT reaches 35ºC, the human body cannot cool itself by sweating and even fit people sitting in the shade can die within six hours.

As is fast becoming evident, migrations and the walls meant to prevent migrants from entering are becoming more and more intertwined with ecological disturbances like global warming, so that the ecological apocalypse and the refugee apocalypse are increasingly overlapping in what is aptly named "climate apartheid": "As extreme weather events such as droughts, floods, and hurricanes become more frequent, the world's poorest people will be forced to choose between starvation and migration. "We risk a 'climate apartheid' scenario where the wealthy pay to escape overheating, hunger and conflict while the rest of the world is left to suffer," said Philip Alston, the UN Special Rapporteur on extreme poverty and human rights. "Perversely, while people in poverty are responsible for just a fraction of global emissions, they will bear the brunt of climate change, and have the least capacity to protect themselves."[18] Add to this the prospect of total digital control and the picture of the mess we are in begins to emerge.

The predominant Rightist reaction to the warnings about the looming apocalypse is that they are part of the desperate radical Leftist strategy to sustain its revolutionary zeal after the triumph of capitalism in the 1990s. What the Left cannot accept is that, in spite of all the problems, we live in a relatively peaceful and prosperous era: there never were so few wars, poverty is diminishing even in the least developed countries, life will go on as usual and even get better for most of us. The only way for the radical Left, with its vision of the need for radical change, to survive is to construct a new apocalyptic threat that would replace the old Marxist vision of the proletariat that has nothing but its chains to lose, and the obvious candidate for such a catastrophic vision is ecology – today's ecological movement effectively is a "melon" movement (green on the outside, red inside). To maintain a minimum of credibility, such a vision has to cling on to any bad news that comes along: a melting glacier here, a tornado there, a heatwave somewhere else – they are all read as signs of a forthcoming catastrophe. Our reply to this attack should not be just the enumeration of data that confirm apocalyptic predictions; one should also point out the inner inconsistencies of this critique of the Left. Recall that Trump, one of the great proponents of the denial of global warming, proclaimed a national emergency because of the wave of Latino immigrants entering the US. In Europe also, Rightist populists paint a catastrophic vision of our entire civilization as being under threat from Muslim refugees – if today's trends go on, in a decade or so Europe will be the Muslim province of Europastan . . .

And, as it befits every good conspiracy theory, there has to be a secret agent controlling this attack on our way of life: after the failure of the European communist revolutions in the 1920s, the communist center realized that one has first to destroy the moral foundations of the West (religion, ethnic identity, family values), so it founded the Frankfurt School, whose aim was pronounce family and authority as pathological tools of domination, and to undermine every ethnic identity as oppressive. Today, in the guise of different forms of cultural Marxism, their efforts are finally showing results; our societies are caught in eternal guilt for their alleged sins; they are open to an unbridled invasion of immigrants, lost in empty hedonist individualism and lack of patriotism. This is the secret foundation of political correctness, gender theory, and MeToo – there is no contradiction between the support of Muslim fundamentalism and the politically correct attack on our Christian values: they are the two sides of the same coin. Consequently, in exactly the same way as they reproach radical ecologists, anti-immigrant populists desperately cling to bad news: a rape by immigrants here, a fight among them there – all are read as signs of the forthcoming catastrophe. In short, the new Right has its own apocalyptic vision.

But what about those moderate centrists (like today's "rational optimists," from Steven Pinker to Sam Harris) who reject all apocalyptic visions? Even they entertain their own apocalyptic vision, which is, in a paradoxical self-referential twist, the apocalyptic stance itself: for rational optimists, the greatest threat to our well-being is the growth of irrational panic caused by apocalyptic visions, Leftist or Rightist. So where does this panic come from? Why are we not allowed to simply enjoy our welfare? The standard Leftist answer is obvious: authoritarian power can only reproduce itself through our misery, so it is those in power who sabotage our well-being. In *The Pyramid*, Ismail Kadare proposes a nice version of this conspiracy of power. The novel begins with the Pharaoh Cheops announcing to his advisors that he does not want to build a pyramid like his predecessors. Alarmed by this suggestion, the advisors point out that pyramid building is crucial to preserving his authority: some generations earlier, prosperity had made the people of Egypt more independent, and they began to doubt and resist the Pharaoh's authority. When Cheops sees the necessity to destroy this prosperity, his advisors examine different options to radically diminish prosperity: engaging Egypt in a major war with its neighbors; artificially provoking a large natural catastrophy (like disturbing the regular flow of the Nile and thus ruining agriculture), but they are all rejected as being too dangerous (if Egypt loses the war, Pharaoh himself and his elite may lose power; a natural catastrophe may expose the inability of those in power to control the situation and thus generate chaos). So they return to the idea of building a pyramid so large that its construction will mobilize the resources of the country and drain the prosperity out of Egypt – sapping the energies of its populace will keep everyone in line. The project puts the country into a state of emergency for two decades, with the secret police busy discovering sabotages and organizing Stalinist-style arrests, public confessions, and executions by the Pharaoh's secret police. The novel concludes with a report on how the Pharaoh's wise and ingenious insight was practiced again and again throughout later history, most recently and originally in Albania where, instead of one big pyramid, thousands of bunkers did the same job.

But is this explanation strong enough to account for our late capitalist societies in which those who live inside the cupola of the privileged are not enjoined to suffer for a higher cause but are enjoined to consume and enjoy – i.e., in which the very call to a free life of pleasure is what enslaves us to the system? So the true question is: why does the very call to free pleasure turn into its opposite and produce a life of self-destructive misery? The cult film *The Matrix* provides a hint in this direction – toward the end of the film, Smith, the agent of the Matrix, gives a properly Freudian explanation of our predicament in the Matrix:

Did you know that the first Matrix was designed to be a perfect human world? Where no one suffered, where everyone would be happy? It was a disaster. No one would accept the program. Entire crops of the humans serving as batteries were lost. Some believed we lacked the programming language to describe your perfect world. But I believe that, as a species, human beings define their reality through suffering and misery. The perfect world was a dream that your primitive cerebrum kept trying to wake up from. Which is why the Matrix was re-designed to this: the peak of your civilization.

The agent Smith (let us not forget: not a human being as others, but the direct virtual embodiment of the Matrix itself) is the stand-in for the figure of the psychoanalyst in the universe of the film; his lesson is that the experience of an insurmountable obstacle is a positive condition for us, humans, to perceive something as reality – reality is ultimately that which *resists*. Freud referred to this dimension as the "death drive," a kind of primordial masochism that defines being human: something in ourselves forever resists too much pleasure, and our most intense enjoyments are always in one way or another enjoyments in pain. This is also what is wrong with the latest Leftist ideological dream, that of "fully automated luxury communism" (FALC), "an opportunity to realise a post-work society, where machines do the heavy lifting and employment as we know it is a thing of the past."[19] What we get here is an exemplary case of abstract reasoning that ignores the complexity of the actual situation: not only is there another (much darker) side to fully automated society (new modes of digital control and domination); one confronts here also some much more difficult questions. Will people really just enjoy a peaceful affluent life in FALC, or will new violent tensions emerge in it?

So what is going on? We are increasingly becoming aware of the ultimate uncertainty of our survival: a devastating earthquake, a big asteroid hitting earth, a deadly heatwave, and it's all over. Gilbert Keith Chesterton wrote: "Take away the supernatural and what you are left with is the unnatural." We should endorse this statement, but in the opposite sense, not in the sense intended by Chesterton: we should accept that nature is "unnatural," a freak show of contingent disturbances with no inner rhythm. But there is more, much more, going on.

The lesson of global warming is that the freedom of humankind was possible only against the backdrop of stable natural parameters of life on earth (temperature, composition of the air, sufficient water and energy supply, etc.): humans can "do what they want" only insofar as they remain marginal enough, so that they don't seriously perturb the parameters of life on earth. The limitation of our freedom that becomes palpable with global warming is the paradoxical outcome of the very exponential growth of our freedom and power – i.e., of our growing ability to transform nature around us to the point of destabilizing the very basic geological parameters of life on earth. "Nature" thereby literally becomes a sociohistorical category – recall the famous lines from *The Communist Manifesto*:

> Constant revolutionizing of production, uninterrupted disturbance of all social conditions, everlasting uncertainty and agitation distinguish the bourgeois epoch from all earlier ones. All fixed, fast-frozen relations, with their train of ancient and venerable prejudices and opinions are swept away, all new-formed ones become antiquated before they can ossify. All that is solid melts into air, all that is holy is profaned.

Things went much further here than Marx could have imagined – he couldn't have imagined that the capitalist dynamics of dissolving all particular identities would also affect ethnic and sexual identities; that, concerning sexual practices, "one-sidedness and narrow-mindedness become more and more impossible," and that "all that is solid melts into air, all that is holy is profaned," so that capitalism tends to replace standard normative heterosexuality with a proliferation of unstable shifting identities and/or orientations. Things also go much further in another direction. Science and technology today no longer aim only at understanding and reproducing natural processes, but at generating new forms of life that will surprise us; the goal is no longer just to dominate nature (the way it is), but to generate something new, greater, stronger than ordinary nature, including ourselves – exemplary here is the obsession with artificial intelligence, which aims at producing a brain stronger than the human brain. The dream that sustains the scientific-technological endeavor is to trigger a process with no return, a process that would exponentially reproduce itself and go on on its own. The notion of "second nature" is therefore today more pertinent than ever, in both its main meanings. First, literally, as the artificially generated new nature: monsters of nature, deformed cows and trees, or – a more positive dream – genetically manipulated organisms, "enhanced" in the direction that fits us. Then, the "second nature" in the more standard sense of the autonomization of the results of our own activity: the way our acts elude us in their consequences, the way they generate a monster with a life on its own. It is this horror at the unforeseen results of our own acts that causes shock and awe, not the power of nature over which we have no control. What is new today is the short circuit between these two senses of "second nature": "second nature" in the sense of objective Fate, of the autonomized social process, and "second nature" in the sense of artificially created nature, of natural monsters. The process that threatens to run out of control is no longer just the social process of economic and political development, but new forms of natural processes themselves, from the unforeseen nuclear catastrophe to global warming and the unforeseen consequences of biogenetic manipulations. Can one even imagine what can be the unforeseen result of nanotechnological experiments: new life forms reproducing themselves out of control in a cancer-like way.

We are thus entering a new phase in which it is simply nature itself that melts into air: the main consequence of the scientific breakthroughs in biogenetics is the end of nature. This compels us to give a new twist to Freud's title *Unbehagen in der Kultur* – discontent, uneasiness, in culture. With the latest developments, the discontent shifts from culture to nature itself: nature is no longer "natural," the reliable "dense" background of our lives. It now appears as a fragile mechanism, which, at any point, can explode in a catastrophic direction. How are we to prevent this explosion?

Perhaps, a Scandinavian TV series can give us the first lead. In the superb *The Killing*, one of the two central figures is the autistic Swedish police detective Sarah Lund, who lives alone; rather than becoming engaged in serious relationships, she picks up men in bars for casual sex. Her poor social skills, her difficulty in empathizing, and her inability to channel her emotions make her appear cold, insensitive, and blunt, but she is completely honest and forthright in all aspects. The final (third) season ends with an ethical act so shocking that it perplexed many of the series' most avid followers. Saga (superbly played by Sofie Gråbøl) finally confronts the serial killer Reinhardt, a corporate manager with high political connections. When the two of them are alone in a car, he coldly confesses to her his brutal murders but mockingly claims that she will never succeed in prosecuting him; desperate for her impotence, she executes him with a gun. Is her illegal act a crime or an ethical act – or both? This is the profoundly feminine "toxic masculinity" at its best: breaking the law as an act of ethical duty.

There must be something Scandinavian in this kind of radically ethical feminine stance, since another Swedish girl acted similarly in real life: 15-year-old Greta Thunberg, who, after realizing that the only way to do something about global warming is civil disobedience, instigated a wave of children's school strikes, which spread all around Europe. The fact that she was diagnosed with autism acquires an unexpected political meaning here: far from being a disturbing factor, it is what gives her strength. The definition of autism is "a developmental disorder characterized by difficulty in social interaction and communication and by restricted or repetitive patterns of thought and behavior," and this is exactly what is needed if we are to confront global warming: repetitively insisting on scientific results and ignoring all the rhetorical tricks that obfuscate the scientific message.

When, as happened in recent months, children all around the world go on strike to protest our (adults') ignorance of ecological dangers, we should support them unconditionally, and reject all claims that children "don't understand the complexity of the situation," etc. The most disgusting reaction was that of a Belgian politician: instead of striking, children should rather stay in school and learn . . . Learn what? How to ruin our chances of a future the way their elders (those who are teaching them) did? The second most disgusting reaction came from Angela Merkel, who hinted that children like Greta could not themselves organize such a large strike movement – there must be some dark force pulling the strings behind them, such as Putin . . .

True, children "don't see the complexity" – namely, the complexity of how our politicians are desperately trying to water down the emergency of our predicament. They seem to be the only ones who take seriously (which means here: literally) what scientists are telling us again and again. Greta is fully aware of the logic of fetishist disavowal that determines our predominant reaction to global warming: adults are "always talking about how we should turn off lights, save water, not throw out food. I asked why and they explained about climate change. And I thought this was very strange. If humans could really change the climate, everyone would be talking about it and people wouldn't be talking about anything else. But this wasn't happening."[20] They (adults) know very well what is going on but . . . they add the usual "but nonetheless . . . ," which prevents us from acting upon our knowledge.

Children just know it. The only really "complex" thing are the emperor's new clothes, and children simply see that the emperor is naked, and demand from us that we act upon it.

What does this amount to, concretely? Among other things, it means that, obscene as this may sound, the Left should not be afraid to also learn from Trump. How does Trump operate? Many perspicuous analysts pointed out that, while (mostly, at least) he does not violate explicit laws or rules, he exploits to the extreme the fact that all these laws and rules rely on a rich texture of unwritten rules and customs that tell us how to apply explicit laws and rules – and he brutally disregards these unwritten rules. The latest (and, till now, the most extreme) example of this procedure is Trump's proclamation of a national emergency. His critics were shocked at how he applied this measure, clearly intended only for major catastrophes like a threat of war or natural disaster, in order to build a border to protect US territory from an invented threat. However, it was not only Democrats who were critical of this measure, some Rightists were also alarmed by the fact that Trump's proclamation sets a dangerous precedent: what if a future Leftist Democratic president were to proclaim a national emergency on behalf of, say, global warming? My point is that a Leftist president should do something like this precisely to legitimize fast extraordinary measures – global warming effectively *is* a (not only national) emergency. Proclaimed or not, we *are* in a state of emergency. In view of the latest news about global warming, which makes clear that it progresses much faster than even the pessimists expected, some commentators quite appropriately draw a parallel with World War II – nothing less than a similar global mobilization is needed.

When we ignore the need for such mobilization, we act just like the patient (from a medical joke) who lies in a crowded hospital room and complains to a nurse: "Patients on the other beds are crying and moaning all the time – could you ask them to be more quiet?" The nurse replies: "You have to understand them, they are terminal cases." The patient snaps back: "Ok, but why, then, do you not put them in a special room for terminal cases?" "But this is a room for terminal cases." Is it not the same with all those "realists" who claim that that radical ecologists complain too much about our predicament, acting as if we – humanity – are a terminal case? What they are ignoring is that we *are* indeed a terminal case.

So what will happen in the in-between time, before the catastrophe strikes with full force? Cyril Ramaphosa, current president of South Africa, made back in the early 1990s a comparison between boiling a frog and the new ANC government's strategy for dealing with the whites: "it would be like boiling a frog alive, which is done by raising the temperature very slowly. Being cold-blooded, the frog does not notice the slow temperature increase, but if the temperature is raised suddenly, the frog will jump out of the water. [Ramaphosa] meant that the black majority would pass laws transferring wealth, land, and economic power from white to black slowly and incrementally, until the whites lost all they had gained in South Africa, but without taking too much from them at any given time to cause them to rebel or fight."[21] Ramaphosa is one of the wealthiest South African businessmen, worth more than half a billion US dollars, so if we are talking about redistributing wealth, should he not also be thrown into the pot to boil slowly? Or do we aim only at replacing the old white ruling class with the new black one, with the black majority stuck in the same poverty?

There is, however, another much more interesting use of Ramaphosa's rather unfortunate metaphor: does it not render perfectly how (until now and in the developed countries) we experience the ecological threat? While we are quite literally boiled in the process of global warming, it seems that cruel Mother Nature is playing with us, humans, the same game of slowly heating the water (and the air); the process of global warming is slow and full of ambiguities exploited by the deniers - for example, it generates local effects of extreme cold spells, enabling stable geniuses like Trump to claim that we need more warm weather. One of the effects of global warming may be that the Gulf Stream will change course and no longer reach Northwestern Europe, leading to a new ice age from France to Scandinavia. It is as if the "global warming project" is executed in such a way that it makes sure that the majority of people will remain skeptical and refuse to do anything about it. Just as a reminder that things are maybe serious, we are from time to time hit by a heatwave or an unexpected tornado, but such calamities are quickly interpreted as freakish accidents. In this way, even if we are aware of the threat, the subtle message of our media is that we should just go on living the way we do, with no great changes. Recycle your trash, put your Coke cans into one bag and old newspapers into another, and you did your duty . . .

There is another use of Ramaphosa's metaphor that is no less pertinent with regard to our survival as humans: is something similar not going on with the threat of the digital control of our lives? We are definitely entering the era of a digital police state: in one way or another, digital machines are registering all our personal facts and acts, from health to shopping habits, from political opinions to amusement, from business decisions to sexual practices. With today's supercomputers, this vast amount of data can be neatly categorized and organized in individual files, and all the data made accessible to state agencies and private corporations. However, the true game changer is not digital control as such but the pet project of brain scientists: digital machines that will be able to directly read our minds (without us knowing it, of course).

The agents of this process - i.e., those in power - rely on a series of strategies to keep us in the position of the frog, unaware that the water is getting hotter and hotter. One is to dismiss the threat as utopian; we are still far from it: being controlled by mind-reading machines is just liberal-Leftist paranoia. Another is to put forward the potential (mostly medical) benefits of this process: if a machine can read the mind of a guy who is totally crippled, it will make everyday life for him much easier; for example, he can inform those around him what he wants by just clearly thinking about it. More generally, our media repeatedly point out how much easier everyday life will be for us in a digitally controlled society. My favorite story here is the one about eye scanning when we enter a department store: the machine identifies us by scanning our eye, contacts our bank account, and establishes our purchase power; in addition, it automatically registers what we have when we exit the store, so that we have to do nothing. The store becomes a place where we just enter, take what we want or need and leave.

With both global warming and the exploding digital control, changes are gradual, so that, except for brief emergencies, we are able to ignore the effects in our daily lives – until, all of a sudden, it will be too late, and we will realize that we lost it all. But there is a difference between boiling a frog and global warming or digital control: in both the ecological threat and the threat of digital control, there is no one else, no inhuman agent gradually raising the temperature or enhancing digital control. We are doing it to ourselves; we are raising the heat gradually, thereby enabling us to ignore the threat. We ourselves are the frogs gradually boiling ourselves to death.

So what will happen? Nothing, probably. We need more (hopefully not too big) catastrophes to awaken us and make ready to proclaim a true state of emergency, to fight the war against ourselves that lies ahead. This is how communism will eventually enter the stage: not through a simple parliamentary electoral process, of course, but through a state of emergency enforced on us by an apocalyptic threat. Resistance against this radicalization is extremely strong, as we can see in the latest fictional example of the radical feminine political agent, Daenerys in *Game of Thrones*. The last season of the series gave rise to public outcry which culminated in a petition (signed by almost one million outraged viewers) to disqualify the entire season and shoot a new one. The ferocity of the debate is in itself proof that the ideological stakes must be high.

The dissatisfaction turned around a couple of points: a bad scenario (under pressure of quickly ending the series, the complexity of the narrative got simplified), bad psychology (Daenery turning into the Mad Queen is not justified by her character development), etc. One of the few intelligent voices in the debate was that of Stephen King, who noted that dissatisfaction was not generated by the bad ending but by the ending as such – in this epoch of series which, in principle, go on indefinitely, the idea of a narrative closure becomes intolerable. It is true that, in the series' swift denouement, a strange logic takes over, a logic that does not violate credible psychology but rather the narrative presuppositions of a TV series. In the last season, it's just the preparation for a battle, mourning and destruction after the battle, and the battle itself in all its meaninglessness – much more realistic for me than the usual gothic melodramatic plots.

The universe of *Game of Thrones* is (like that of *Lord of the Rings*) spiritualized but godless: there are supernatural forces, but they are part of nature, with no higher gods or priests serving them. Within this frame, the outline of Season 8 is deeply consistent: it stages three consecutive struggles. The first is between humanity and its inhuman Others (the Night Army from the North led by the Night King); between the two main groups of humans (the evil Lannisters and the coalition against them led by Daenerys and the Starks); the inner conflict between Daenerys and the Starks. This is why the battles in Season 8 follow a logical path from an external opposition to the inner split: the defeat of the inhuman Night Army, the defeat of the Lannisters and the destruction of the King's Landing; the last struggle the Starks and Daenerys – ultimately between traditional "good" nobility (Starks) faithfully protecting their subjects from bad tyrants, and Daenerys as a new type of a strong leader, a kind of progressive bonapartist acting on behalf of the underprivileged. The stakes of the final conflict are, thus, to put it in a simple way: should the revolt against tyranny be just a fight for the return of the old kinder version of the same hierarchic order, or should it develop into the search for a new order needed?

The dissatisfied viewers have a problem with this last struggle – no wonder, since it combines the rejection of a radical change with an old anti-feminist motif at work in Hegel, Schelling, and Wagner. In his *Phenomenology of Spirit*, Hegel introduces his notorious notion of womankind as "the everlasting irony of the community": womankind "changes by intrigue the universal end of the government into a private end, transforms its universal activity into a work of some particular individual, and perverts the universal property of the state into a possession and ornament for the family."[22] These lines fit perfectly the figure of Ortrud in Wagner's *Lohengrin*: for Wagner, there is nothing more horrible and disgusting than a woman who intervenes in political life, driven by the desire for power. In contrast to male ambition, a woman wants power in order to promote her own narrow family interests or, even worse, her personal caprice, incapable as she is of perceiving the universal dimension of state politics. How are we not to recall F.W.J. Schelling's claim that "the same principle carries and holds us in its ineffectiveness which would consume and destroy us in its effectiveness?"[23] – a power that, when it is kept in its proper place, can be benign and pacifying, turns into its radical opposite, into the most destructive fury, the moment it intervenes at a higher level, the level that is not its own. The same femininity that, within the close circle of family life, is the very power of protective love, turns into obscene frenzy when displayed at the level of public and state affairs. The lowest point of the dialogue is the moment when Daenerys tells Jon that if he cannot love her as a queen then fear should reign – the embarrassingly vulgar motif of a sexually unsatisfied woman who explodes into destructive fury.

But – let's bite our sour apple now – what about Daenerys's murderous outbursts? Can the ruthless killing of the thousands of ordinary people in King's Landing really be justified as a necessary step to universal freedom? Yes, this is inexcusable – but at this point, we should remember that the scenario was written by two men. Daenerys as the Mad Queen is strictly a male fantasy, so the critics were right when they pointed out that her descent into madness is psychologically unjustified. The view of Daenerys with a mad furious expression flying on a dragon and burning houses and people is simply the expression of patriarchal ideology with its fear of a strong political woman.

The final destiny of leading women in *Game of Thrones* fits these coordinates. Central is the opposition between Cersei and Daenerys, the two women in/of power, and the message of their conflict is clear: even if the good one wins, power corrupts a woman. Arya (who saved them all by single-handedly killing the Night King) also disappears, sailing to the West of the West (as if to colonize America). The one who remains (as the queen of the autonomous kingdom of the North) is Sansa, a type of women beloved by today's capitalism: she combines feminine softness and understanding with a good dose of spirit of manipulation, and thus fully fits the new power relations. This marginalization of women is a key moment of the general liberal conservative lesson of the finale: revolutions are destined to go wrong and lead to new tyrannies.

Does the same not hold for Christopher Nolan's *The Dark Knight Rises*, the final part of his Batman trilogy? Although Bane is the official villain, there are indications that he, much more than Batman himself, is the film's authentic hero distorted as its villain: he is ready to sacrifice his life for his love, ready to risk everything for what he perceives as injustice, and this basic fact is occluded by superficial and rather ridiculous signs of destructive evil. And in *Black Panther*, is not Killmonger the true hero? He prefers to die free than to be healed and survive in the false abundance of Wakanda – the strong ethical impact of Killmonger's last words immediately ruin the idea that he is a simple villain. The liberal conservative lesson is best imparted by the following words of Jon to Daenerys:

> I never thought that dragons will exist again; no one did. The people who follow you know that you made something impossible happen. Maybe that helps them believe that you can make other impossible things happen: build a world that's different from the shit one they've always known. But if you use them [dragons] to melt castles and burn cities, you're no different. You're just more of the same.

Consequently, Jon kills out of love (saving the cursed woman from herself, as the old male-chauvinist formula says), the only social agent in the series who really fought for something new, for a new world that would put an end to old injustices. So no wonder the last episode was well received: justice prevailed – what kind of justice? Each person is allocated to his/her proper place, Daenerys who disturbed the established order killed and flown away to eternity by her last dragon. The new king is Bran: crippled, all-knowing, who wants nothing – with the evocation of the insipid wisdom that the best rulers are those who do not want power. In a supremely politically correct ending, a disabled king now rules, helped by a dwarf, and chosen by the new wise elite. (A nice detail: the laughter that ensues when one of them proposes a more democratic selection of the king.) And one cannot but note that those faithful to Daenerys to the end are more ethnically diverse, while the new rulers are clearly white Nordic. The radical queen who wanted more freedom for everyone irrespective of their social standing and race is eliminated, things are back to normal, the people's misery leavened by a resigned wisdom (just remember that the first measures envisaged by the new ruling council are the restoration of the army and brothels . . .).

And is Greta not our Daenerys? Is she not the same Mad Queen who wants real change? And is not the answer of our establishment to her acts not the same cynical wisdom as displayed by the ruling council at the end of *Game of Thrones*?

7

They Are Both Worse!

When I try to explain to students what "free association" means in psychoanalytic treatment, I regularly refer to the well-known saying: "Don't throw the baby out with the dirty bathwater!" When the psycho-analyst asks his patient to "freely associate," i.e., to suspend control of his conscious ego and say anything that comes to mind, does he not demand from him to do almost the exact opposite? The analyst asks the patient to "throw out the baby" (his ego) and keep only the "dirty water" (of his free associations). The idea is, of course, that this "dirty water" will bring out the hidden truth of the sane and healthy ego itself. Don't forget that the dirt in the water comes from the baby, not from outside!

Does the same not hold also for many fake ecologists? They are obsessed by healthy "sustainable" dwellings in a clean green habitat, ignoring the dirty water that freely floats in the polluted surroundings. If one wants to deal with pollution in a serious way, the first thing to do is to focus on the dirty surroundings and to analyze how our isolated "sustainable" habitats merely export the pollution to their environs. Perhaps we should adopt the opposite approach, along the lines of what they are doing in Japan: concentrate as much pollution and pop-ulation in big cities, so that they function as dirty babies in (relatively) clean water.

Another example: the sheer number of pedophiliac crimes that have been taking place in the Catholic Church all around the world, from Ireland and Pennsylvania to Australia, crimes committed by members of the institution that claims to be the moral compass of our society, compels us to reject the easy idea that the Church should throw out the dirty pedophiliac water but keep the sane body of its good priests. This abuse is not something that happens because the institution has to accommodate itself to the pathological realities of libidinal life in order to survive, but something that the institution itself needs in order to reproduce itself.

What this means is that, when we see how a system is confronted with its dark side, we should not simply support its good side; we should also inquire into how and why did this good side gives birth to the bad side – in some sense, both sides are worse. Back in the late 1920s, Stalin was asked by a journalist which deviation is worse, the Rightist one (Bukharin and company) or the Leftist one (Trotsky and company), and he snapped back: "They are both worse!" It is a sad sign of our predicament that, when we are confronted with a political choice and asked to take a side, even if it is only the less bad one, quite often the reply that imposes itself is: "But they are both worse!" This, of course, does not mean that both poles of the alternative simply amount to the same – in concrete situations, we should, for example, conditionally support the protests of the "yellow vests" (*les gilets jaunes*) in France or make a tactical pact with liberals to block fundamentalist threats to our freedoms (say, when fundamentalists want to limit abortion rights or pursue an openly racist politics). But what it does mean is that most of the choices imposed on us by the big media are false choices – their function is to obfuscate a true choice. The sad lesson to be drawn from this is: if one side in a conflict is bad, the opposite side is not necessarily good.

Let's take today's situation in Venezuela: Maduro or Guaido? They are both worse, although not in the same sense. Maduro is "worse" because his reign brought Venezuela to a complete economic fiasco with a majority of the population living in abject poverty, a fiasco that cannot be attributed only to the sabotage of internal and external enemies. It is enough to bear in mind the indelible damage that the Maduro regime did to the idea of socialism: for decades to come, we will have to listen to variations on the theme "You want socialism? Look at Venezuela . . . ." However, Guaido is no less "worse": when he assumed his virtual presidency, we were without doubt witnessing a well-prepared coup orchestrated by the US, not an autonomous popular insurgency (which is precisely the "better" third term missing in the choice between Maduro and Guaido, who are "both worse").

And we should not shirk from applying the same logic to the struggle between populists and establishment liberals which characterizes Western democracies. With regard to US politics, this means that the answer to "Who is worse, Trump or Clinton (or now Pelosi)?" our answer should be: they are both worse! Trump is "worse," of course: an agent of "socialism for the rich," systematically undermining the norms of civilized political life, dismantling the rights of minorities, ignoring threats to our environment, etc. However, in another sense, the democratic establishment is also "worse": we should never forget that it was the immanent failure of the democratic establishment that opened up the space for Trump's populism. The first step in defeating Trump is therefore a radical critique of the democratic establishment. Why can Trump and other populists exploit ordinary people's fears and grievances? Because they felt betrayed by those in power.

Let's now move to a more complex case. Western liberal universalism versus the assertion of ("anti-Eurocentric") particular identities. In this choice also, both terms are worse – why? The Jewish joke we quoted in the chapter on nomadic proletarians makes clear what the problem is with fake Left-liberal "antiracists." In their zeal for identity politics, they all support the effort of the black communities to retain and strengthen their cultural identity; they worry that black communities will lose their specific identity and get drowned in the global universe defined by white categories, a world in which they are a priori in a subordinated position. However, the reason white liberal "antiracists" support black identity is a much more murky affair: what they really fear is that the blacks will leave behind their particular identity, assume "being nothing" and formulate their own universality as different from the universality imposed by hegemonic white culture and politics. *This* option is the "better" one, the one with regard to which both terms of the original choice (liberal universalism or marginal particular identities) are "worse." Malcolm X saw this in an exemplary way: instead of searching for particular black roots and identity, he accepted the X (the lack of ethnic roots) as a unique chance to assert a universality different from the one imposed by whites.

And here is our last, even more problematic, example of "both are worse." In 2018, a video clip went viral on the web. It shows a tense scene near the Lincoln Memorial in Washington: at the end of Indigenous Peoples March, an elderly Native American man steadily beats his drum while singing a song of unity urging participants to "be strong" against the ravages of colonialism that include police brutality, poor access to healthcare, and the ill effects of climate change on reservations. He is surrounded by a group of young, mostly white teenage boys, several of them wearing "Make America Great Again" caps; one of them stands about a foot from the drummer's face wearing a relentless smirk. Now we know who these two are: the Native American is Nathan Phillips, an Omaha elder, a veteran in the indigenous rights movement, and the smirking young boy is Nick Sandmann, a student at a Catholic high school.

The video of this confrontation fully deserves its fame: it provides a kind of condensed index of our ideological predicament. As expected, the predominant liberal reaction to it focused on Nick's insolent smirk, seeing in it a pure expression of alt-Right racism, mocking not only protests against our injustices but also authentic displays of the minority cultures. I fully endorse this view. For me, Nick's smirk stands for the worst of Americanism, so when I saw the clip, I was personally disgusted by the expression of Nick's face, and I was haunted for days by its ignorantly brutal self-satisfaction. (Nick is now defending his actions, claiming that he was just trying to defuse the tension: "I was not intentionally making faces at the protester. I did smile at one point because I wanted him to know that I was not going to become angry . . . ." The absurdity of this counter-claim is breathtaking: if his smirk expresses benevolence, then it is the most arrogant and patronizing benevolence the world has ever seen, similar to that of a father trying to contain his wild child.)

However – this is my professional deformation as a philosopher – I feel compelled to take a critical look also at the opposite side. As it was reported in the media, Phillips is not only a veteran of Native American protest movements, but is also a Vietnam war veteran, which means that, for him, maintaining his authentic cultural roots posed no obstacle to his becoming involved in the most efficient modern military machine. We can easily presume that, sincere as it undoubtedly was, his continuing immersion into Native American culture even made his participation easier. There are many similar examples of an "authentic" traditional cultural practice rendering possible the efficient participation in modern war at its most brutal. (According to some sources, Phillips never actually served in Vietnam – but if this proved to be true, presenting himself as a Vietnam veteran makes his identification with the US Army military operations even stronger: not something that he regrets, but a declaration of faith.)

Anyone acquainted by the recent history of Zen Buddhism in Japan knows how, in the era of brutal military expansion of Japan (the 1930s and 1940s), the large majority of the Buddhist establishment actively supported war efforts, even providing justification for them. For example, D.T. Suzuki, well known in the hippy times as the ultimate popularizer of Zen, wrote in 1930s a series of texts in which he tried to demonstrate how the experience of Zen enlightenment makes a soldier more efficient – if you are aware that you don't have a stable Self and that the world is just a dance of fleeting phenomena, it is much easier to kill. In Suzuki's own words, when a soldier attacks an enemy with a sword, "it is really not he but the sword itself that does the killing. He had no desire to do harm to anybody, but the enemy appears and makes himself a victim. It is as though the sword performs automatically its function of justice, which is the function of mercy."

How far authentic Buddhism is from our usual notion of compassion for the suffering of others is made clear by the story concerning a disciple who once asked Buddha: "Master, should we be compassionate to others?" After a few moments of contemplation, Buddha answered: "There are no others." This is the only consequential answer from the Buddhist standpoint of denying any substantial reality of human Selves: we suffer insofar as we perceive ourselves as substantial Selves, so the true overcoming of our suffering resides not in getting rid of what our Self perceives as an obstacle to its happiness but in getting rid of the Self itself. No wonder that Buddhism quickly abandoned this radical stance – it all began to go wrong with the Mahayana turn. The main split of Buddhism is the one between Hinayana ("the small wheel") and Mahayana ("the great wheel"). The first is elitist and demanding, trying to maintain fidelity to Buddha's teaching, focusing on the individual's effort to get rid of the illusion of the Self and attain Enlightenment. The second, which arose through the split from the first one, subtly shifts the accent onto compassion for others: its central figure is bodhisattva, the individual who, after achieving Enlightenment, decides out of compassion to return to the world of material illusions in order to help others to achieve Enlightenment – i.e., to work to end the suffering of all sentient beings. It is easy to locate the inconsistency of the Mahayana move, which cannot but lead to fateful consequences: when a bodhisattva returns to the life of illusory passions out of compassion for all those who are still caught in the Wheel of Craving in order to help them achieve Enlightenment and enter nirvana, there is a simple question to be raised: if, as radical Buddhists emphatically point out, entering nirvana does not mean that we leave this world and enter another higher reality – in other words, if reality remains as it is and all that changes in nirvana is the individual's attitude toward it – why, then, in order to help other suffering beings, must we *return* to our ordinary reality? Why can't we do it while dwelling in the state of Enlightenment in which, as we are taught, we remain living in this world? There is thus no need for Mahayana, for the "larger wheel": the small (Hinayana) wheel is large enough to allow for the Enlightened one in helping others. In other words, is the very concept of bodhisattva not based on a theologico-metaphysical misunderstanding of the nature of nirvana? Does it not underhandedly change nirvana into a higher metaphysical reality? No wonder Mahayana Buddhists were the first to give a religious twist to Buddhism, abandoning Buddha's original agnostic materialism, his explicit indifference toward the religious topic.

If proof were needed of the violent potential of Buddhism, here is the latest case:

Myanmar police have issued an arrest warrant for Ashin Wirathu, a firebrand monk known as the "Buddhist Bin Laden." Wirathu has long been accused of inciting sectarian violence against Myanmar's Muslims, in particular the Rohingya community, through hate-filled, Islamaphobic speeches. While Buddhism espouses non-violence, Wirathu has openly said he is "proud to be called a radical Buddhist" and in a 2013 sermon said of Muslims in Myanmar: "You can be full of kindness and love, but you cannot sleep next to a mad dog."[24]

Maybe, this brings us to one of the most accurate characterizations of the authentic Buddhist stance that avoids such dangers: the truly enlightened person is the one who can sleep next to a mad dog.

What this means is that, to put it in a brutal (and for some people undoubtedly "insensitive") way, in spite of my full sympathy for and solidarity with Phillips, I unconditionally want to assert my right to consider performing such "authentic" rituals stupid, inefficient, and even counterproductive. Yes, of course, we should fight people like Sandmann, but not primarily by way of drumbeating accompanied by ritualistic chanting – if anything, our almost hypnotic immersion into the numb rhythm of such performances deactivates our critical rational thinking, which, today, is needed more than ever. We don't have to become animists in order to fight military imperialism.

Not all our choices, luckily, are of this sort, where both sides are worse. Just think about the latest case of toxic masculinity, the autistic Greta from Sweden who triggered a series of school strikes against global warming. The lesson of her acts is not just political; it also demonstrates that one should reject the standard series of oppositions between masculine and feminine (order versus chaos, reason versus emotion, hierarchy versus cooperation, relations with objects versus interpersonal relations, etc.). It is much more appropriate to talk about two different combinations of order versus chaos, etc.: feminine "toxic masculinity" detectable in the line that runs from Antigone to Greta Thunberg is different from its masculine version, which is an offspring of patriarchal authority in decay. The latter is the (constitutive) exception to the paternal Law (the explosion of violence that counteracts the perceived impotence of the male master), while the feminine "toxic masculinity" is immanent to the sense of justice, it is an act of fidelity to justice.

8

A Desperate Call for (T)Reason

The latest news from the border of Ukraine and Russia indicates that we already live in a prewar situation – so what should we, ordinary people, do when the explosion of global madness looms? Perhaps, our first reaction should be to confront such dark news with another series of even more catastrophic news. Recent scientific reports make it clear that our global food system is broken: according to 130 national academies of science and medicine across the world, billions are either underfed or overweight and our food production is driving the planet toward climate catastrophe. To provide an environmentally friendly diet for all of us will require a radical transformation of the system.

But it's not just the global food system that is out of joint. As we learned abundantly from the latest environmental reports, the scientific diagnosis of our predicament is very simple and straight: if we don't cut greenhouse gas emissions by 45 percent in the next 12 years, coastal cities will be inundated, food will run short, etc. And, again, to do it, a rapid radical social transformation is needed that will deeply affect all spheres of our life. So how to achieve this? Apart from rapidly phasing out carbon-intensive fuels, another more dramatic approach is considered: SRM (solar radiation management), the continuous massive dispersal of aerosols into our atmosphere to reflect and absorb sunlight and thus cool the planet. However, SRM is extremely risky: it could decrease crop yields, irreparably alter the water cycle, not to mention many other "unknown unknowns" - we cannot even imagine how the fragile balance of our earth functions, and in what unpredictable ways such geoengineering can disturb it. Plus, it is easy to guess why SRM is so popular with many corporations: instead of a painful social change, it offers the prospect of a straight technological fix of our biggest problem. We are in a real deadlock: if we do nothing we are doomed, and whatever we do involves mortal risks. Who will make the decisions here? Who is even qualified to do it?[25] Decisions are to be made here that are to a large extent based on scientific reasoning, not on direct perceptions of interests: even if we already feel and experience effects of ecological disturbances, our daily lives are not yet truly shattered.

Phenomena like global warming make us aware that, with all the universality of our theoretical and practical activity, we are at a certain basic level just another living species on planet Earth. Our survival depends on certain natural parameters that we automatically take for granted. "Nature" thereby literally becomes a sociohistorical category, but not in the exalted Marxist sense (the content of what is - or counts for us as - "nature" is always overdetermined by historical conditions that structure our horizon of our understanding of nature). It becomes a sociohistorical category in the much more radical and literal sense; nature is not just a stable background of human activity, but is affected by this activity in its very basic components.

In short, the prospect of geoengineering implies that we are knee-deep in "Anthropocene," a new epoch in the life of our planet in which we, humans, cannot any longer rely on the Earth as a reservoir ready to absorb the consequences of our productive activity. Earth is no longer the impenetrable background/horizon of our productive activity; it emerges as a(nother) finite object that we can inadvertently destroy or transform to make it unlivable. Therein resides the paradox of

Anthropocene: humanity became aware of its self-limitation as a species precisely when it became so strong that it influenced the balance of the entire life on Earth. It was able to dream of dominating and exploiting nature as long as its influence on nature (Earth) was marginal – that is, against the background of stable nature. The paradox is thus that the more the reproduction of nature depends on human activity, the more it escapes our control. What eludes us is not just the hidden side of nature but, above all, the impenetrable consequences of our own activity.

So yes, we are in a deep mess: there is no simple "democratic" solution here. The idea that people themselves (not just governments and corporations) should decide sounds deep, but it begs an important question: even if their comprehension is not distorted by corporate interests, what qualifies them to pass a judgment in such a delicate matter? But what we can do is at least set the priorities straight and admit the absurdity of our geopolitical war games when the very planet for which wars are fought is under threat.

The logic of nation-state competition is extremely dangerous because it runs directly against the urgent need to establish a new mode of relating to our environs, a radical politico-economic change called by Peter Sloterdijk "the domestication of the wild animal Culture." Until now, each culture disciplined/educated its own members and guaranteed civic peace among them in the guise of state power, but the relationship between different cultures and states was permanently under the shadow of potential war, with each state of peace nothing more than a temporary armistice. The entire ethic of a state culminates in the highest act of heroism, the readiness to sacrifice one's life for one's nation-state, which means that the wild barbarian relations between states serve as the foundation of the ethical life within a state. Is today's North Korea, with its ruthless pursuit of nuclear weapons and rockets set to hit distant targets, not the ultimate example of this logic of unconditional nation-state sovereignty?

However, the moment we fully accept the fact that we live on a Spaceship Earth, the task that urgently imposes itself is that of civilizing civilizations themselves, of imposing universal solidarity and cooperation among all human communities, a task rendered all the more difficult by the ongoing rise of sectarian religious and ethnic "heroic" violence and readiness to sacrifice oneself (and the world) for one's specific Cause.

Reason thus compels us to commit treason here: to betray our Cause, to refuse to participate in the ongoing war games. If we really care for the fate of the people who make up our nation, our motto should be: "America last, China last, Russia last . . ." Half a century ago, Huey Newton, the founder and theorist of the Black Panther Party, saw clearly the limitation of local (national) resistance to the global reign of capital. He even took a key step further and rejected the term "decolonization" as being inappropriate – one cannot fight global capitalism from the position of national unities. Here are his statements from a singular dialogue with the Freudian psychoanalyst Erik Erikson from 1972:

We in the Black Panther Party saw that the United States was no longer a nation. It was something else; it was more than a nation. It had not only expanded its territorial boundaries, but it had expanded all of its controls as well. We called it an empire. Now at one time the world had an empire in which the conditions of rule were different – the Roman Empire. The difference between the Roman and the American empires is that other nations were able to exist external to and independent of the Roman Empire because their means of exploration, conquest, and control were all relatively limited. But when we say "empire" today, we mean precisely what we say. An empire is a nation-state that has transformed itself into a power controlling all the world's lands and people.

We believe that there are no more colonies or neocolonies. If a people is colonized, it must be possible for them to decolonize and become what they formerly were. But what happens when the raw materials are extracted and labor is exploited within a territory dispersed over the entire globe? When the riches of the whole earth are depleted and used to feed a gigantic industrial machine in the imperialists' home? Then the people and the economy are so integrated into the imperialist empire that it's impossible to "decolonize," to return to the former conditions of existence. If colonies cannot "decolonize" and return to their original existence as nations, then nations no longer exist. Nor, we believe, will they ever exist again. And since there must be nations for revolutionary nationalism or internationalism to make sense, we decided that we would have to call ourselves something new.[26]

Is this not our predicament today, much more than in Newton's time? One can question Newton's name for the new dimension – "revolutionary intercommunalism" – but still fully endorse his basic communist insight. How many of today's Leftists, caught in the quagmire of "decolonization" and other items of identity politics, are ready to act upon Newton's diagnosis?

The last meeting of the heads of G20 in Osaka (June 2019) and the surrounding events provided a sad view of the emerging New World Order: Trump exchanging love messages with Kim Yong Un and inviting him to the White House; Putin jovially clapping hands with

Mohammad bin Salman, and so on, while Merkel and Tusk, the two voices of old European reason, were marginalized and mostly ignored. This *now* is very tolerant: they are all respecting each other, no one is imposing on others' imperialist Eurocentrist notions like women's rights. This new spirit is best encapsulated by the interview Putin gave to the *Financial Times* on the eve of the Osaka summit, in which, as expected, he lambasted the "liberal idea," claiming that it had "outlived its purpose." Riding on the wave of the "public turn against immigration, open borders and multiculturalism," Putin's evisceration of liberalism,

> chimes with anti-establishment leaders from US president Donald Trump to Hungary's Viktor Orbán, Matteo Salvini in Italy, and the Brexit insurgency in the UK. "[Liberals] cannot simply dictate anything to anyone just like they have been attempting to do over the recent decades," he said. Mr Putin branded Chancellor Angela Merkel's decision to admit more than 1m refugees to Germany, mainly from war-ravaged Syria, as a "cardinal mistake." But he praised Donald Trump for trying to stop the flow of migrants and drugs from Mexico. "This liberal idea presupposes that nothing needs to be done. That migrants can kill, plunder and rape with impunity because their rights as migrants have to be protected." He added: "Every crime must have its punishment. The liberal idea has become obsolete. It has come into conflict with the interests of the overwhelming majority of the population."[27]

There is no surprise here, and the same holds for how Donald Tusk, the European Council president, reacted to Putin: "What I find really obsolete is authoritarianism, personality cults and the rule of oligarchs" – a toothless assertion of empty principles that avoids the roots of the crisis. Liberal optimists desperately cling to good signs here and there (the strong Leftist turn of the US younger generation; the fact that Trump got three million fewer votes than Clinton and that his victory was more the result of manipulations within electoral districts; the re-emergence of the European liberal Left in countries like Slovakia . . .), but they are not strong to affect the basic global trend.

The only interesting feature of Putin's interview, the point at which one can feel how he really speaks from his heart, occurs when he solemnly declares his zero tolerance for spies who betray their country: "Treason is the gravest crime possible and traitors must be punished. I am not saying that the Salisbury incident is the way to do it . . . but traitors must be punished." It is clear from this outburst that Putin has no personal sympathy for Snowden or Assange: he just helps them to annoy his enemies, and one can only imagine the fate of an eventual Russian Snowden or Assange. One can only wonder at some Western Leftists who continue to claim that, in spite of his socially conservative stance, Putin still nonetheless poses an obstacle to US world domination and should for this reason be viewed with sympathy.

Every authentic Leftist should ferociously oppose the claim that treason (the betrayal of one's own nation-state) is the gravest crime possible: no, there are circumstances when such treason is the greatest act of ethical fidelity. Today, such treason is personified by names like Assange, Manning, and Snowden.

The West . . .

9

Democratic Socialism and
Its Discontents

Now that Alexandria Ocasio-Cortez has joined Bernie Sanders as the public face of the left wing of the Democratic Party, with others waiting in the shadows to explode onto the US national scene, it is no surprise that, amongst the wide scope of reactions, the term "democratic social-ism" gained (limited) acceptability in one of the two US main parties. Republican media predictably spread fear: democratic socialists plan to abolish capitalism, introduce Venezuelan-style state terror, and bring poverty, etc. In a more restrained way, centrist Democrats warn about the non-intended catastrophic economic consequences of democratic socialist proposals: how should money be raised for universal health-care, for example. (Incidentally, one should recall here how even the most daring proposals of today's democratic socialists do not come even close to moderate European social democracy of half a century ago – proof of how the center of gravity of the entire political field has shifted to the right.) Even on the liberal Left side of the Democratic Party, there are bad surprises. In the long list of Obama's endorsements of the Democratic candidates for the mid-term elections (more than 80 names), one looks in vain for Ocasio-Cortez. Echoing Nancy Pelosi, who stated "I have to say, we're capitalists, that's just the way it is," even the "Leftist" Elisabeth Warren declared herself "capitalist to my bones."

The latest – and morally most problematic – fad in this series is the charge of anti-Semitism addressed at anyone who deviates to the Left from the acceptable Left-liberal establishment. Until recently, the label "anti-Semitism" was used against any critique of the state of Israel and the way it deals with Palestinians; now, it is mobilized more and more to disqualify anyone on the Left perceived as "too radical," from Corbyn in the UK to Ocasio-Cortez in the US. Anti-Semites in one's own country (Poland, Hungary, Baltic states) are tolerated insofar as they turn into Zionist supporters of Israeli politics in the West Bank, while Leftists who sympathize with West Bank Palestinians, but who also warn against the resurgent anti-Semitism in Europe, are denounced all the time. This rise of the weird figure of anti-Semitic Zionists is one of the most worrying signs of our decay.

However, while these external enemies and attacks can only bolster democratic socialists' readiness to fight, much more fatal limitations lurk in the very heart of the democratic socialist project. Today's democratic socialism is infinitely superior to the academic radicals who flourished in past decades, for the simple reason that it stands for an actual political movement that mobilizes hundreds of thousands of ordinary people, registering and articulating their dissatisfaction. Problems begin when we raise the simple question: what do democratic socialists effectively want? The Rightist reproach against them is that, beneath their innocent-sounding concrete proposals to raise taxes, improve healthcare, etc., there is a dark project to destroy capitalism and its freedoms. My fear is exactly the opposite one: that beneath their concrete welfare state proposals there is nothing, no great project, just a vague idea of more social justice. The idea is simply that, through electoral pressure, the center of gravity will move back to the Left.

But is, in the (not so) long term, this enough? Do the challenges that we face, from global warming to refugees, from digital control to biogenetic manipulations, not require nothing less than a global reorganization of our societies? Whatever happens, two things are sure: none of this will be enacted by some new version of a Leninist communist party, but nor will it happen as part of our parliamentary democracy. It is not just a matter of one political party winning more votes and enacting social democratic measures.

This brings us to the fatal limitation of democratic socialists. Back in 1985, Félix Guattari and Toni Negri published a short book in French, *Les Nouveaux Espaces de liberté*, whose title was changed for the English translation into *Communists Like Us*. The implicit message of this change was the same as that of democratic socialists: "Don't be afraid, we are ordinary guys like you, we don't pose any threat, life will just go on when we will win . . . ." This, unfortunately, is not the option. Radical changes are needed for our survival, and life will *not* go on as usual, we will have to change even in our innermost life.

So we should of course fully support democratic socialists; if we just wait for the right moment to enact a radical change, this moment will never arrive, we have to begin with where we are. But we should do this without illusions, fully aware that our future will demand much more than electoral games and social democratic measures. We are at the beginning of a dangerous voyage on which our survival depends.

And, finally, this brings me back to my "controversial" stance toward Trump. Since his election to the presidency, I have often been asked by friends and "friends" whether I still stand by my preference for Trump over Clinton, or do I now admit that I was terribly wrong. My answer is easy to guess: not only do I stand by what I said, but I think recent events fully confirmed my choice. Why? The growing lack of agreement on the basics in US politics comes from two sides. First, Trump broke the established order from the side of the populist Right, and then Left democrats (Sanders and others) broke it from the Left. These two ruptures are not symmetrical. The struggle between Trump and the liberal establishment is a cultural-ideological struggle within the same space of global capitalism, while the Left Democrats began to question this global capitalist order itself. This is why the only true struggle going on today is taking place within the Democratic Party itself.

Liberals who are panicked by Trump dismiss the idea that his victory can start a process out of which an authentic Left would emerge – their counterargument is basically a comparison with Hitler's rise to power. Many German communists welcomed the Nazi takeover as a new chance for the radical Left ("now the situation is clear, democratic illusions have vanished, we are confronted by the true enemy"), but, as we know, their appreciation was a catastrophic mistake. The question is: are things the same with Trump? Is Trump a danger that could bring together a broad front akin to anti-fascist popular fronts, a front where "decent" conservatives will fight together with mainstream liberal progressives and (whatever remains of) the radical Left? Such a broad front against Trump is a dangerous illusion: it would amount to the capitulation of the new Left, to its surrender to the liberal establishment. The fear that a Trump victory would turn the US into a fascist state is a ridiculous exaggeration: the US has a rich enough texture of divergent civic and political institutions so that their direct fascist *Gleichschaltung* cannot be enacted (in contrast to, say, France, where the victory of Le Pen would have been much more dangerous). What happened in the US is that the Trump victory triggered a process of radicalization within the Democratic Party, and this process is our only hope. Saritha Prabhu's opinion piece recently published in the *Tennessean* deserves to be quoted here – it moved me almost to tears with its description of a simple truth:

> Brace yourself; there is a civil war coming soon in the Democratic Party. At the heart of today's Democratic Party is an identity crisis

and an ideological struggle. For starters, is the Democratic Party a party of the rich or a party of the little guy? For many years, they've been the party of the rich playing a good game of pretending to be for the little guy. And the Democratic establishment does it in insidious ways that are too clever by half: they are for the marginalized guy or gal in the race, gender, and sexuality issues because, hey, that doesn't hurt their and their affluent constituents' pocketbook much. But in the economic issues that matter, they often sock it to the average Democratic working-class voter: in the global trade deals that've offshored jobs and have decimated the American manufacturing base; in their looking the other way as illegal immigrants depress the wages of working-class Americans, and more. But as long as they talk and talk and talk some more – about abortion and transgender rights and racism (not that these aren't relevant issues), they can have their cake and eat it too. But all this worked until 2016, but can't be pulled off anymore. The Democratic establishment wing is still either clueless or stubborn, but they want good ol' Joe Biden to come to the rescue and Make Oligarchic America Great Again. When you rip off their mask, what is revealed is troubling: the Party of Davos masquerading as the Party of Scranton, Pennsylvania, that essentially hoodwinks much of the electorate.[1]

Yes, "all this worked" until 2016 – until Trump appeared. Let's make it clear: it was the rise of Trump that triggered the "civil war" in the Democratic Party – and, by the way, the proper name of this "civil war" is class struggle. So let's not lose nerves, let's rather use the opportunity inadvertently opened up by Trump. The only way to really defeat Trump is for the Left to win the civil war in the Democratic Party.

10

Is Donald Trump a Frog Embracing a Bottle of Beer?

A couple of decades ago, a charming publicity spot for a beer was shown on British TV. Its first part staged the well-known fairytale anecdote: a girl walks along a stream, sees a frog, takes it gently into her lap, kisses it, and, of course, the ugly frog miraculously turns into a beautiful young man. However, the story wasn't over yet: the young man casts a covetous glance at the girl, draws her toward himself, kisses her – and she turns into a bottle of beer, which the man holds triumphantly in his hand. For the woman, the point is that her love and affection (signaled by the kiss) turn a frog into a beautiful man, a full phallic presence; for the man, it is to reduce the woman to what Freud called a partial object, the true cause of his desire. (Incidentally, many women told me that their experience was rather the opposite one: they kissed what appeared to them a beautiful man, and on close contact they became aware that he is really a sleazy frog.) So we have either a woman with a frog or a man with a bottle of beer – what we can never obtain is the "natural" couple of the beautiful woman and man. Why not? Because the fantasmatic (imagined but impossible) support of this "ideal couple" would have been the inconsistent figure of a frog embracing a bottle of beer.

This same tasteless fantasy offers a model for Donald Trump's politics. After the Singapore meeting with Kim Yong-un, where Trump declared his intention to invite Kim to the White House, I was haunted by a dream – not the noble Martin Luther King one but a much weirder one (which will be much easier to realize than Luther's dream). Trump, who had already revealed his love for military parades, proposed to organize one in Washington, but Americans seem not to like the idea, so what if his new friend Kim were to give him a helping hand? What if he were to return the invitation and prepare a spectacle for Trump at the big stadium in Pyongyang, with hundreds of thousands of well-trained North Koreans waving colorful flags to form gigantic moving images of Kim and Trump smiling? Is this not the shared fantasy that underlies the Trump–Kim link, the frog-like Trump embracing the can-of-beer-like Kim? (In a rather distasteful step further, we can even imagine Trump kissing Melania and then gleefully observing how she changes into a can of beer.)

Another case in the same series: in a CNN interview in June 2018, Steve Bannon declared his political ideal to be the unity of Right and Left populism against the old political establishment. He praised the coalition of the Rightist Northern League and the Leftist populist Five Star movement which now rules Italy as the model for the world to follow, and as proof that politics is moving beyond Left and Right – again, the fantasy is that of a frog-like alt-Right embracing the Sanders movement and turning it into a bottle of beer. The stake of this (politically and aesthetically) disgusting idea is, of course, to obfuscate the basic social antagonism, which is why it is condemned to fail – although it can cause a lot of misfortunes before its final failure.

While any pact between Sanders and Bannon is excluded for obvious reasons, a key element of the Left's strategy should be to ruthlessly exploit division in the enemy camp and fight for Bannon followers. To cut a long story short, there is no victory of the Left without the broad alliance of all anti-establishment forces. One should never forget that our true enemy is the global capitalist establishment and not the new populist Right, which is merely a reaction to its impasses. If we forget this, then the Left will simply disappear from the map, as it is already happening with the moderate social democratic Left in much of Europe (Germany, France, etc.), or, as Slawomir Sierakowski put it: "As leftwing parties have collapsed, the sole option remaining for voters is conservatism or rightwing populism."

This is the reason why, to the consternation of many of my friends (who, of course, are now no longer my friends), I claimed that, apropos the US 2016 presidential elections, a victory for Trump is better for the future of progressive forces than a victory for Clinton. Trump is dangerous scum, of course, but his election may open possibilities and move the liberal-Left pole to a new, more radical position. I was surprised to learn that David Lynch adopted the same position: in an interview in June 2018, Lynch (who voted for Bernie Sanders in the 2016 Democratic primary) said that Trump "could go down as one of the greatest presidents in history because he has disrupted the thing so much. No one is able to counter this guy in an intelligent way." While Trump may not be doing a good job himself, Lynch thinks, he is opening up a space where other outsiders might. "Our so-called leaders can't take the country forward, can't get anything done. Like children, they are. Trump has shown all this."

One should further take into account how the aestheticization of politics is exploding today: on the surface (and this surface is essential), political battles are less about "real issues" than about images, values, attitudes.[2] For example (and this, of course, is *the* example today), "Trump" does not stand only for a set of economic and ideological measures; he is also an (anti-)aesthetic phenomenon, the personification of a certain vulgar style – and the same goes for Boris Johnson in the UK. It is precisely this aesthetic style that enables Trump (as well as Boris Johnson in the UK) to attract voters from the opposite social strata (rich and poor). They identify with Trump at this aesthetic level. Let's take Trump at his lowest, when he boasted about daring to grab women by their "pussies": this tasteless phrase is not only a clear indication of Trump's male chauvinist sexism; it also began to function as a metaphor for his "America first" politics. In his ruthless defense of US interests, Trump grabs other countries (like China) by their pussy, at their weakest point, where it hurts, to make them comply with his wishes.

The ongoing trade war between the US and China, the latest example of Trump grabbing pussies, cannot but fill us with dread: how will it affect our daily lives? Will it result in a new global recession or even geopolitical chaos? To orient ourselves in this mess, we should bear in mind some basic facts.

The trade conflict with China is just the culmination of a war that began a few years ago when Trump fired the opening shot aimed at the US's biggest trading partners by deciding to levy tariffs on imports of steel and aluminum from the EU, Canada, and Mexico. Trump was here playing his own populist version of class warfare: his professed goal was to protect the American working class (and are metal workers not one of the emblematic figures of the traditional working class?) from "unfair" European competition, and thereby save American jobs. Now he is doing the same with China.

Trump's impulsive decisions are not just expressions of his personal quirks: they are reactions to the end of an era in the global economic system. An economic cycle is coming to an end, a cycle that began in the early 1970s, the time when what Yanis Varoufakis calls the "Global Minotaur" was born, the monstrous engine that was running the world economy from the early 1970s to 2008. By the end of the 1960s, the US economy was no longer able to continue the recycling of its surpluses to Europe and Asia: its surpluses had turned into deficits. In 1971, the US government responded to this decline with an audacious strategic move: instead of tackling the nation's burgeoning deficits, it decided to do the opposite, to *boost deficits*. And who would pay for them? The rest of the world! How? By means of a permanent transfer of capital that rushed ceaselessly across the two great oceans to finance America's deficits.

This growing negative trade balance demonstrates that the US became the non-productive predator: in recent decades, it had to suck up an influx of one billion dollars daily from other nations to buy for its consummation and is, as such, the universal Keynesian consumer that keeps the world economy running. (So much for the anti-Keynesian economic ideology that seems to predominate today!) This influx, which is effectively like the tithe paid to Rome in Antiquity (or the gifts sacrificed to Minotaur by the Ancient Greeks), relies on a complex economic mechanism: the US is "trusted" as the safe and stable center, so that all others, from the oil-producing Arab countries to Western Europe and Japan, and now even China, invest their surplus profits in the US. Since this "trust" is primarily ideological and military, not economic, the problem for the US is how to justify its imperial role – it needs a permanent threat of war, offering itself as the universal protector of all other "normal" (not "rogue") states.

From 2008 on, however, this world system has been breaking down. In the Obama years, Paul Bernanke, Chairman of the Federal Reserve, gave another breath of life to this system. Ruthlessly exploiting the fact that the US dollar is the global currency, he financed imports by massively printing money. Trump decided to approach the problem in a different way. Ignoring the delicate balance of the global system, he focused on elements that may be presented as "injustice" for the US:

gigantic imports are reducing domestic jobs, etc. But what he decries as "injustice" is part of a system that profited the US: the US was effectively "robbing" the world by importing stuff and paying for it by debts and printing money.

Consequently, in his trade wars, Trump cheats: he wants the US to continue to be a global power, but he refuses to pay even the nominal price for it. He follows the "America first" principle, ruthlessly privileging US interests, while still acting as a global power. Even if some of the US arguments against China and its trade may appear reasonable, they are ridiculously one-sided: the US profited from the situation decried by Trump as unjust, and Trump wants to keep on profiting in the new situation. The only way out left to others is therefore that they should, at some basic level, unite to undermine the central role of the US as a global power secured by its military and financial might. This does not mean that the sins of those who oppose the US should be forgiven. It is typical that Trump proclaimed he is not interested in the democratic protests in Hong Kong (which started in March 2019), dismissing it as China's internal affair. While we should support the protests, we should just be careful that it is not used as an argument for the US trade war against China – we should always bear in mind that Trump is here on the side of China.

So should we nonetheless be glad that the ongoing trade war is just an economic war? Should we find solace in the hope that it will end with some kind of truce negotiated by managers of our economies? No way: geopolitical rearrangements that are already discernible can easily explode into (at least local) real wars. Trade wars are the stuff real wars are made of. Our global situation increasingly resembles that of Europe in the years before World War I – it is just not yet clear where our Sarajevo will be, the place where the war will explode: Ukraine, South Chinas Sea, or . . .

To prevent this catastrophe, one should be as ruthless as Trump in his struggle. Our predicament can only be stabilized by the collective imposition of a new world order no longer led by the US. The way to beat Trump is not to imitate him with "China first," "France first," etc., but to oppose him globally and treat him as an embarrassing outcast. Will the Left gather the strength to use this opening, or will it continue to defend the status quo? The Left's answer to Trump's fantasy of a frog embracing a bottle of beer should be simply a couple eating fried frog legs and drinking beer.

11

Better Dead than Red!

A series of things took place lately: suspicious packages sent to outstanding liberal democrats, the Pittsburgh synagogue shooting, the sharpening of Trump's rhetoric – from characterizing the main public media in the US as being enemies of the people to hints that, if Republicans lost the midterm elections, he would not recognize them since they would be based on fraud. Since all these phenomena occurred on the Republican side of the US political space, and since the color of the Republican Party is red, one can see how the old anti-communist motto from the days of the Cold War, "Better dead than red!," acquires an unexpected new meaning today. But one should be more precise here: what really goes on in this eruption of vulgarity in our political space? As Yuval Harari noted:

> People feel bound by democratic elections only when they share a basic bond with most other voters. If the experience of other voters is alien to me, and if I believe they don't understand my feelings and don't care about my vital interests, then even if I am outvoted by a hundred to one, I have absolutely no reason to accept the verdict. Democratic elections usually work only within populations that have some prior common bind, such as shared religious beliefs and national myths. They are a method to settle disagreements between people who already agree on the basics.[3]

When this agreement on basics falters, the only procedure at our disposal (outside outright war, of course) is negotiation. That's why the Middle East conflict cannot be solved by elections, but only by war or negotiations. And that's why every democracy is limited from within: it silently defines the limited scope of its validity. Liberals of all colors like to repeat Rosa Luxembourg's critical stab at the Bolsheviks: "Freedom is freedom for those who think differently." And, to spice it up, they like to include Voltaire's maxim: "I disapprove of what you say, but I will defend to the death your right to say it." Does, however, our recent (and not so recent) experience not show that freedom for those who think differently is acceptable only within the constraints of the predominant social pact? We can see this clearly today when the social pact that determines the limits of what is acceptable is breaking apart, and different visions compete to impose themselves as hegemonic. Years ago, Noam Chomsky caused a scandal when he followed Voltaire's maxim to its extreme: he defended the Holocaust denier Jean Faurisson's right to publish his book; Chomsky's argumentation even appeared in Faurisson's book as an afterword. Today such a gesture would be immediately identified as anti-Semitic. Holocaust denial is today not only criminalized, but the terms of its criminalization are sometimes even numerically circumscribed – for example, an idea circulated a decade or so ago that it should be punishable to set the number of Holocaust victims at lower than five million. Other mass crimes are then added to the list: France made it illegal to deny the Armenian genocide, for example. Even if something is not legally criminalized, it can be submitted to de facto criminalization. Typical here is the fate of Heidegger's thought: after his *Black Notes* was published, a group of liberal critics made a coordinated campaign to academically criminalize his thought. The idea was that, given his direct links with Nazi ideology, Heidegger doesn't even deserve to be the topic of serious philosophical debate; he should simply be dismissed as unworthy of such an approach, since, as Emmanuel Faye put it, Heidegger not only supported Nazism, his thought is nothing but the introduction of Nazism into philosophy.

This procedure of not-legal criminalization reaches its peak in today's politically correct version of MeToo. Sometimes it looks as if its devotees care more about a couple of affluent women who were shocked when comedian Louis CK showed them his penis than they do about the hundreds of poor girls being brutally raped. In replying to those who insisted on a difference between Harvey Weinstein and Louis CK, MeToo activists claimed that those who say this have no idea about how male violence works and is experienced, and that masturbation in front of women can be experienced as no less violent than physical imposition. Although there is a moment of truth in these claims, one should nonetheless pose a clear limit to the logic that sustains this argumentation: the limits of freedom are set so narrow here that even a modest debate about different grades of abuse is considered unacceptable. Is freedom (of debate) here not de facto reduced to the freedom for those who think like us? Not only do we have to accept the general (PC) consensus and then limit our debate to minor details, but even the scope of the details one is allowed to debate is very narrow.

Am I then a diehard liberal who pleads for total openness? No, prohibitions are necessary, limits should be set. One has to be very realist here, which means that one should discard platitudes like "When you begin by burning books, you will end by burning people" – what if there are situations where the only way to prevent burning people is to burn books (those who incite readers to burn people)? I just hate those hypocrites who don't admit the obvious fact that, in some sense, freedom effectively *is* freedom for those who basically think like us.

Supporters of the criminalization of "hate speech" predictably try to concoct a way out of this paradox; their usual line of argumentation is: hate speech deserves criminalization because it effectively deprives its victims of their freedom and humiliates them, so the exclusion of hate speech effectively widens the scope of actual freedom. True, but problems arise with the PC procedure of prohibiting even an open debate on this topic, so that an arbitrary exclusion (like the prohibition of Louis CK) is itself excluded from debate.

The argument evoked against defenders of Louis CK is the same as the one evoked by those who accuse the British Labour Party of tolerating anti-Semitism: who are we to judge if the complaints of the self-proclaimed victims are justified or not? It is up to the victims to decide this – if they feel hurt, then this is it . . . really? Let's take the case of anti-Semitism: so we should take seriously the complaints of Jews in the UK, but are they ready to take seriously the complaints of the West Bank Palestinians, or is this just a different example of a complaint where the victim's word is not to be trusted? A nice proof that the claims of one's own victimization are never to be taken at face value but always coldly analyzed. As Gilles Deleuze put it decades ago, politics that relies on a unique experience of a limited group is always reactionary.

However, the growing lack of agreement on the basics in the US and elsewhere does not concern primarily ethnic or religious diversity: it cuts across the entire body politic. It confronts two visions of social and political life, populist nationalist and liberal democratic. This confrontation mirrors class struggle, but in a displaced way: Rightist populists present themselves as the voice of the oppressed working class, while Left liberals are the voice of the new elites. Ultimately, no resolution of the tensions through negotiation is possible: one side has to win or the entire field has to be transformed.

A rupture is thus taking place in what philosophers call the "ethical substance" of our life. This rupture is getting too strong for "normal" democracy, and it is gradually drifting toward a kind of civil cold war. Trump's perverted "greatness" is that he effectively acts – he is not afraid to break the unwritten (and written) rules to impose his decisions. Our public life is regulated by a thick web of unwritten customs, rules that teach us how to practice the explicit (written) rules. While Trump (more or less) sticks to explicit legal regulations, he tends to ignore the unwritten silent pacts that determine how we should practice these rules – the way he dealt with Brett Kavanaugh was just the latest case of it. Instead of just blaming Trump, the Left should learn from him and do the same. When a situation demands it, we should shamelessly do the impossible and break the unwritten rules. Unfortunately, today's Left is, in advance, terrified of any radical acts; even when in power, it worries all the time: "If we do this, how will the world react? Will our act cause panic?" Ultimately, this fear means: "Will our enemies be mad and react?" In order to act in politics, one has to overcome this fear and assume the risk, take a step into the unknown.

Politicians like Andrew Cuomo are making desperate appeals for a return to civility, but this is not enough: it doesn't take into account the fact that the rise of "brutal" populism filled in the gap opened up by the failure of the liberal consensus. So what are we to do? We should quote Samuel Beckett here; in his novel *Malone Dies*, he wrote: "Everything divides into itself, I suppose." The basic division is not, as Mao Zedong claimed, that of the One that divides into Two; it's the division of a nondescript thing into One and its rest. Till the recent populist explosion, the "One" into which our societies divided was the liberal consensus with respect for established unwritten customs of democratic struggle shared by all; the excluded "rest" were the so-called extremists on both sides – they were tolerated, but precluded from participating in political power. With the rise of alt-Right populism, the hegemony of the liberal center was undermined, and a different political logic (not so much with regard to its content but primarily with regard to its style) asserted itself as part of the mainstream.

Such a situation cannot last indefinitely; there is a need for a new consensus, the political life of our societies should divide itself into a new One, and it is not determined in advance what this One will be. The situation comes with real dangers – who can guess the consequences of the victory of Bolsonaro in Brazil, not only for Brazil but for all of us – however, instead of losing nerves and resigning ourselves to panic, we should gather the courage and use this dangerous moment as an opportunity. To quote Mao Zedong again: "There is great chaos under heaven – the situation is excellent."

The One, the new common space, that the Left should offer is simply modern Europe's greatest economico-political achievement, the social democratic welfare state. According to Peter Sloterdijk, our reality is – in Europe, at least – "objective" social democracy, as opposed to "subjective" social democracy: one should distinguish between social democracy as the panoply of political parties and social democracy as the "formula of a system," which "precisely describes the political economic order of things, which is defined by the modern state as the state of taxes, as infrastructure state, as the state of the rule of law, and, not least, as the social state and the therapy state." "We encounter everywhere a phenomenal and a structural social democracy, a manifest and a latent one, one that appears as a party and another that is more or less irreversibly built into the very definitions, functions, and procedures of the modern statehood as such."[4]

Are we thereby just returning to the old? No: the paradox is that, in today's new situation, to insist on the old social democratic welfare state is an almost revolutionary act. The proposals of Bernie Sanders and Jeremy Corbyn are often less radical than those of a moderate social democracy half a century ago, but they are nonetheless decried as socialist radicals.

Although the populist Right is nationalist, it is much better than the Left at organizing itself as an international network. So the new Leftist project can only come alive if it matches populist internationalism and organizes itself as a global movement. The emerging pact between Sanders, Corbyn, and Yanis Varoufakis is a first step in this direction. The reaction of the liberal establishment will be violent – the campaign against Corbyn's alleged anti-Semitism is just a first indication of how the entire movement will be the victim of a campaign to discredit it. But there is no other way – risks will have to be taken.

In this sense, the image of Donald Trump is also a fetish: the last thing a liberal sees before confronting class struggle. That's why liberals are both so fascinated and so horrified by Trump: to avoid the class topic. Hegel's motto "Evil resides in the gaze which sees evil everywhere" fully applies here: the very liberal gaze that demonizes Trump is also evil because it ignores how its own failures opened up the space for Trump's type of patriotic populism. If one really wants to leave Rightist populism behind, the first thing to do is to avoid anti-populist arrogance, i.e., the line of thought that argues that the rational public space is falling apart, that voters more and more (re)act emotionally, propelled by hatreds and fears instead of by rational self-interest. The solution offered by this line of thought is a mixture of carrots and sticks: we should diminish poverty, provide free education and healthcare – and ruthlessly fight hate speech, up to directly criminalizing it. What this line of thought misses is that Trump voters *are* in some sense quite rational: their behavior can be easily explained by their own perception of self-interest; they respond to actual problems that were effectively neglected by the establishment. The problem is not the exploding new "irrationality": the problem is the failure of the (ideological) rationality threatened by the populist wave.

Who, then, wants Trump really to lose? During the heated Democratic primary debate on July 30, 2019, former Colorado governor John Hickenlooper warned that "you might as well FedEx the election to Donald Trump" if the party were to adopt Bernie Sanders's "Medicare for All" plan, the Green New Deal, and other radical initiatives. The ensuing passionate exchange clearly distinguished two camps in the Democratic Party: the "moderates" (representatives of the party establishment whose main face is Joe Biden), and the more "radical" democratic socialists (Bernie Sanders, maybe Elizabeth Warren, plus the four young congresswomen dubbed by Trump "the Squad," and whose most popular face is now Alexandria Ocasio-Cortez). This struggle is arguably the most important political struggle taking place today anywhere in the world.

It may appear that the moderates have a convincing argument. Are democratic socialists not simply too radical to win over the majority of voters? Is the true battle not the battle for the undecided moderate voters who will never endorse a Muslim Ilhan Omar with her hair covered? And did Trump himself not count on this when he brutally attacked the Squad, thereby obliging the entire Democratic Party to solidarize with the four women, elevating them to the symbol of the party? For Democrat moderates, the important thing is to get rid of Trump and bring back the normal liberal democratic hegemony that he destroyed.

Unfortunately, this strategy is already tested: Hillary Clinton followed it, and the large majority of the media thought she could not lose since Trump was unelectable. Even Bush father and son, the two previous Republican presidents, said they would vote for her, but she lost and Trump won. Trump's victory undermined the establishment from the Right – isn't it time for the Left to do the same? Like Trump in 2016, they have a serious chance of winning.

And it is this prospect that throws the entire establishment, inclusive of Trump's pseudo-alternative to it, into panic. Mainstream economists predict the economic collapse of the US in the case of a Sanders victory; mainstream political analysts fear the rise of totalitarian state socialism; moderate Left liberals sympathize with the goals of the democratic socialists but warn that, unfortunately, they are out of touch with reality. And they are right to be in panic: something entirely new is emerging in the US.

What is so refreshing about the Leftist wing of the Democratic Party is that it left behind the stale waters of political correctness and MeToo excesses. While firmly standing with antiracist and feminist struggles, it focuses on social issues like universal healthcare, ecological threats, etc. Far from being crazy socialists who want to turn the US into a new Venezuela, the left wing of the Democratic Party simply gave to the US the taste of good old authentic European social democracy. A quick look at their program makes it abundantly clear that they pose no greater threat to Western freedoms than did Willy Brandt or Olof Palme.

But what is even more important is that this is not only the voice of the radicalized young generation. Already the public faces – four young women and an old white man – tell a different story. Yes, they clearly demonstrate that the majority of the younger generation in the US is tired of the establishment in all its versions, that they are skeptical about the ability of capitalism as we know it to deal with the problems we are facing, and that the word "socialism" is for them no longer taboo. However, the true miracle is that they joined forces with "old white men" like Sanders, who stand for the older generation of ordinary workers, people who often tended to vote Republican or even for

Trump. What is going on here is something that all supporters of culture wars and identity politics considered impossible: antiracists, feminists, and ecologists joining forces with what was the "moral majority" of ordinary working people. Bernie Sanders, not the alt Right, is the true voice of moral majority, if this term has any positive meaning.

So no, the eventual rise of the democratic socialists will not guarantee Trump's reelection. It was Hickenlooper and other moderates who were actually FedExing a message to Trump from the debate. Their message was: we may be your enemies, but we all want Bernie Sanders to lose. So don't worry, if Bernie or someone like him is to be the Democratic candidate, we will not stand behind him - we secretly prefer you to win . . .

12

"There Is Disorder Under Heaven, the Situation Is Excellent"

At the beginning of his presidency, Donald Trump visited three places: Brussels, where he met key European leaders; London, where he met then prime minister Theresa May (plus the Queen); and Helsinki, where he met Vladimir Putin. Everybody noted the strange fact that Trump was much friendlier to (those perceived as) America's enemies than he was to its friends – but such facts should not surprise us too much; our attention should turn in another direction. As is often the case with Trump, reactions to his acts are more important than what he actually did or said.

Let us begin by comparing what Trump said with what his partners said. When Trump and May were asked by a journalist what they thought about the flow of immigrants to Europe, Trump brutally and honestly reiterated his populist anti-immigrant position: immigrants are a threat to the European way of life, they are destabilizing the safety of our countries, bringing violence and intolerance, so we should keep them out. A careful listener might easily notice that Theresa May said exactly the same thing, just in a more diplomatic and "civilized" way: immigrants bring diversity, they contribute to our welfare, but we should carefully check whom we let in. We got here a clear taste of the choice that is increasingly the only one presented to us: direct populist barbarism or a more civilized version of the same politics – barbarism with a human face.

Generally, global reactions to Trump from all across the spectrum, including both Republicans and Democrats in the US, were one of shock and awe bordering on panic pure and simple: Trump is unreliable, he brings chaos. First, he reproached Germany for relying on Russian gas and thus making themselves vulnerable to the enemy; days later he boasted of his good relations with Putin. He doesn't even have good manners (horror: when meeting the Queen, he violated the protocol of how to behave in the presence of a monarch!); he doesn't really listen to his democratic partners in a dialogue; he is much more open to the charm of Putin, America's big enemy. The way he acted at a press conference with Putin in Helsinki was not only an unheard-of humiliation (just think of it – he didn't behave as Putin's master), and some of his statements could even be considered outright acts of treason. Rumors reappeared of how Trump acts as Putin's puppet because Putin must have some hold over him (the famous photos of prostitutes urinating on Trump in Moscow?), and parts of the US establishment, Democrats and some Republicans, began to consider a quick impeachment, even if that meant getting Pence as his replacement. The conclusion was simply that the President of the United States is no longer the leader of the free world. But was the President of the United States really ever such a leader? Here our counterattack should begin.

Let us first note that some truths here and there can be found in the overall confusion of Trump's statements. Wasn't he in some sense right when he said that it is in our interest to have good relations with Russia and China so as to prevent war? Wasn't he partially right to present his tariff war also as a protection of the interests of US workers? The fact is that the existing order of international trade and finance is far from just, and that the European establishment that is hurt by

Trump's measures should also look at its own sins. Have we already forgotten how the existing financial and trade rules that privilege the strong European states, especially Germany, brought devastation to Greece?

Concerning Putin, I believe most of the accusations against him are true – for example, with regard to his meddling in the US elections: probably, yes, Putin was caught doing . . . what? What the US also does, regularly and on a massive scale, except that, in their case, they call it defense of democracy. So yes, Trump is a monster, and when he designated himself as a "stable genius," we should read this as a direct reversal of the truth – he is an unstable idiot who disturbs the establishment. But as such, he is a symptom, an effect of what is wrong with the establishment itself. The true monster is the very establishment shocked by Trump's actions.

The panicky reaction to Trump's latest acts demonstrates that he is undermining and destabilizing the US political establishment and its ideology. So our conclusion should be: yes, the situation is dangerous, there is uncertainty as well as elements of chaos in international relations – but it is here that we should remember Mao's old motto: "There is great disorder under the sky, so the situation is excellent!" Let's not lose our nerve, let's exploit the confusion by systematically organizing another anti-establishment front from the Left. Signs are clear here: the surprising electoral victory of Alexandria Ocasio-Cortez, a self-proclaimed democratic socialist, against ten-term House incumbent Joe Crowley in a New York congressional primary was, with luck, the first in the series of shocks that will transform the Democratic Party. People like her, not the well-known faces from the liberal establishment, should be our answer to Trump.

No wonder the establishment in all its guises is reacting so violently to this threat. After Bernie Sanders announced his bid for the presidency, attacks on him instantly arose from all sides. Not only from Trump, who referred to him as a "wacko," not only from the usual bunch of conservative commentators, who proposed dozens of variations on the motif "You want Sanders as President? Look at Venezuela today!" – but also from his more centrist Democratic opponents. Reading these last attacks, one is immediately overwhelmed by the feeling of déjà vu – we have lived through this situation before, in the time of the Democratic primaries marked by the conflict between Sanders and Clinton.

Arguably, the Clinton campaign against Sanders reached its lowest point when, campaigning for Hillary, Madeline Albright said: "There's a special place in hell for women who don't help each other!" (Meaning: who will vote for Sanders instead of Clinton.) Maybe we should amend this statement: there is a special place in hell for women (and men) who think half a million dead children is an affordable price for a military intervention that ruins a country (as Albright said in support of the massive bombing of Iraq back in 1996), while wholeheartedly supporting women's and gay rights at home. Is this comment of Albright's not infinitely more obscene and lewd than all Trump's sexist banalities?

We are not yet there, but we are slowly approaching it. Liberal attacks on Sanders for his alleged rejection of identity politics rose from the dead again, ignoring the fact that Sanders is doing the exact opposite, insisting on a link between class, race, and gender. One has to support him unconditionally when he rejects identity in itself as a reason to vote for someone: "It is not good enough for somebody to say, I'm a woman, vote for me. What we need is a woman who has the guts to stand up to Wall Street, to the insurance companies, to the drug companies, to the fossil fuel industry." As expected, for this very statement, Sanders was attacked as a white male chauvinist advocating "class reductionism." One should not be surprised if this were soon to be denounced as an expression of toxic masculinity.

If we disregard straightforward lies (like the claim, proven false, that the young Sanders did not work with Martin Luther King in the civil rights struggle), the strategy of those who privilege Warren over Sanders is a rather simple one. First, they claim that the difference between their respective economic programs is minimal and negligible. (One is tempted to add here: yes, minimal, like the fact that Sanders proclaims himself a democratic socialist, while Warren insists she is a capitalist to her bones. It is sad to hear Warren describing herself thus when even top corporate managers like Bill Gates, Elon Musk, and Mark Zuckerberg talk about how capitalism, at least the way it functions now, cannot survive.) Then, the critics claim that, in contrast to Sanders's exclusive focus on economic injustice, Warren also brings in gender and race injustices, so her advantage over Sanders is clear: only Warren can unite a broad progressive front against Trump. Ultimately, critics of Sanders end up with a kind of electoral affirmative action: Sanders is a man and Warren is a woman, so . . . Two key facts get obfuscated here: the democratic socialism of Sanders is much more radical than Warren's, which remains firmly within the Democratic establishment, plus it is simply not true that Sanders ignores the race and gender struggles – he just brings out their links with the economic struggle.

Warren is not, as her defenders claim, a third way between centrist Democrats and democratic socialists, the synthesis of what is best in race/gender identity politics and in the struggle for economic justice. No, she is just Hillary Clinton with a slightly more human face. Even defenders of Warren admit that her claim to Native American roots was a mistake – but was it really just an innocent mistake? The Cherokee Nation's secretary of state, Chuck Hoskin Jr., responded to the test showing Warren was between 1/64th and 1/1,024th Native American: "A DNA test is useless to determine tribal citizenship. Current DNA tests do not even distinguish whether a person's ancestors were indigenous to North or South America." Hoskin was right, and what one should add is that proving that you have a little bit of exotic ancestry in one ethnic group to legitimize your popular roots has nothing whatsoever to do with the actual fight against racism. But the main point is that Warren applied (for a "progressive") cause the same procedure that the Nazis applied to identify those suspected of having Jewish blood.

In today's market, we find a whole series of products deprived of their malignant property: coffee without caffeine, cream without fat, beer without alcohol . . . And the list goes on: what about virtual sex as sex without sex? What about contemporary politics – the art of expert administration – as politics without politics? Do the "Leftist" Democrats attacking Sanders not offer something similar – socialism without socialism, deprived of the features that make it a threat to the establishment?

What is arguably more problematic than these pseudo-feminist critiques of Sanders are a few pseudo-radical Leftists who claim that Sanders is a social democrat who just wants to moderately modify the system to make it more efficient instead of aiming at a true socialist revolution (socialization of the means of production, etc.). What makes such "radicalism" especially disgusting is that its proponents are well aware of how such a "radical" stance has no chance of mobilizing people and is, as such, serving only the establishment: it dissuades people from engaging in the only mass movement that mobilizes them on behalf of socialism. Of course, Sanders's program is not more radical than that of a typical European social democracy half a century ago. However, the very fact that advocacy of what was, half a century ago, the standard program of social democracy is today decried as a totalitarian threat says a lot about the triumph of capitalist ideology in the last decades. This fact indicates that even such classic social democratic demands pose a threat to today's system, so we should begin with them, fully aware that, in the course of their realization, further radical measures will impose themselves.

Back to our main line, the message to those who are critical of the turn taken by political correctness is thus clear: vote Sanders!

13

Soyons Réalistes, Demandons l'Impossible!

The protests of the "yellow vests" (*gilets jaunes*) in France have been going on for months. They began as a grassroots movement that grew out of widespread discontent with a new eco-tax on petrol and diesel, seen as hitting hardest those living and working outside metropolitan areas, where there is no public transport. More recently, the movement has grown to include a panoply of demands, including "Frexit" (the exit of France from the EU), lower taxes, higher pensions, and an improvement in ordinary French people's spending power. The movement offers an exemplary case of Leftist populism, of the explosion of people's wrath with all its inconsistencies: lower taxes and more money for education and healthcare; cheaper petrol and ecological struggle. Although the new petrol tax was obviously an excuse or, rather, a pretext – not what the protests are "really about" – it is significant to note that what triggered them was a measure intended to act against global warming. No wonder Trump enthusiastically supported the yellow vests (even claiming that some of the protesters were shouting "We want Trump!"), noting that one among the demands was for France to step away from the Paris agreement. In a hotel room, you can hang a sign on the door saying either "Please clean the room!" or "Please do not disturb!" Whenever I see this sign, I imagine a sign saying: "Please do not disturb while cleaning the room!" Are the demands of yellow vests not a similar combination of contradictory demands? "Please protect our environment while providing cheaper fuel!"

The yellow vest protests embody the weird reversal that characterizes today's global situation. The old antagonism between "ordinary people" and the financial capitalist elites is back with a vengeance, with "ordinary people" exploding in protests against the elites accused of being blind to their suffering and demands; however, what is new is that the populist Right proved to be much more adept than the Left in channeling these explosions in its direction. Alain Badiou was thus fully justified to say apropos the yellow vests: "Tout ce qui bouge n'est pas rouge" – all that moves (leads to unrest) is not red. Today's populist Right participates in the long tradition of popular protests which were predominantly Leftist. Yes, *tout ce qui bouge n'est pas rouge*, but even when it is Right populism that *bouges*, the Left should learn to ruthlessly exploit the crack opened up in the edifice of the existing ideological hegemony by the unrest to promote its own cause.

The yellow vest movement fits the specific French Left tradition of large public protests targeting political elites (more than business or financial elites). However, in contrast to the protests of 1968, the yellow vests are much more characteristic of a movement from *la France profonde*, a revolt against big metropolitan areas, which means that its Leftist orientation is much more blurred. (Both Marine le Pen and Jean-Luc Mélenchon support the protests.) As expected, commentators are asking which political force will appropriate the movement's energy, le Pen or a new Left, with purists demanding that it remains a "pure" protest movement, at a distance from established politics. One should be clear here: in all the explosion of demands and expressions of dissatisfaction, it is clear the protesters don't really know what they want; they don't have a vision of a society they want, just a mixture of demands that are impossible to be met within the system, although they address them to the system. This feature is crucial: their demands express their interests rooted in the existing system.

One should not forget that they are addressing these demands at the (political) system at its best, which, in France, means Emmanuel Macron. The protests mark the end of the Macron dream. Recall the enthusiasm about Macron offering new hope not only of defeating the Rightist populist threat but of providing a new vision of progressive European identity, which brought philosophers as opposed as Habermas and Sloterdijk to support him. Recall how every Leftist critique of Macron, every warning about the fatal limitations of his project, were dismissed as "objectively" supporting Marine le Pen. Today, with the ongoing protests in France, we are brutally confronted with the sad truth of the pro-Macron enthusiasm. Macron's TV address to the protesters on December 10 was a miserable performance, half-compromise, half-apology, which convinced no one and stood out by its lack of vision. Macron may be the best of the existing system, but his politics are located within the liberal democratic coordinates of the enlightened technocracy.

As everyone who has trouble with constipation knows, the suppository is a solid medical cone that is inserted into the rectum to facilitate defecating. I always found it strange that such a noble philosophical sounding term is used for a rather disgusting task. Is it not the same with the way many of our economic experts talk when they call rather brutal measures that hurt ordinary people "stabilization" or "regulation"? Macron remains within this expert frame and that's why his reaction to the protests caused uproar.

We should therefore give the protests a conditional "yes" – conditional, since it is clear that Left populism does not provide a feasible alternative to the system. That is to say, let's imagine that the protesters somehow win, take power, and act within the coordinates of the existing system (like Syriza did in Greece). What would have happened then? Probably some kind of economic catastrophe. This doesn't mean that we simply need a different socioeconomic system, a system that would be able to meet the protesters' demands; the process of radical transformation would also give rise to different demands and expectations. Say, with regard to fuel costs, that what is really needed is not just cheap fuel; the true goal is to diminish our dependency on oil for ecological reasons, to change not only our transportation but our entire way of life. The same holds for lower taxes plus better healthcare and education: the whole paradigm will have to change.

The same holds for our big ethico-political problem: how do we deal with the flow of refugees? The solution is not just to open the borders to anyone who wants to come in, and to ground this openness in our generalized guilt ("colonization is our greatest crime, which we will have to repay forever"). If we remain at this level, we serve perfectly the interests of those in power who foment the conflict between immigrants and the local working class (which feels threatened by them) and retain their superior moral stance. (The moment one begins to think in this direction, the politically correct Left instantly cries "fascism" – see the ferocious attacks on Angela Nagle for her outstanding essay "The Left Case against Open Borders."[5]) Again, the "contradiction" between advocates of open borders and populist anti-immigrants is a false "secondary contradiction" whose ultimate function is to obfuscate the need to change the system itself: the entire international economic system that, in its present form, gives rise to refugees.[6]

The stance of generalized guilt provides a clinically perfect example of the superego paradox confirmed by how fundamentalist immigrants react to Left liberal guilt feeling: the more European Left liberals admit responsibility for the situation that creates refugees, and the more they demand that we should abolish all walls and open our gates to immigrants, the more they are despised by fundamentalist immigrants. There is no gratitude in it – the more we give, the more we are reproached for not giving enough. It is significant that the countries that are most attacked are not those with an open anti-immigrant stance (Hungary, Poland, e.g.) but precisely those that are the most open. Sweden is reproached for not really wanting to integrate immigrants, and every detail is seized upon as proof of its hypocrisy ("You see: they still serve pork at meals in the schools! They still allow their girls to dress provocatively! They still don't want to integrate elements of sharia in their legal system!"), while every demand for symmetry (but where are the new Christian churches in Muslim countries with a Christian minority?) is flatly rejected as European cultural imperialism. Crusades are mentioned all the time, while the Muslim occupation of large parts of Europe is treated as normal. The underlying premise is that a kind of radical sin (of colonization) is inscribed into the very existence of Europe, a sin incomparable with others, so that our debt to others cannot ever be repaid. However, beneath this premise it is easy to discern its opposite, the stance of scorn – they loath us for our guilt and responsibility, they perceive it as a sign of our weakness, of our lack of self-respect and trust in ourselves. The ultimate irony is that some Europeans then perceive such an aggressive stance as Muslim "vitality" and contrast it to Europe's "exhaustion" – again turning this into the argument that we need the influx of foreign blood to regain our vitality. We in Europe will only regain the respect of others by learning to impose limits, to fully help others not from a position of guilt and weakness, but from a position of strength.

What do we mean by this strength?[7] Precisely such a strength was displayed by Angela Merkel when she extended the invitation to refugees to come to Germany. Her invitation demonstrated faith that

Germany could do it, that it is strong enough to accept refugees *and* retain its identity. Although anti-immigrant patriots like to pose as strong defenders of their nation, it is their position that betrays panic and weakness – how little trust they must have in the German nation when they perceive a couple of hundred new immigrants as a threat to German identity. Crazy as it may sound, Merkel acted as a strong German patriot, while anti-immigrants are miserable weaklings.

What happened in Egypt during the so-called Arab Spring is a kind of symptom of our times, a formula of how things go wrong. A popular revolt overthrew the hated dictator and gave rise to democracy, but, in the free elections that followed, the Muslim Brotherhood (not the people who organized the protests but their passive onlookers) were brought to power. The army soon organized a coup against the Brotherhood, with the half-support of the protesters. The circle was thus closed. The cause of these reversals is the gap between the enlightened middle-class minority that organized the revolt and the fundamentalist majority that made their preference known in the elections – an indication that there is no deeper wisdom in the minds of ordinary people. Against this idea (which runs from Mao to Podemos populists), one should fearlessly admit that the majority of ordinary people are not to be trusted, that there is nothing, no privileged authentic knowledge, to be learned from them – not because they are stupid but because, as Lacan put it, there is no thirst for knowledge (what Freud called *Wissenstrieb*, the drive to know) but only the desire not to know. Knowledge doesn't bring happiness or power: knowledge hurts.

Does this mean that we should patiently wait for a big change? No, we can begin right now by measures that appear modest but nonetheless undermine the foundations of the existing system like the patient subterranean digging of a mole. What about the overhaul of our entire financial system, which would affect the rules of how credits and investments work? What about imposing new regulations that would prevent the exploitation of the least developed countries from which refugees come?

The old 1968 motto, *"Soyons réalistes, demandons l'impossible!"* remains fully relevant – on condition that we take note of the shift to which it has to be submitted. First, there is "demanding the impossible" in the sense of bombarding the existing system with demands that it cannot meet: open borders, better healthcare, higher wages, etc. Here we are today, in the midst of a hysterical provocation of our masters (technocratic experts). This provocation has to be followed by a key step further: not demanding the impossible from the system, but demanding the "impossible" changes of the system itself. Although such changes appear "impossible" (unthinkable within the coordinates of the system), they are clearly required by our ecological and social predicament, offering the only realist solution.

At this point, we should be very clear. To accomplish this key step, a shift from the hysteric to the Master has to occur: a new Master is needed. Here we encounter the fatal limitation of the much-praised "leaderless" character of the French protesters, of their chaotic self-organization: it is not enough for a leader to listen to the people and formulate what they want, their interests, into a program. The old Henry Ford was right when he remarked that, in offering the serially produced car, he wasn't following what people wanted. As he put it succinctly, if asked what they wanted, the people would have answered: "A better and stronger horse to pull our carriage!" This insight finds an echo in Steve Jobs's infamous motto: "A lot of times, people don't know what they want until you show it to them." In spite of any criticisms one might have concerning the activities of Jobs, he was close to an authentic Master in how he understood his motto. When he was asked how much research went into finding out what customers want from

Apple, he snapped back: "None. It's not the customers' job to know what they want . . . we figure out what we want." Note the surprising turn of this argumentation: after denying that customers know what they want, Jobs doesn't go on with the expected direct reversal "it is our task (the task of creative capitalists) to figure out what customers want and then 'show it to them' on the market." Instead, he continues "we figure out what we want" – this is how a true Master works: he doesn't try to guess what people want; he simply obeys his own desire so that it is up to the people to decide whether they will follow him or not. In other words, his power stems from his fidelity to his vision, from not compromising it.

And the same goes for a political leader that is needed today. The famous motto of the three musketeers, "All for one and one for all" can be read in two fundamentally different ways. It can simply mean that each person should contribute to the whole (whenever there is trouble, every single person should do its part to help out), so that nobody will be left behind (when one person is in trouble, this should be a problem for the whole community – to put it simply, the whole of us relies on each one of us, and each one of us can rely on the whole of us). But there is a much more ominous reading: not all individuals are at the same level; there is one who is in an exceptional position – a Leader – so that all people should work for this one who stands for the whole and works for all, for the common good of everybody. The trick is, of course, that the two "alls" don't really coincide: the first "all" (in "all for one") is the collection of individuals who are solicited to work for the Leader, while the second "all" (in "one for all") is the mythic-ideological "all" ("the real interest of the people"), embodied in (and also defined by) the one, the Leader, who knows better than we, ordinary people, what is in our real interest. The key point here is that the first reading cannot really work in political reality: it has to revert to the second reading, where the "all" is embodied in an exceptional "one."

Protesters in France want a better (stronger and cheaper) horse – in this case, ironically, cheaper fuel for their cars. They should be given the vision of a society where the price of fuel no longer matters, in the same way that, after cars, the price of horse fodder no longer matters. A possible counterargument is that the "chaotic" leaderless and decentralized character of the yellow vest protests is precisely their strength: instead of a clear agent addressing demands to state power and thereby offering itself as a partner in dialogue, we get a polymorphous popular pressure, and what puts those in power in a panic is precisely that this pressure cannot be localized in a clear opponent but remains a version of what Antonio Negri called multitude. If such a pressure expresses itself in concrete demands, these demands are not what the protest is really about. However, at some point, hysterical demands have to translate themselves into a political program (or they disappear), and we should perhaps read the protesters' demands as the expression of a deeper dissatisfaction with the very liberal democratic capitalist order, in which demands can only be met through the process of parliamentary political representation. In other words, the protests contain a deeper demand for a different logic of economico-political organization, and here a new leader is needed to operationalize this deeper demand.

14

Catalonia and the End of Europe

One of the reliable signs of political opportunism is what, in parallel with particle physics, one may call political correlationism. Let's imagine that I and my enemy both hold in our hand a ball, which can be either white or black, and neither of us knows its color (I am also not allowed to look into my own folded palm). We have here four possibilities: white–white, black–black, black–white, and white–black. Now let's suppose that, for some reason, we both know that the two balls (the one in my hand and in the one in my enemy's hand) are opposite in color. In this case, there are only two possibilities (black–white and white–black), and if by some luck I get to know the color of the ball in the hand of my enemy, then I automatically know the color of my ball – the two are correlated. (This happen when particles are split and their spins remain correlated – if I measure the spin of one particle, I know automatically the spin of the other.) Something similar often happens (and happened) in (mostly Leftist) politics. I am not sure which position we should take in a particular political struggle, but when we learn the position of our enemy, we automatically assume that our position should be the opposite one. One should add that Lenin provided a scathing critique of this stance (ironically, his target was Rosa Luxembourg). Such was the case in the cultural Cold War: when, in late 1940s, Western culture was perceived as promoting universalist cosmopolitanism (under Jewish influence), pro-Soviet communists (from the USSR to France) decided to turn patriotic, promoting their own cultural tradition and attacking imperialism for destroying it.

Was not something similar going on in the reaction to the Catalonia referendum? Remember how Putin proclaimed the disintegration of the Soviet Union a mega-catastrophe – but now he supports Catalonian independence. The same holds for all those European Leftists who opposed the disintegration of Yugoslavia as the result of a dark German–Vatican plot; now, however (as with Scotland), separation is OK. And Western centrist liberals are no better: always ready to support any separated movement that threatens the geopolitical power of Russia, they now warn against the threat to the unity of Spain (hypocritically deploring the police violence against Catalonian voters, of course). In Slovenia, my own country, this confusion reached its peak: the old Left, which was to the end mostly against Slovene independence, pleading for a renewed more open Yugoslavia, is not organizing petitions and demonstrations for Catalonia, while the nationalist Right, which fought for full Slovene independence, is now discreetly for the unity of Spain (since their conservative colleague Mariano Rajoy is the Spanish prime minister). We can only say: shame on the European establishment – obviously, some have the right to sovereignty and others not, depending on geopolitical interests.

One argument against Catalonian independence nonetheless seems rational: is Putin's support of Catalonian independence not obviously part of his strategy to strengthen Russia by way of working for the disintegration of European unity? Should then partisans of a strong united Europe not advocate the unity of Spain? Here, one should dare to turn this argument round. Support for the unity of Spain is also part of the ongoing struggle to assert the power of nation-states against European unity. What we need in order to accommodate new local sovereignties (of Catalonia, of Scotland, maybe, etc.) is thus simply a stronger European Union: nation-states should accustom themselves to a more modest role as intermediators between regional autonomies and united Europe. In this way, Europe can avoid the debilitating conflicts between states and emerge as a much stronger international agent, on a par with other large geopolitical blocks.

The failure of the EU to take a clear stance on the Catalonian referendum is just the latest in a series of blunders, the biggest being the total lack of coherent policies toward the flow of refugees from the Middle East and North Africa into Europe. The confused reaction to the flow of refugees failed to take into account the basic difference between (economic) immigrants and refugees: immigrants come to Europe to search for work, to meet the demands for workforces in the developed European countries; refugees don't primarily come to work, but simply to look for a safe place to survive – they often don't even like the new country they find themselves in. Refugees who used to gather in Calais are paradigmatic here: they didn't want to stay in France, but to move on to the UK. The same holds for the countries that most resist accepting refugees (the new "axis of evil" Croatia/Slovenia/Hungary/ Czech Republic/Poland/Baltic countries) – they are definitely not the places where refugees want to settle. But perhaps the most absurd effect of this confusion is that Germany, the only country that behaved in a half-decent way to refugees, became the butt of many critics, not only of the Rightist defenders of Europe but also of the Leftists, who, in a typical superego turn, focused on the best element in the chain, attacking it for not being even better.

The most worrying aspect of the Catalonian crisis is thus the inability of Europe to take a clear stand: to allow its member states either to adopt their own politics with regard to separatism or refugees, or to adopt efficient measures against those who don't want to apply the common decisions. Why is this so important? Europe is supposed to work as a minimal unity, supporting single states, providing a frame, a safety network for their tensions. Only such a Europe can be an important agent in the emerging New World Order, where powerful agents are less and less single states. It is clearly in the interest of the US and Russia to weaken the EU or to even trigger its disintegration: such a disintegration will create a power vacuum that will be filled in by new alliances of single European states with Russia or with the US. Who in Europe would like to see this?

15

Which Idea of Europe Is Worth Defending?

In January 2019, a group of 30 writers, historians and Nobel laureates – including Bernard-Henri Lévy, Milan Kundera, Salman Rushdie, Orhan Pamuk, Mario Vargas Llosa, Adam Michnik – published a manifesto in several newspapers all around Europe, including the *Guardian* in the UK. They claim that Europe as an idea is "coming apart before our eyes." "We must now will Europe or perish beneath the waves of populism," they wrote. "We must rediscover political voluntarism or accept that resentment, hatred and their cortege of sad passions will surround and submerge us."[8]

This manifesto is deeply flawed: just carefully reading it makes it clear why populists are thriving. Its signatories – the flower of European liberal intelligence – ignore the unpleasant fact that the populists also present themselves as the saviors of Europe.

In an interview on July 15, 2018, just after attending a stormy meeting with EU leaders, Trump mentioned the European Union as the first in the line of "foes" of the US, ahead of Russia and China. Instead of condemning this claim as irrational ("Trump is treating the allies of the US worse than its enemies," etc.), we should ask a simple question: what is it about the EU that bothers Trump so much? Which Europe is Trump talking about? When he was asked by journalists about immigrants flowing into Europe, he answered as befits the anti-immigrant populist that he is: immigrants are tearing apart the fabric of European mores and ways of life, they pose a danger to European spiritual identity – in short, it was people like Orbán or Salvini who were talking through him. One should never forget that they also want to defend Europe.

So which Europe bothers both Trump and the European populists? It is the Europe of transnational unity, the Europe vaguely aware that, in order to cope with the challenges of our moment, we should move beyond the constraints of nation-states? Is it the Europe that also desperately strives to somehow remain faithful to the old Enlightenment motto of solidarity with victims, the Europe aware of the fact that humanity is today One, that we are all in the same boat (or, as we say, on the same Spaceship Earth), so that others' misery is also our problem?

This idea that underlies a united Europe got corrupted, half-forgotten, and it is only in a moment of danger that we are compelled to return to this essential dimension of Europe, to its hidden potential. Europe lies within the vast pincers of America on the one side and Russia on the other, both of which want to dismember it: Trump and Putin both support Brexit; they support Euroskeptics in every corner, from Poland to Italy. What is it that bothers them about Europe, given that we all know the misery of the EU, which fails again and again at every test: from its inability to enact a consistent politics about immigrants to its miserable reaction to Trump's tariff war? It is obviously not this actual existing Europe, but the idea of a Europe that flares up against all the odds and in moments of danger. The problem for Europe is how to remain faithful to its emancipatory legacy, which is threatened by the conservative populist onslaught?

In his *Notes Towards a Definition of Culture*, the great conservative

T.S. Eliot remarked that there are moments when the only choice is the one between heresy and nonbelief, when the only way to keep a religion alive is to perform a sectarian split from its main corpse. This is what has to be done today: the only way to really defeat populists and to redeem what is worth saving in liberal democracy is to perform a sectarian split from liberal democracy's main corpse. Sometimes, the only way to resolve a conflict is not to search for a compromise but to radicalize one's position.

Back to the letter of the 30 liberal luminaries: what they refuse to admit is that the Europe whose disappearance they deplore is already irretrievably lost. The threat does not come from populism: populism is merely a reaction to the failure of Europe's liberal establishment to remain faithful to Europe's emancipatory potential, offering a false way out of ordinary people's troubles. So the only way to really defeat populism is to submit the liberal establishment itself, its actual politics, to a ruthless critique which can sometimes also take an unexpected turn. For example: does Europe needs its own army? Yes, it needs it more than ever. But why, when we all know that the most sickening excuse for joining the arms race is that, when our prospective enemies are arming themselves, the only way to deter war and protect peace is for us to also get ready for war?

Already, for a decade or so, the arms race between three superpowers (US, Russia, and China) has been exploding at a frantic pace. The entire arctic area is becoming militarized; billions are being invested in military supercomputers and biogenetics. In October 2018, Trump announced that the US would pull out of the nuclear arms treaty with Russia. Chinese military journals openly debate the need for China to engage in real war (while the US and Russian military has recently been tested by conflicts in Iraq, Syria, etc., the Chinese army has avoided a real fight for decades). And Russia? Addressing members of the Russian Parliament, Vladimir Putin said on March 1, 2018: "The missile's test-launch and ground trials make it possible to create a brand-new weapon, a strategic nuclear missile powered by a nuclear engine. The range is unlimited. It can maneuver for an unlimited period of time. No one in the world has anything similar," he said to applause and concluded: "Russia still has the greatest nuclear potential in the world, but nobody listened to us. Listen to us now."

Yes, we should listen to these words, but we should listen to them as to the words of a madman joining the duet of the other two madmen, Trump and Xi. Each side can, of course, claim that all it wants is peace and is only reacting to the threat posed by others (for example, Putin immediately added that he is simply reacting to Trump's claims that, due to its protective shields, the US can win a nuclear war against Russia) – true, but what this means is that the madness is in the whole system itself, in the vicious cycle we are caught in once we participate in the system. The structure here is similar to that of the supposed belief where also all individual participants act rationally, attributing irrationality to the other who reasons in exactly the same way. From my youth in socialist Yugoslavia, I remember a weird incident with toilet paper. All of a sudden, a rumor started to circulate that there was not enough toilet paper in the stores. The authorities promptly issued assurances that there was enough toilet paper for normal consumption, and, surprisingly, this was not only true but people mostly even believed it to be true. However, an average consumer reasoned in the following way: I know there is enough toilet paper and the rumor is false, but what if some people take this rumor seriously and, in a panic, start to buy and stockpile toilet paper, thereby causing an actual lack of toilet paper? So I had better go and buy reserves of it myself. It is not even necessary to believe that some others take the rumor seriously; it is enough to presuppose that some others believe that there are people who take the rumor seriously – the effect is the same, namely, a real lack of toilet paper in the stores.

Already in December 2016, this madness reached an almost unimaginably ridiculous peak: both Trump and Putin emphasized the chance for new, more friendly relations between Russia and the US, and simultaneously asserted their full commitment to the arms race – as if peace among the superpowers can only be provided by a new Cold War. Alain Badiou wrote that the contours of the future war are already drawn:

> The United States and their "Western–Japanese" clique on one side, and China and Russia on the other side, with nuclear weapons everywhere. So all we can do is remember what Lenin said: "Either revolution will prevent war or war will trigger revolution." Thus, the highest aspiration of future political work could be defined as follows: that for the first time in history it may be the former possibility – revolution will prevent war – that becomes a reality, and not the latter – war will lead to revolution. Indeed, it was the latter possibility that materialized itself in Russia in the context of the First World War and in China in the context of the Second. But at what a price! And with what long-term consequences![9]

So why should Europe join this crazy dance? Because it is clearly an exception: it doesn't fit the world of the struggle for domination between America-first, Russia-first, and China-first. Not building an army would just make Europe the playground of the battle for domination between the big three (which Europe is already becoming). The US and Russia both work hard to destroy European unity, while China retains an ambiguous distance. Europe is increasingly an anomaly, standing alone, with no allies. The only way for Europe to maintain autonomy is to become even more united and signal this unity through united armed forces.

16

The Right to Tell the Public
Bad News

Today, in our era of digital media's escalating control, we should remember the origin of the internet: in the US army, they were wondering how to maintain communication among surviving units in a scenario where global nuclear war were to destroy the central command, and the idea emerged of laterally connecting these dispersed units and bypassing the (destroyed) center. From the very beginning, the internet thus contained a democratic potential, since it stood for a multiple direct exchange between individual units bypassing central control and coordination - and this democratic potential presented a threat to those in power. Their main reaction to this threat was to control the digital "clouds" that mediate communication between individuals. "Clouds" in all their forms are, of course, presented to us as facilitators of our freedom: clouds make it possible for me to sit in front of my PC and freely surf; everything is out there at our disposal - however, those who control the clouds also control the limits of our freedom.

The most direct form of this control is, of course, direct exclusion: individuals as well as entire news organizations (teleSUR, RT, Al Jazeera) disappear from social media (or their accessibility is limited - try getting Al Jazeera on the TV screen in a US hotel!) without any reasonable explanation being given – usually pure technicalities are evoked. While in some cases (like direct racist excesses) censorship is justified, what is dangerous is that it just happens in a nontransparent way. The minimal democratic demand should be that such limitations of access are done in a transparent way and with public justification. These justifications can also be cheating and ambiguous, concealing their true reason. In an additional perverse twist, control and censorship can be justified as a mode of protecting individuals from traumatic experiences that threaten to disturb their happiness.

At one conference, I described the strange case of Bradley Barton from Ontario, Canada, who, in March 2016, was found not guilty of first-degree murder of Cindy Gladue, an indigenous sex worker who bled to death at the Yellowhead Inn in Edmonton, having sustained an 11-centimetre wound on her vaginal wall. The defense argued that Barton accidentally caused Gladue's death during rough but consensual sex, and the court agreed. This case doesn't just counteract our basic moral intuitions – a man brutally murders a woman during sexual activity, but he walks free because "he didn't mean it . . ." The most disturbing aspect of the case is that, conceding to the demands of the defense, the judge allowed Gladue's preserved pelvis to be admitted as evidence: brought into court, the lower part of her torso was displayed for the jurors (incidentally, this is the first time a portion of a body had been presented at a trial in Canada). Why would hard copy photos of the wound not be enough? But my point here is that I was repeatedly attacked for my reporting of this case: the reproach was that, by describing the case, I reproduced it and thus repeated it symbolically – although I described it with strong disapproval, I secretly enabled my listeners to find perverse pleasure in it. These attacks on me exemplify nicely the politically correct need to protect people from traumatic or disturbing news and images. My counterpoint to it is that, in order to fight such crimes, one has to present them in all their horror, one has to be shocked by them. In his preface to *Animal Farm*, George Orwell wrote that if liberty means anything, it means "the right to tell people what they do not want to hear" – *this* is the liberty that we are deprived of when our media are censored and regulated.

We are caught in the progressive digitalization of our lives: most of our activities (and passivities) are now registered in some digital cloud that also permanently evaluates us, tracing not only our acts but also our emotional states. When we experience ourselves as free to the utmost (surfing on the web where everything is available), we are totally "externalized" and subtly manipulated. The digital network gives new meaning to the old slogan "the personal is political." And it's not only the control of our intimate lives that is at stake: everything is today regulated by some digital network, from transport to health, from electricity to water. That's why the web is our most important commons today, and the struggle for its control is *the* struggle today. The enemy is the combination of privatized and state-controlled commons, corporations (Google, Facebook) and state security agencies (NSA).

The digital network that sustains the functioning of our societies as well as their control mechanisms is the ultimate figure of the technical grid that sustains power, and that's why regaining control over it is our first task. Wikileaks was here just the beginning, and our motto here should be a Maoist one: "Let a hundred Wikileaks blossom."

. . . And the Rest

17

It's the Same Struggle, Dummy!

The ongoing attacks on the UK Labour Party for the alleged anti-Semitism of some of its prominent members is not only extremely biased; in the long term, it also obfuscates the true danger of anti-Semitism today, the danger perfectly illustrated by a caricature published back in July 2008 in the Viennese daily *Die Presse*: two stocky Nazi-looking Austrians sit at a table, one of them holding in his hands a newspaper and commenting to his friend: "Here you can see again how a totally justified anti-Semitism is being misused for a cheap critique of Israel!" This joke turns around the standard argument against critics of the policies of the State of Israel: like every other state, the State of Israel can and should be judged and eventually criticized, but critics misuse the justified critique of Israeli policy for anti-Semitic purposes. When today's Christian fundamentalist supporters of Israeli politics reject Leftist critiques of Israeli policies, is their implicit line of argumentation not uncannily close to the caricature from *Die Presse*?

What this means is that, when approaching the Israeli-Palestinian conflict, one should stick to ruthless and cold standards, suspending the urge to try to "understand" the situation: one should unconditionally resist the temptation to "understand" Arab anti-Semitism (where we really encounter it) as a "natural" reaction to the sad plight of the Palestinians, or to "understand" the Israeli measures as a "natural" reaction against the background of the memory of the Holocaust.

There should be no "understanding" of the fact that, in many, if not most, of the Arab countries, from Saudi Arabia to Egypt, Hitler is still considered a hero, the fact that, in primary school textbooks, all the traditional anti-Semitic myths, from the notorious forged Protocols of the Zion Elders to the claims that Jews use the blood of Christian (or Arab) children for sacrificial purposes, are attributed to them. To claim that this anti-Semitism articulates in a displaced mode the resistance against capitalism in no way justifies it (the same goes for the Nazi anti-Semitism: it also drew its energy from the anti-capitalist resistance): displacement is not here a secondary operation, but the fundamental gesture of ideological mystification.

So we should not interpret or judge singular acts "together"; we should excise them from their historical texture. The present actions of the Israeli Defense Forces in the West Bank should *not* be judged "against the background of the Holocaust"; the fact that many Arabs celebrate Hitler or that synagogues are desecrated in France and elsewhere in Europe should *not* be judged as an "inappropriate, but understandable, reaction to what Israelis are doing in the West Bank." When any public protest against the Israel Defense Forces activities in the West Bank is flatly denounced as an expression of anti-Semitism, and – implicitly, at least – put in the same line with the defenders of the Holocaust, that is to say, when the shadow of the Holocaust is permanently evoked in order to neutralize any criticism of Israeli military and political operations, it is not enough to insist on the difference between anti-Semitism and the critique of particular measures of the State of Israel. One should go a step further and claim that it is the State of Israel that, in this case, is desecrating the memory of the Holocaust victims, ruthlessly manipulating them, instrumentalizing them into a means to legitimize present political measures.

What this means is that one should flatly reject the very notion of any logical or political link between the Holocaust and the present Israeli-Palestinian tensions; these are two thoroughly different phenomena: the one part of the European history of Rightist resistance to the dynamics of modernization, the other one of the last chapters in the history of colonization. On the other hand, the difficult task for the Palestinians is to accept that their true enemies are not Jews but the Arab regimes themselves, which manipulate their plight in order, precisely, to prevent this shift – i.e., the political radicalization in their own midst. Part of today's situation in Europe effectively is the growth of anti-Semitism – say, in Malmö, Sweden, where the aggressive Muslim minority harasses Jews so that they are afraid to walk in the streets in their traditional dress.[1] Such phenomena should be clearly and unambiguously condemned. The struggle against anti-Semitism and the struggle against Islamophobia should be viewed as two aspects of the *same* struggle. Far from standing for a utopian position, this necessity of a common struggle is grounded in the very fact of the far-reaching consequences of extreme suffering. In a memorable passage in *Still Alive: A Holocaust Girlhood Remembered*, Ruth Klüger describes a conversation with "some advanced PhD candidates" in Germany:

One reports how in Jerusalem he made the acquaintance of an old Hungarian Jew who was a survivor of Auschwitz, and yet this man cursed the Arabs and held them all in contempt. How can someone who comes from Auschwitz talk like that? the German asks. I get into the act and argue, perhaps more hotly than need be. What did he expect? Auschwitz was no instructional institution . . . . You learned nothing there, and least of all humanity and tolerance. Absolutely nothing good came out of the concentration camps, I hear myself saying, with my voice rising, and he expects catharsis, purgation, the sort of thing you go to the theatre for? They were the most useless, pointless establishments imaginable.[2]

In short, the extreme horror of Auschwitz did not make it into a place that purifies its surviving victims into ethically sensitive subjects who got rid of all petty egotistic interests; on the contrary, part of the horror of Auschwitz was that it also dehumanized many of its victims, transforming them into brutal insensitive survivors, making it impossible for them to practice the art of balanced ethical judgment. The lesson to be drawn here is a very depressing and sad one: we have to abandon the idea that there is something emancipatory in extreme experiences, that they enable us to clear the mess and open our eyes to the ultimate truth of a situation. Or, as Arthur Koestler, the great anti-communist convert, put it concisely: "If power corrupts, the reverse is also true; persecution corrupts the victims, though perhaps in subtler and more tragic ways."

18

The Real Anti-Semites and Their Zionist Friends

A very important event that happened recently was largely ignored by the big media, although it allows us to understand in a new light the ongoing campaign against Jeremy Corbyn in the UK and "democratic socialists" in the US, accusing them of anti-Semitism.

In January 2019, our media abundantly reported that the Polish Sejm (the lower house of parliament), dominated by the populist PiS (Law and Justice) party, had endorsed an amendment according to which attributing blame to Poland for World War II-era Nazi crimes (the Holocaust) is punishable by three years in prison. This amendment caused great outcry around the world and gave rise to tensions between Poland and Israel, since it was perceived as being in accordance with the strong anti-Semitic tradition in Poland. So it looked just another chapter in the long feud between Christian nationalists and their "cosmopolitan" Jewish opponents.

But then, the (largely ignored) second act of this affair followed, noted only by a few commentators, my honorable Polish friend Slawomir Sierakowski among them.[3] At an abruptly convened session in late June, the Sejm rushed through another amendment, effective immediately, reversing the first amendment – writing about Polish people's responsibility for the Holocaust is no longer punishable. In line with the PiS ideology, this amendment nonetheless emphasizes the large number of Poles who heroically helped Jews, so that, as they say, PiS kept the cake and ate it; the message was, basically, "you can write about it because there is nothing to write about."

The first puzzle here is the mysterious way this reconciliation between Polish populists and Israel was accomplished. The entire process was carried out in secret, to the point that Israeli–Polish relations were mediated by the countries' respective intelligence agencies. Netanyahu, himself a populist, was eager to resolve the conflict with fellow populist PiS government because he did not want to alienate Israel's most loyal ally within the European Union.

But how can Poland, with its tradition of anti-Semitism, be Israel's most loyal ally? We should remember that Poland is no exception here: relations between Netanyahu and Viktor Orbán (his Fidesz party and its allies are also permeated by Christian nationalist anti-Semitism) are also more than cordial, not to mention Donald Trump himself who, in the US, is supported by the anti-Semitic alt-Right, while internationally he is a staunch supporter of Zionist expansionism (moving the US embassy to Jerusalem, e.g.). The extreme version of this Zionist anti-Semitism was propagated by Anders Breivik, the Norwegian anti-immigrant mass murderer: he was anti-Semitic, but pro-Israel, since the State of Israel was, in his view, the first line of defense against Muslim expansion – he even wanted to see the Jerusalem Temple rebuilt. In short, Jews are OK as long as there aren't too many of them – or, as Breivik wrote in his "Manifesto": "There is no Jewish problem in Western Europe (with the exception of the UK and France) as we only have 1 million in Western Europe, whereas 800,000 out of these 1 million live in France and the UK. The US on the other hand, with more than 6 million Jews (600% more than Europe) actually has a considerable Jewish problem." This figure thus encapsulates the ultimate paradox of a Zionist anti-Semite.

And the really depressing fact is that Netanyahu and his followers act as allies of this tendency – one among the clear signs (the other being the new Israeli law on citizenship, which installs direct apartheid, transforming non-Jews into secondary citizens) that Israel is becoming just another Middle Eastern fundamentalist country, an ally of Egypt and Saudi Arabia. This rise of the weird figure of anti-Semitic Zionism, one of the most worrying signs of our decay, is increasingly linked to the growing panic in our political establishment at the growth of the new Left: the charge of anti-Semitism is now addressed at anyone who deviates to the Left from the acceptable Left-liberal establishment.

One should not be surprised to learn that the push within Israel to condemn Poland's memory law did not come from Zionist fundamentalists – it was launched by the Israeli anti-fundamentalist opposition, and Netanyahu had only gone along with it because he had no other choice. A new political line of division is thus emerging among Jews themselves: anti-Semitic Zionists against those who fight aggressive Zionism *and* anti-Semitism on behalf of the Jewish emancipatory legacy itself. They should be our allies; they are one of the few glimmers of hope in today's confused time of false divisions.

The privileged role of Jews in the establishment of the sphere of the "public use of reason" hinges on their subtraction from every state power – this position of the "part of no-part" of every organic nation-state community, not the abstract universal nature of their monotheism, makes them the immediate embodiment of universality. No wonder, then, that, with the establishment of the Jewish nation-state, a new figure of the Jew emerged: a Jew resisting identification with the State of Israel, refusing to accept the State of Israel as his true home, a Jew who "subtracts" himself from this state, and who includes the State of Israel among the states toward which he insists on maintaining a distance, to live in their interstices – and it is this uncanny Jew who is the object of what one cannot but designate as "Zionist anti-Semitism," the foreign excess disturbing the nation-state community. These Jews, the "Jews of the Jews themselves," worthy successors of Spinoza, are today the ones who continue to insist on the "public use of reason," refusing to submit their reasoning to the "private" domain of the nation-state.

I admit that I always had a problem with BDS, the Boycott, Divestment, and Sanctions movement that promotes various forms of boycott against Israel until it meets its obligations under international law (withdrawal from the occupied territories, removal of the separation barrier in the West Bank, full equality for Arab-Palestinian citizens of Israel). While I fully support these goals, my reluctance was based on two main reasons. First, in the current situation, when anti-Semitism really is alive in Europe, it is dangerous to play with the idea of a boycott. Second, why should we not also boycott China for what the Chinese state is doing to Uyghurs? Or, closer to Israel, why not boycott Saudi Arabia (instead of Iran)? The cynical reply of my BDS friends is: because in the case of China it would not work and here it might work. Really? Plus, such reasoning implies a weird ethics: punish the soft ones, not the really bad ones.

Here is an example of the excess of BDS. When, a couple of years ago, I visited the Jerusalem film festival to promote the pro-Palestinian film of my friend Udi Aloni, I was attacked for participating in a state-sponsored event. A BDS fanatic asked me whether I was aware that my visit to Jerusalem was the same as a visit to Berlin in 1938? There was even an "Open letter" circulating on the web that criticized me for accepting the invitation. My reply was: the visit was paid for by me and Udi; I was presented by Udi as his personal guest, not as the Festival's guest. Plus, if we leave aside the problematic nature of the parallel between Jerusalem and Nazi Berlin, then yes, if I had been invited to Berlin in 1938 to promote a film celebrating Jewish resistance to the Nazis, I would have gladly accepted it . . .

However, when, in May 2019, the German Bundestag passed a non-binding resolution declaring BDS anti-Semitic, my alarm bells began to ring. BDS anti-Semitic? All my links to BDS are with my Jewish friends who are part of it, and that was the idea from the beginning: a joint action of West Bank Palestinians with Israeli Jews who oppose the occupation of the West Bank. Obviously, something else is going on here: an obscene diabolical pact between Zionists and true European racists. The sacred memory of the Holocaust is mobilized to legitimize the corrupted politics of today, the apartheid practiced against Palestinians. Those who do it are the true desecrators of the Holocaust. When, in March 2019, (the German band) Rammstein published a video version of their new song "Deutschland," in which the group members appear dressed as Auschwitz inmates, the Israeli foreign ministry protested against such misuse of Holocaust imagery for commercial purposes. The answer should be not only an unconditional defense of Rammstein as an authentic Leftist band reflecting on the difficulties of their German identity; we should also add that the misuse of Holocaust memory for the legitimization of what the State of Israel is doing in the West Bank is an infinitely more repulsive act.

On May 26, 2019, Germany's government commissioner on anti-Semitism suggested that Jews should not always wear the traditional kippah cap in public, in the wake of a spike in the number of anti-Jewish attacks.[4] How seriously are we to take this recommendation? Although anti-Semitism is rising all around Europe, this warning is also in the service of the establishment's strategy of prohibiting the critique of Israeli politics as anti-Semitic.

Furthermore, the claim that the targeting of the State of Israel, conceived as a Jewish collectivity, is also anti-Semitic raises many problems. If we accept this claim, we can easily see how, precisely, a legitimate critique of the politics of the State of Israel can be dismissed as anti-Semitic. Until recently, the two-state solution was officially endorsed by the UN, the US, and Israel. What is replacing it is more and more openly signaled by big media. Caroline B. Glick (author of *The Israeli Solution: A One-State Plan for Peace in the Middle East*) claimed in 2014, in a *New York Times* article, "There Should Be No Palestinian State," that those who propose to recognize Palestine as a state

> know that in recognizing "Palestine" they are not helping the cause of peace. They are advancing Israel's ruin. If they were even remotely interested in freedom and peace, the Europeans would be doing the opposite. They would be working to strengthen and expand Israel, the only stable zone of freedom and peace in the region. They would abandon the phony two-state solution, which . . . is merely doublespeak for seeking Israel's destruction and its replacement with a terror state.
>
> With strategic blindness and moral depravity now serving as the twin guideposts for European policy toward Israel, Israel and its supporters must tell the truth about the push to recognize "Palestine." It isn't about peace or justice. It's about hating Israel and assisting those who most actively seek its obliteration.[5]

What was (and still is) official international policy is thus openly denounced as a receipt for Israel's ruin, and as an expression of brutal anti-Semitism. And it is clear that, far from standing as an extremist minority view, this stance just renders explicit the strategic orientation of the gradual colonization of the West Bank in the last decades:

the disposition of new settlements (with a large number of them in the east, close to the Jordanian border) makes it clear that a West bank Palestinian state is out of the question. Furthermore, if we accept that "the targeting of the state of Israel, conceived as a Jewish collectivity" is per se anti-Semitic, should we not also renounce every criticism of new legal measures that introduce a kind of apartheid, clearly treating only Jews as citizens with full rights, since any such criticism in some sense effectively targets "the State of Israel, conceived as a Jewish collectivity"?

As for the so-called "Macpherson principle" ("a racist incident is one perceived to be racist by the victim"), one should simply ask: if it holds that anti-Semitic incidents are those perceived by Jews as anti-Semitic, does the same not hold for Palestinians and their protests? Should we also not say that the racist measures against Palestinians are those perceived by them as such? So what about the denial of Palestinian nationhood as the standard procedure of Zionists? Plus, the final obvious argument against the principle "a racist incident is one perceived to be racist by the victim": anti-Semites perceive themselves as victims of Jewish domination (Jews secretly control the world, etc.) – in this case, for sure, the "victim's perception" is false!

19

Yes, Racism Is Alive and Well!

Our media widely reported on the results of a recent CNN poll: anti-Semitism is alive and well in Europe, a third of the people think Jews have too much influence, younger generations are less and less aware of the Holocaust, etc. While one should without any restraints condemn and fight all forms of anti-Semitism, one should nonetheless add some observations on the results of this poll. First, it would be interesting to learn how the percentage of those with a negative stance toward Jews compares to the percentage of those with a negative stance toward Muslims and Blacks – just to make sure that we don't find some forms of racism unacceptable and other forms normal. Second, one should raise here the paradox of Zionist anti-Semitism: quite a few European (and American) anti-Semites just don't want too many Jews in their own country, even while they fully support the expansion of Israel into the West Bank – how do we count them? This brings us to the key question: how do we measure anti-Semitism? Where does the legitimate criticism of Israeli politics in the West Bank end and anti-Semitism begin?

To clarify this point, a brief detour into philosophy is required. After quoting a key passage from Hegel about how the Universal "determines itself, and so is itself the particular; the determinateness is its difference; it is only differentiated from itself. Its species are therefore only (a) the universal itself and (b) the particular," Todd MacGowan provides its interpretation:

The particular concept relies on the determination of the universal through the form of an opposing particular. The case of Nazism perfectly illustrates Hegel's point here. The attempt to assert German particularity establishes an opposition between two particulars (German and Jew), but one of these particulars must take on the form of the universal in order to define the other. In an ironic twist, however, it is not German that takes on this role. The two particular species of the universal are Jew and German, but the opposing particular, Jew, is the one that comes to act as universal because it provides the basis through which one can identify oneself as a German. The oppressed group in a struggle of competing particulars will always represent the universal, even as it is degraded by the oppressor."[6]

In short, if every opposition of particulars is the self-determining of the universal, this means that, in the opposition of two particulars, one always stands for the Universal. MacGowan immediately applies this logical proposition to the status of the Jews: "Rosenberg labels Jewishness an 'anti-race' without any particularity of its own. Nazi identity depends on the universality of the Jew, but this dependence only augments Nazi hatred."[7] Effectively, in the Nazi imaginary, Jews are not just another race that should be put to its proper (subordinated) place in the hierarchy of races; they are "anti-race" in the sense of lacking a firm ethnic inner form, which is why they tend to corrode every (other particular) race they come into contact with.

What the fact of Jews functioning as an anti-race implies is not only that they – precisely insofar as they are the foreign body that resists being transformed into a particular race – stand for the nonracial universality of humanity. It also implies that, in every conflict between two particular races, one of the two implicitly stands for the universal and the other for the particular. It is here that one should apply Hegel's idea that every genus ultimately has only two species, itself and the particular (species). In short, a racial conflict is never just a conflict between two particular entities: it is, of course, the oppressed race that stands for the universal.

For some time, in the mid-1930s, the Nazis thought that it would be eventually possible to reduce the Jews to a particular group with their proper land and state, which is why they supported their immigration to Palestine. Not only do today's European anti-Semites follow the same line (Jews are bad here, in our midst, but they are good there, defending us from Muslims); it is even today's Zionism of the State of Israel, which seems to be trying to realize this program of creating a strong Jewish nation-state on their own land, thereby transforming the Jews from anti-race into a race proper.

This brings us back to our problem. One of the best indications of the gradual disappearance of the sense of irony in our public space was the repetition of a certain metaphor about the negotiations between the State of Israel and Palestinians in the span of a decade or so. About a decade ago, when some kind of negotiations were still ongoing, the Palestinian negotiator compared the talks with the Israelis – the fact that, even as Israel was negotiating how to divide the West Bank, it was gradually building more and more settlements there – with two guys at a table negotiating over how to split a pizza between them: as the debate goes on and on, one of the guys is all the time eating parts of the pizza. In a recent documentary report about the West Bank, a settler mentions the same anecdote, but with no sad irony, just brutal satisfaction: "Our negotiations with Palestinians are like debating about how to cut a pizza while we are all the time eating slices of it," accompanied by a mischievous smile.

There is something truly disturbing in the way the TV documentary from which we quoted the remark on eating pizza presents the West Bank settlements. We learn that, for the majority of the new settlers, what brought them to move there was not a Zionist dream but a simple wish to live in a nice clean habitat close to a large city (Jerusalem, in this case). They describe their life there as much better than living in a suburb of Los Angeles: green surroundings, clean air, cheap water and electricity, big city easily accessible by special highways, all the local infrastructure (schools, shopping centers, etc.), but cheaper than in the US, built and sustained by the Israeli state. And the Palestinian cities and villages which surround them? They are basically invisible, present in two main forms: cheap labor for building the settlements, occasional acts of violence treated as a nuisance. In short, the majority of settlers live in invisible cupolas, isolated from their surroundings, behaving as if what goes on outside their cupolas belongs to another world that doesn't really concern them.

The dream that underlies this politics is best rendered by the wall that separates a settler's town from the Palestinian town on a nearby hill somewhere in the West Bank. The Israeli side of the wall is painted with the image of the countryside beyond the wall – but without the Palestinian town, depicting just nature, grass, trees – is this not ethnic cleansing at its purest, imagining the outside beyond the wall as it should be, empty, virginal, waiting to be settled?

So should we doubt that Israel sincerely wants peace in the Middle East? Of course it does – colonizers and occupiers in general always want peace, after they've got what they want, because peace means they can enjoy, in peace, what they grabbed. No doubt that, after Germany occupied most of Europe in 1941, it also sincerely wanted peace (and ruthlessly fought all resistance as terrorists . . .). (As for the use of the term "colonization," one should recall that the early Zionists themselves used it to designate their endeavor a century ago.)

And, to conclude, if anyone who just read these lines considers them anti-Semitic, then, I think, he (or she) is not only totally wrong but also poses a threat to what is most valuable in the Jewish tradition.

20

What Is To Be Done When Our Cupola Is Leaking?

Columns of refugees from Honduras approach the US border through Mexico; African refugees break the barriers and enter the small Spanish territory of Ceuta on the northern tip of Africa . . . Although the numbers are comparatively small, they do signal a basic geopolitical fact: the network of borders on which the fragile balance of our world relies is seriously disturbed.

In *In the World Interior of Capital*, Peter Sloterdijk demonstrates how, in today's globalization, the capitalist system came to determine all conditions of life. The first sign of this development was the Crystal Palace in London, the site of the first world exhibition in 1851. Its structure rendered palpable the exclusivity of globalization as the construction and expansion of a world interior whose boundaries are invisible, yet virtually insurmountable from without, and which is now inhabited by one and a half billion winners of globalization; three times this number are left standing outside the door. Consequently, "the world interior of capital is not an agora or a trade fair beneath the open sky, but rather a hothouse that has drawn inwards everything that was once on the outside."[8] This interior, built on capitalist excesses, determines everything: "The primary fact of the Modern Age was not that the earth goes around the sun, but that money goes around the earth."[9]

After the process that transformed the world into the globe, "social life could only take place in an expanded interior, a domestically and artificially climatized inner space."[10]

What Sloterdijk correctly pointed out is that capitalist globalization does not stand only for openness, conquest, but also for a self-enclosed globe separating the Inside from its Outside. The two aspects are inseparable: capitalism's global reach is grounded in the way it introduces a radical class division across the entire globe, separating those protected by the sphere from those outside its cover. The flow of refugees is a momentary reminder of the violent world outside our cupola, a world which, for us, insiders, appears mostly on TV reports about distant violent countries, not as part of our reality but encroaching on it. Our ethico-political duty is not just to become aware of the reality outside our cupola, but to fully assume our co-responsibility for the horrors there. The hypocrisy of the reactions to the brutal murder of Jamal Khashoggi provides a nice example of how this cupola works. In a broader sense, he was one of us, well located within the cupola, so we are shocked and outraged. But our care is ridiculously displaced: the true scandal is that the murder in Istanbul created so much greater a scandal than in Yemen, where Saudi Arabia is destroying an entire country. In (probably) ordering the murder, Mohammad Bin Salman forgot the lesson of Stalin: if you kill one person, you are a criminal; if you kill thousands, you are a hero. So Mohammad Bin Salman should have gone on killing thousands in Yemen . . .

So, back to our Leninist question: what is to be done? The first and (sadly) predominant reaction is one of protective self-enclosure: the world out there is in a mess, let's protect ourselves by all kinds of walls. A New World Order is emerging in which the only alternative to the "clash of civilizations" remains the peaceful coexistence of civilizations (or "ways of life," a more popular term today): forced marriages and homophobia (or the idea that a woman going alone to a public place calls for rape) are OK, just as long as they are confined to another country that is otherwise fully included in the world market.

The New World Order that is emerging is thus no longer the Fukuyamaist one of global liberal democracy, but a new world order of the peaceful coexistence of different politico-theological ways of life – coexistence, of course, against the background of the smooth functioning of global capitalism. The obscenity of this process is that it can present itself as a progress in anticolonial struggle: the liberal West will no longer be allowed to impose standards on others, all ways of life will be treated as equal . . . It is no wonder that Robert Mugabe displayed sympathy for Trump's slogan "America first!" – "America first!" for you, "Zimbabwe first!" for me, "India first!" or "North Korea first!" for them. This is already how the British Empire, the first global capitalist empire, functioned: each ethnic religious community was allowed to pursue its own way of life, Hindus in India were safely burning widows, etc., and these local "customs" were either criticized as barbaric or praised for their premodern wisdom, but were tolerated since what mattered is that they were economically part of the Empire.

The sad truth that sustains this new "tolerance" is that today's global capitalism can no longer afford a positive vision of emancipated humanity, even as an ideological dream. Fukuyamaist liberal democratic universalism failed because of its own inherent limitations and inconsistencies, and populism is the symptom of this failure, its Huntington's disease. But the solution is not populist nationalism, Rightist or Leftist. The only solution is a new universalism – it is demanded by the problems confronted by humanity today, from ecological threats to refugee crises.

The second reaction is global capitalism with a human face, personified in socially responsible corporate figures like Bill Gates and George

Soros. But even in its extreme form – open up our borders to refugees, treat them like one of us – the problem with this solution is that it only provides what in medicine is called a symptomatic treatment. Therapy leaves the basic global situation intact; it affects only its symptoms, not its cause. Such treatment is aimed at reducing the signs and symptoms for the comfort and well-being of the patient – but, in our case, this is obviously not enough since the solution is obviously not that all the wretched of the world will move into the safety of the cupola. We need to move from the humanitarian focus on the wretched of the Earth to the wretched Earth itself.

The third reaction is therefore to gather courage and envisage a radical change that imposes itself when we fully assume the consequences of the fact that we live in *one* world. "Anthropocene" describes a new age in the life of our planet: we can no longer rely on the Earth as a receptacle for the consequences of our productive activity; we can no longer afford to ignore the side effects (collateral damage) of our productivity; they can no longer be reduced to the background of the figure of humanity. At the very moment when we become powerful enough to affect the most basic conditions of our life, we have to accept that we are just another animal species on a small planet. A radical politico-economic change is necessary, what Sloterdijk calls "the domestication of the wild animal Culture."

Is such a change a utopia? No, the true utopia is that we can survive without such a revolution.

21

Is China Communist or Capitalist?

The ideologist and perpetrator of the Christchurch, NZ, terrorist attacks in March 2019 wrote a short collection of texts, "The Great Replacement," in which he answers the question "Were/are you a fascist?"; after declaring himself "an Eco-fascist by nature," he writes: "The nation with the closest political and social values to my own is the People's Republic of China."[11] It is important that he says this when he is challenged to define his basic stance and principles, so we cannot reduce it to his (probable) admiration of how the Chinese government is dealing with its Uyghur Muslim minority. Is this just a crazy reference, unfairly exploited in the critique of today's China? What *is* today's China?

Official Chinese social theorists paint a picture of today's world, which, to put it simply, basically remains the same as that of the Cold War: the worldwide struggle between capitalism and socialism carries on unabated, the fiasco of 1990 was just a temporary setback, so that today, the big opponents are no longer the US and the USSR, but the US and China, which remains a socialist country. The explosion of capitalism in China is read as a gigantic case of what in the early Soviet Union they called New Economic Policy, so that what we have in China is a new "socialism with Chinese characteristics" – but it is still socialism: the Communist Party remains in power and tightly controls and directs market forces. Domenico Losurdo, the Italian Marxist who died in 2018, elaborated on this point in detail, arguing against a "pure" Marxism that wants to establish a new communist society directly after the revolution, and for a more "realist" view that advocates a gradual approach with turnarounds and failures. Roland Boer evokes the memorable image of Losurdo drinking a cup of tea on a busy Shanghai street in September 2016: "In the midst of the bustle, traffic, advertising, shops, and clear economic drive of the place, Domenico said, 'I am happy with this. This is what socialism can do!' To my quizzical look, he replied with a smile, 'I am strongly in favour of the reform and opening up'."[12]

Boer then goes on to resume the argument for this "opening up": "Most efforts had been directed at the relations of production, focusing on socialist equality and collective endeavor. This is all very well, but if everyone is equal simply because they are poor, few would see the benefit. So Deng and those working with him began to emphasize another dimension of Marxism: the need to unleash the forces of production."[13] For Marxism, however, "unleashing the forces of production" is not "another dimension" but the very goal of transforming relations of production – here is Marx's classic formulation:

At a certain stage of development, the material productive forces of society come into conflict with the existing relations of production or – this merely expresses the same thing in legal terms – with the property relations within the framework of which they have operated hitherto. From forms of development of the productive forces these relations turn into their fetters. Then begins an era of social revolution.[14]

The irony is that while, for Marx, communism arises when capitalist relations of production became an obstacle to the further development of the means of production, so that this development can be secured only by a (sudden or gradual) progress from a capitalist market economy to a socialized economy, Deng Hsiao-Ping's "reforms" turn Marx around – at a certain point, one has to return to capitalism to enable the economic development of socialism. There is a further irony here that is difficult to surpass. The twentieth-century Left was defined by its opposition to two fundamental tendencies of modernity: the reign of capital with its aggressive individualism and alienating dynamics and authoritarian bureaucratic state power. What we get in today's China is exactly a combination of these two features in its extreme form: a strong authoritarian state, wild capitalist dynamics – and this should be the most efficient form of socialism today. Orthodox Marxists liked to use the term "dialectical synthesis of the opposites": a true progress takes place when we bring together the best of both opposing tendencies. It looks as if China succeeded by way of bringing together what we considered the worst in both opposing tendencies (liberal capitalism and communist authoritarianism).

From this standpoint, the economic success of China in recent decades is not interpreted as proof of the productive potential of capitalism, but as proof of the superiority of socialism over capitalism. To sustain this view, which also counts Vietnam, Venezuela, Cuba, and even Russia as socialist countries, one has to give this new socialism a strong socially conservative twist – and this is not the only reason why such a rehabilitation of socialism is blatantly non-Marxist, totally ignoring the basic Marxist point that capitalism is defined by capitalist relations of production, not by the type of state power.[15] (Incidentally, all those who have any illusions about Putin should note the fact that he elevated to the status of his official philosopher Ivan Ilyin, a Russian political theologist who, after being expelled from the Soviet Union in the early 1920s on the famous "philosophers' steamboat," advocated against Bolshevism and Western liberalism his own version of Russian fascism: the state as an organic community led by a paternal monarch.)

One must nonetheless concede a partial truth in this Chinese position: even in the wildest versions of capitalism, it matters who controls the state apparatuses. Classical Marxism and the ideology of neoliberalism both tend to reduce the state to a secondary mechanism that obeys the needs of the reproduction of capital; they both thereby underestimate the active role played by state apparatuses in economic processes. To what extent can we then imagine a non-capitalist state with capitalists playing a strong role in the economy? While the Chinese model, for sure, cannot serve as a model for emancipatory struggle – it combines immense social inequalities with a strong authoritarian state – one should nonetheless not exclude a priori the possibility of a strong non-capitalist state that resorts to elements of capitalism in some of the domains of social life: it is possible to tolerate limited elements and domains of capitalism without allowing the logic of capital to become the overdetermining principle of social totality.

Years ago, a Chinese social theorist with links to Deng Hsiao-Ping's daughter told me an interesting anecdote. When Deng was dying, an acolyte asked him what he thought his greatest act had been, expecting the usual answer: namely that he would mention his economic reforms, which had brought such development to China. To the surprise of the questioner, Deng answered: "No, it was that, when the leadership decided to open up the economy, I resisted the temptation to go all the way and open up also political life to multiparty democracy." (According to some sources, this tendency to go all the way was pretty strong in some Party circles and the decision to maintain Party control was in no way preordained.) We should resist here the liberal temptation to dream about how, had China also opened up to political democracy, its economic progress would have been even faster: what if political democracy had generated new instabilities and tensions that would have hampered economic progress? What if this (capitalist) progress was feasible only in a society dominated by a strong authoritarian power? Recall the classical Marxist thesis on early modern England: it was in the bourgeoisie's own interest to leave political power in the hands of the aristocracy and keep for itself economic power. Maybe something homologous is going on in today's China: it was in the interest of the new capitalists to leave political power to the Communist Party.

Chinese political theorists, of course, claim that their system is also democratic, but in a different way from Western parliamentary democracies: they characterize their own system as "deliberative democracy." One should take this self-designation and just see what it actually implies. When huge decisions are made, the Party does not simply decree them: people are asked to deliberate, voice their opinions . . . but the Party then decides.

Peter Sloterdijk remarked that if there is one person to whom they will build monuments a hundred years from now, it is Lee Quan Yew, the Singapore leader who invented and realized so-called "capitalism with Asian values" (which, of course, has nothing to do with Asia and all to do with authoritarian capitalism). The virus of this authoritarian capitalism is slowly but surely spreading around the globe. Before setting in motion his reforms, Deng Hsiao-Ping visited Singapore and expressly praised it as a model that all of China should follow. This change has a world-historical meaning: until now, capitalism seems inextricably linked with democracy – there were, of course, from time to time, recourses to direct dictatorship, but, after a decade or two, democracy again imposed itself (just recall the cases of South Korea and Chile). Now, however, the link between democracy and capitalism is broken. So it is quite possible that our future will be modeled upon

Chinese capitalist socialism – definitely not the socialism we were dreaming about.

But cracks are already appearing in this model. Today's Cambodia is the emblem of the antagonisms of the "developing" part of our world. A short time ago, they condemned the last surviving Khmer Rouge leaders for their crimes – but where is Cambodia now, after (officially, at least) it settled accounts with the horrors of the Khmer Rouge? Full of sweatshops, with child prostitution all around and foreigners owning most of the restaurants and hotels – one form of misery replaced by another, which is maybe just marginally better. But is China not caught in a similar, although less extreme, predicament? Remember what one may call the strange case of the disappearing Marxist students.

In dealing with critical voices, Chinese authorities seem increasingly to resort to a particular procedure: someone (an ecological activist, a Marxist student, the chief of Interpol, a religious preacher, a Hong Kong publisher, even a popular movie actress) just disappears for a couple of weeks (before reappearing in public with specific accusations raised against them), and this protracted period of silence delivers the key message: power is exerted in an impenetrable way, where nothing has to be proven, legal reasoning comes afterward when this basic message has been taken in. But the case of disappearing Marxist students is nonetheless specific: while all disappearances concern individuals whose activities can be somehow characterized as a threat to the state, the missing students legitimize their critical activity by reference to the official ideology itself.

In recent years, the Chinese leadership decided to reassert ideological orthodoxy: there is less tolerance for religion; texts of Marx, Lenin, and Mao are extensively reprinted, etc. However, the message that comes with it is: don't take it seriously! The disappeared students were doing exactly this: action upon official ideology, solidarity with overexploited workers (plus ecology, plus women's rights . . .). Two of the best-known examples (at least in our media reports) are those of Zhang Shengye and Yue Xin. While strolling through the Beida campus at Peking University, Zhang, a graduate student, was all of a sudden surrounded by a group of men in black jackets from a black car, who, after beating him heavily, pushed him into a car and drove away. (Other students who filmed the event on their mobile phones were also beaten and compelled to erase the recordings.) From that moment, nobody heard anything about Zhang. Yue Xin, a 22-year-old female student at the same university, who led the campaign to clarify the suicide of a student raped by a high Party functionary, also disappeared, and when her mother tried to unearth what happened to her, she too disappeared. Yue was a member of a Marxist circle that combined struggle for workers' rights with ecological concerns, and a Chinese version of MeToo. She joined dozens of other students from different universities who went to Shenzhen to support workers in a local robot factory in their demand for an independent trade union; in a brutal police crackdown, 50 students and workers disappeared.

What triggered such a panicky reaction in the Party leadership was, of course, the specter of a network of self-organization emerging through direct horizontal links between groups of students and workers, and based in Marxism, with sympathy in some old Party cadres and even parts of the army. Such a network directly undermines the legitimacy of Party rule and denounces it as an imposture. No wonder, then, that, in recent years, many "Maoist" websites were closed down and many Marxist debate groups at universities were prohibited – the most dangerous thing to do today in China is to believe in and take seriously the official ideology itself.

Even when, today, China appears to repeat some old Maoist measures, one should read carefully the justification:

China is planning to send millions of youth "volunteers" back to villages, raising fears of a return to the methods of Chairman Mao's brutal Cultural Revolution of 50 years ago. The Communist Youth League has promised to despatch more than 10 million students to "rural zones" by 2022 in order to "increase their skills, spread civilisation and promote science and technology," according to a Communist party document.[16]

One cannot but note that the justification here is the very opposite of the old Maoist one: students are not sent to rural zones to learn from the people's wisdom, but to teach them, to spread modern "civilization" among them.

However, the trap to avoid here is to throw all our sympathy at the Marxist students, hoping they will somehow win, or at least compel the Party to change its line into taking workers' concerns more seriously. We (and they) should rather raise a more basic and disturbing question: how is it that states where Marxism was elevated to the official ideology are precisely those states where any independent workers' movement is most brutally crushed and exploitation of workers is given free rein? It is not enough just to regret that the Chinese party is not effectively faithful to its Marxist ideology. What if there is something wrong with this ideology itself, at least in its traditional form?

22

Venezuela and the Need for
New Clichés

Back in the early 1970s, in a note to the CIA advising them how to undermine the democratically elected Chilean government of Salvador Allende, Henry Kissinger wrote succinctly: "Make the economy scream." High US representatives are openly admitting that today the same strategy is being applied in Venezuela. Former US Secretary of State Lawrence Eagleburger said on Fox News:

> [Chavez's] ability to appeal to the Venezuelan people only works so long as the population of Venezuela sees some ability for a better standard of living. If at some point the economy really gets bad, Chavez's popularity within the country will certainly decrease and it's the one weapon we have against him to begin with and which we should be using, namely the economic tools of trying to make the economy even worse so that his appeal in the country and the region goes down. . . . Anything we can do to make their economy more difficult for them at this moment is a good thing, but let's do it in ways that do not get us into direct conflict with Venezuela if we can get away with it.

The least one can say is that such statements give credibility to the theory that the economic difficulties faced by the Chavez government (major product and electricity shortages nationwide, etc.) are not only the result of the ineptness of its own economic politics. Here we come to the key political point, difficult to swallow for some liberals: we are clearly not dealing with blind market processes and reactions (say, shop owners trying to make more profit by keeping some products off the shelves), but with an elaborate and fully planned strategy.

However, even if it is true that the economic catastrophe in Venezuela is, to a large extent, the result of the conjoined action of Venezuelan big capital and US interventions, and that the core of the opposition to the Maduro regime consists of far-Right corporations and not the popular democratic forces, this insight just raises further and even more troublesome questions. In view of these reproaches, why was there no Venezuelan Left to provide an authentic radical alternative to Chavez and Maduro? Why was the initiative in the opposition to Chavez taken by the extreme Right, which triumphantly hegemonized the oppositional struggle, imposing itself as the voice of (even) the ordinary people who suffer the consequences of the Chavista mismanagement of economy?

So when the Left blames the US boycott and support of the internal opposition for the economic woes of Venezuela, one should point out that this is not the whole story: the ultimate cause of these woes is not the external imperialist plot but the inner antagonisms and insufficiency of the Chavista project itself. If we just blame the external enemy, we commit the same mistake as the fascists who ignore inherent antagonisms of their society and blame the crisis on external enemies who are not part of the organic social body – Jews, communists . . . No wonder that even Chavez himself committed a couple of anti-Semitic slips (for which he had to apologize later under the instigation of Fidel Castro).

Chavez was not just a populist throwing around oil money. What is largely ignored in the international media are the complex and often inconsistent efforts undertaken to overcome the capitalist economy by experimenting with new forms of the organization of production, forms that endeavor to move beyond the alternatives between private and state property: farmers and workers cooperatives, worker participation, control and organization of production, different hybrid forms between private property and social control and organization, etc. (Say, factories not used by the owners are given to the workers to run them.) There are many hits and runs on this path – for example, after some attempts, giving ownership of nationalized factories to workers, distributing stocks among them, was abandoned. Although we are dealing here with genuine attempts, in which grassroots initiatives interact with state proposals, we must also note many economic failures, inefficiencies, widespread corruption, etc. The usual story is that after (half) a year of enthusiastic work, things go downhill.

In the first years of Chavismo, we were clearly witnessing a broad popular mobilization. However, the big question remains: how does or should this reliance on popular self-organization affect the running of a government? Can we even imagine today an authentic communist power? What we get is disaster (Venezuela), capitulation (Greece), or a full return to capitalism (China, Vietnam). As Julia Buxton put it, the Bolivarian Revolution "has transformed social relations in Venezuela and had a huge impact on the continent as a whole. But the tragedy is that it was never properly institutionalized and thus proved to be unsustainable."[17] It is all too easy to say that authentic emancipatory politics should remain at a distance from the state: the big problem that lurks behind is what to do with the state. Can we even imagine a society outside the state? One should deal with these problems here and now; there is no time to wait for some future situation and, in the meantime, keep a safe distance from the state.

To really change things, one should accept that nothing can really be changed (within the existing system). Jean-Luc Godard proposed the motto *"Ne change rien pour que tout soit différent"* ("change nothing so that everything will be different"), a reversal of "some things must change so that everything remains the same." In our late capitalist consumerist dynamics, we are all the time bombarded by new products, but this very constant change is more and more monotonous. When only constant self-revolutionizing can maintain the system, those who refuse to change anything are effectively the agents of true change: the change of the very principle of change.

Or, to put it in a different way, the true change is not just the overcoming of the old order but, above all, the establishment of a new order. Louis Althusser once came up with a typology of revolutionary leaders worthy of Kierkegaard's classification of humans into officers, housemaids, and chimney sweeps: those who quote proverbs, those who do not quote proverbs, those who invent (new) proverbs. The first are scoundrels (Althusser thought of Stalin); the second are great revolutionaries who are doomed to fail (Robespierre); only the third understand the true nature of a revolution and succeed (Lenin, Mao). This triad registers three different ways to relate to the big Other (the symbolic substance, the domain of unwritten customs and wisdoms best expressed in the stupidity of proverbs). Scoundrels simply reinscribe the revolution into the ideological tradition of their nation (for Stalin, the Soviet Union was the last stage of the progressive development of Russia). Radical revolutionaries like Robespierre fail because they just enact a break with the past without succeeding in their effort to enforce a new set of customs (recall the utter failure of Robespierre's idea to replace religion with the new cult of a Supreme Being). Leaders like Lenin and Mao succeeded (for some time, at least) because they invented new proverbs, which means that they imposed new customs that regulated daily lives. One of the best "Goldwynisms" tells how, after being informed that critics complained that there are too many old clichés in his films, Sam Goldwyn wrote a memo to his scenario department: "We need more new clichés!" He was right, and this is a revolution's most difficult task – to create "new clichés" for ordinary daily life.

One should even take a step further here. The task of the Left is not just to propose a new order, but also to change the very horizon of what appears possible. The paradox of our predicament is thus that, while resistances against global capitalism seem to fail again and again to undermine its advance, they remain strangely out of touch with many trends that clearly signal capitalism's progressive disintegration – it is as if the two tendencies (resistance and self-disintegration) move at different levels and cannot meet, so that we get futile protests in parallel with inherent decay and no way to bring the two together in a coordinated act of capitalism's emancipatory overcoming. How did it come to this? While (most of) the Left desperately tries to protect the old workers' rights against the onslaught of global capitalism, it is almost exclusively the most "progressive" capitalists themselves (from Elon Musk to Mark Zuckerberg) who talk about postcapitalism – as if the very topic of a passage from capitalism as we know it to a new post-capitalist order has been appropriated by capitalism.

In Ernst Lubitch's film *Ninotchka*, the hero visits a cafeteria and orders coffee without cream. The waiter replies: "Sorry, but we've run out of cream. Can I bring you coffee without milk?" In both cases, the customer gets straight coffee, but this coffee is each time accompanied by a different negation, first coffee-with-no-cream, then coffee-with-no-milk. The difference between "plain coffee" and "coffee without milk" is purely virtual, there is no difference in the real cup of coffee – the lack itself functions as a positive feature. This paradox is also rendered nicely by an old Yugoslav joke about Montenegrins (people from Montenegro were stigmatized as lazy in ex-Yugoslavia): why does a Montenegrin guy, when going to sleep, put two glasses, one full and one empty, at the side of his bed? Because he is too lazy to think in advance whether he will be thirsty during the night. The point of this joke is that the absence itself has to be positively registered: it is not enough to have a full glass of water, since, if the Montenegrin is not thirsty, he will simply ignore it – this negative fact itself has to be registered, the no-need-for-water has to be materialized in the void of the empty glass. A political equivalent can be found in a well-known joke from socialist-era Poland. A customer enters a store and asks: "You probably don't have butter, or do you?" The answer: "Sorry, but we're the store that doesn't have toilet paper; the one across the street is the one that doesn't have butter!" Or consider contemporary Brazil, where, during a carnival, people from all classes dance together in the street, momentarily forgetting their race and class differences – but it is obviously not the same if a jobless worker joins the dance, forgetting his worries about how to take care of his family, or if a rich banker lets himself go and feels good about being one with the people, forgetting that he has just refused a loan to the poor worker. They are both the same on the street, but the worker is dancing without milk, while the banker is dancing without cream. In a similar way, East Europeans in 1990 wanted not only democracy-without-communism, but also democracy-without-capitalism.

And this is what the Left should learn to do: to offer the same coffee, with the hope that a coffee without milk has all of a sudden changed into a coffee without cream. Only then can the struggle for cream begin.

23

Welcome to the True New World Order!

The first thing that strikes the eye apropos the 2018 conflict between Canada and Saudi Arabia is the grotesque disproportion between cause and effect: a minor diplomatic protest triggered a set of measures that almost amount to a military conflict. Saudi Arabia finally allowed women to drive, but at the same time arrested women who campaigned for the right to drive. Among the arrested peaceful activists was Samar Badawi, who has family in Canada. The Canadian government demanded her release, but the Saudi government proclaimed this protest a reprehensible interference in its internal affairs and immediately expelled the Canadian ambassador, canceled flights to Canada, froze new trade and investment, began selling Canadian assets, announced the withdrawal of students and patients currently undergoing treatment in Canada back home. All this was done under the guidance of the crown prince who poses as a big reformer, a clear sign that Saudi Arabia remains what it is: not a real state, but a large mafia corporation run by a family, a country that quite reprehensibly interferes in the internal affairs of Yemen, literally ruining that country, and that, incidentally, takes no refugees from the nearby war zones, although it is emmeshed in the conflict up to its knees.

The message of simultaneously allowing women to drive and

arresting those who demanded it is clear and unambiguous, there is no contradiction here: if small changes happen, they must come as an act from above; no protest from below is tolerated. In the same way, there is "absurd overreaction" in the Saudi countermeasures to Canada's protest note – the message is clear: Canada got it wrong, it acted as if we still live in an era of universal human rights. The fact that Egypt and Russia supported Saudi Arabia in its measures, and that even the US and Great Britain, otherwise great protectors of human rights, decided to stay out of the melee, makes it clear that a New World Order is emerging. The crown of this new trend is a newly found Islamophobic respect for Islam: the same politicians who warn of the danger of the Islamization of the Christian West, respectfully congratulated Erdoğan for his last electoral victory – the authoritarian reign of Islam is OK for Turkey, but not for us. Israel, with its new scandalous apartheid laws privileging Jewish citizens, followed the same path. This is the truth of today's multiculturalism: every imposition of universal standards is denounced as colonialist.

Following the formula of Zionist anti-Semitism, there will be no contradiction in imposing on our countries the strictest politically correct feminist rules and simultaneously rejecting a critique of the dark side of Islam as neocolonialist arrogance.

So welcome to the New World Order in which Saudi Arabia leads the anticolonialist struggle! In some crazy formal sense, Saudi Arabia is the least corrupt state in the world: there is no need for (further) corruption, since the existing order is already absolute corruption – the King owns everything, he has already stolen the entire state.

There is something hypocritical about those liberals who criticize the slogan "America first!" – as if this is not what more or less every country is doing, as if America did not play a global role precisely because it fitted its own interests. The underlying message of "America first!" is nonetheless a sad one: the American century is over; America has resigned itself to being just one among the (powerful) countries. The supreme irony is that the Leftists who for a long time criticized the US pretension to be the global policeman may begin to long for the old times when, with all hypocrisy included, the US imposed democratic standards on the world.

24

A True Miracle in Bosnia

A miracle in Bosnia? The first association that pops up is the appearance of the Virgin Mary a couple of decades ago in Medjugorje – it brought millions of pilgrims to the area. However, in the fall of 2018, a much greater and more important miracle took place in Banja Luka, the capital of the Serb part of Bosnia ("Republika Srpska"), and also in other Bosnian cities across the ethnic divide.

The miracles were not the elections that took place in October – as usual, Bosnian elections (with all the accompanying irregularities) were marked by apathy and indifference, and just confirmed the tripartite division of the state along ethnic lines. The Serb part acts, more and more, as a sovereign state; in Muslim Sarajevo, Islamization progresses, to the extent that it is increasingly difficult to get a beer in a restaurant or bar, for example. A specific form of the much-publicized PPP (public–private partnership) is flourishing in all of Bosnia: local political elites intertwined with half-legal private businesses, their rule legitimized as protectors of ethnic entities (Bosnians, Serbs . . .) against the "enemy." In such a situation, where poverty is everywhere and young people are massively migrating to Western Europe in search of jobs, nationalism thrives and defense of our own ethnic identity easily prevails over economic issues.

The problem we are facing in Bosnia is best exemplified by what took place a couple of years ago in Croatia. Two public protest gatherings were announced: trade unions called for a protest against the exploding levels of unemployment and poverty (felt very much by ordinary people); Rightist nationalist announced a gathering in order to protest the reintroduction of the official status of Cyrillic writing in Vukovar (because of the Serb minority there). A couple of hundred people attended the first gathering; there were more than one hundred thousand people at the second protest. For ordinary people, it was poverty, much more than the Cyrillic threat, that was experienced on a daily basis, but trade unions nevertheless failed to mobilize people.

Wise commentators like to evoke such stories to cynically mock Leftist claims that our goal should be to defeat local nationalisms and to bring about a transnational coalition of those who are manipulated and exploited by the ruling ethnic elites. They patiently explain how, especially in an area like The Balkans, "irrational" ethnic hatreds all run too deep to be overcome by "rational" economic concerns – the trans-national coalition of the exploited is a miracle that will never happen. Well, this miracle – compared to which the Medjugorje appearances pale into insignificance – happened last year.

David Dragičević, a young Serb-Bosnian hacker, disappeared on the night of March 17–18, 2018; his body was found in the vicinity of Banja Luka on March 24. It was clear from his heavily disfigured body that he had been killed by protracted brutal torture. From March 26, daily protests took place in the main square of Banja Luka, organized by David's father Davor under the title "Justice for David." Police first declared David's death a suicide, and only after strong public pressure did it begin to investigate it as a case of murder, but with no results as yet. It became clear that David had discovered traces of corruption and other criminal activities in the ruling clique, so he had to disappear. Eventually, the continuous protests erupted into a large mass gathering, with tens of thousands participating, and dozens of buses bringing people from all over Republika Srpska into Banja Luka. The ruling elite reacted with panic: thousands of policemen controlled the streets and blocked entries to the city.

Now comes the true miracle. Unexpectedly, in a wonderful display of transethnic solidarity, similar gatherings took place in other Bosnian cities where Muslims form a majority. In Sarajevo, the capital of Bosnia, hundreds demanded justice for a similar case that happened in their midst: the death of Dženan Memić, who disappeared in the night of February 8–9, 2016, and was never seriously investigated, although his body was also disfigured by traces of torture. Protesters in Banja Luka, Sarajevo, and other Bosnian cities exchanged messages and emphasized their solidarity across their ethnic divides, since they all share the same fate of being run by corrupted PPP elites. Finally, they became fully aware that the true threat does not come from other ethnic groups, but from the corruption within their own group, and that they can get rid of this malignant tumor only by acting together. The impossible and "unimaginable" (for cynical realists) happened.

Of course, one should not expect too much from such uprisings. A similar transethnic movement against economic poverty already took place a couple of years ago, in an echo of the Arab Spring, and gradually dwindled. However, the fire continues to burn beneath the surface, and this fire is the only beacon of hope in Bosnia. It reconfirms the truth of Abraham Lincoln's old saying: you can fool some of the people all the time, and all the people some of the time, but you cannot fool all the people all the time.

Ideology

25

For Active Solidarity, Against Guilt and Self-Reproach

In a recent comment, Laura Kipnis drew out the ethico-political impli-cations of what happened to the film critic David Edelstein.[1] Apropos the death of Bernardo Bertolucci, director of *Last Tango in Paris*, Edelstein made a tasteless "joke" on his private Facebook page: "Even grief is better with butter," accompanied by a still from the movie of Maria Schneider and Marlon Brando (the infamous anal rape scene); he quickly deleted it (before the public outcry broke out, not in reac-tion to it). Actress Martha Plimpton immediately tweeted it to her followers: "Fire him. Immediately." Which is what happened the next day. Fresh Air and NPR announced that they were cutting ties with Edelstein because the post had been "offensive and unacceptable, especially given Maria Schneider's experience during the filming of *Last Tango in Paris*."

So what are the implications (or, rather, the unstated rules) of this incident? First, as Kipnis wrote, "there's nothing inadvertent about inadvertent offense": they cannot be excused as momentary mistakes, since they are treated as revelatory of the true character of the offender. This is why one such offense is a permanent mark against you, how-ever apologetic you might be: "One flub and you're out. An unthinking social media post will outweigh a 16-year track record." The only thing that might help is a long permanent process of self-critical self-examination: "Failure to keep re-proving it implicates you in crimes against women." You have to prove it again and again, since, as a man, you are a priori not to be trusted: "men are not to be believed, they will say anything." Kipnis's bitter conclusion: "Maybe it's time to stop hiding behind the 'speak truth to power' mantra, when women have power aplenty – we can wreck a guy's career with a tweet!" Of course, one has to introduce some further specifications here: *which* women have the power to wreck *which* guys' careers? But the fact remains that we are witnessing an enormous exercise of power that is unchecked by what would otherwise have been considered (fair trial, right to reasonable doubt . . .), and if one just points this out, one is immediately accused of protecting old white men. Plus, the barrier that separates public from private space disappears. Recently, several Icelandic MPs were called on to resign after they were recorded using crude language to describe female colleagues and a disabled activist. They did this in a bar, and an anonymous eavesdropper sent the recording to Icelandic media.[2]

The only parallel that comes to mind here is the brutal swiftness of revolutionary purges – and, effectively, many MeToo sympathizers evoke this parallel and claim that such excesses are understandable in the first moments of radical change. However, it is precisely this parallel that we should reject. Such "excessive" purges are not indications that the revolutionary zeal went too far – on the contrary, they clearly indicate that the revolution was redirected and lost its radical edge.[3] The predominant social form of MeToo and LGBT+, as well as of liberal antiracism, is a model of how to produce spectacular superficial changes without disturbing the actual relations of power and oppression: you can get fired for using the n— word, even if it is in a clearly ironic way; a person demands to be addressed as "ze" or "they"; there are more than two types of toilets in public places so that the gender binary is suspended. It is a paradise allowing big corporations to show their solidarity with victims, while continuing to function the way they always did.

A black woman, Tarana Burke, who created the MeToo campaign more than a decade ago, observed in a recent critical note that in the years since the movement began, it deployed an unwavering obsession with the perpetrators – a cyclical circus of accusations, culpability, and indiscretions: "We are working diligently so that the popular narrative about MeToo shifts from what it is. We have to shift the narrative that it's a gender war, that it's anti-male, that it's men against women, that it's only for a certain type of person – that it's for white, cisgender, heterosexual, famous women."[4] In short, one should struggle to refocus MeToo onto the daily suffering of millions of ordinary working women and housewives. This emphatically can be done – for example, in South Korea, MeToo exploded as tens of thousands of ordinary women demonstrated against their sexual exploitation. Only through the link between the two "contradictions," sexual exploitation and economic exploitation, can we mobilize the majority: men should not be portrayed just as potential rapists; they should be made aware that their violent domination over women is mediated by their experience of economic impotence. The truly radical MeToo is not about women against men but also about the prospect of their solidarity.

What all these complications make clear is that, in our critique of the predominant LGBT+ ideology, it is not enough to proceed in the usual "Marxist" way and focus on the critique of political economy – i.e., the fact that it neglects the socioeconomic causes of sexual domination and exclusion; one should supplement the critique of political economy with what one may call a critique of the libidinal economy, a reading that brings out the inherent antagonisms and inconsistencies of our libidinal lives obfuscated not only by the (till now) hegemonic heterosexual ideology, but also by the predominant versions of sexual emancipation. The antagonism that cuts across MeToo and LGBT+ movements is not to be reduced to an external pressure of "class struggle" and economic exploitation onto the sphere of sexual relations.

Although supporters of LGBT+ like to dismiss psychoanalysis as being out of date, many of them fully participate in the ongoing repression of basic Freudian insights. If psychoanalysis has taught us anything, it is that human sexuality is immanently perverted, traversed by sadomasochist spins and power games, that in it, pleasure is inextricably interlinked with pain. What we get in many LGBT+ ideologists is the opposite of this insight, the naive view that, if sexuality is not distorted by patriarchal/binary etc. pressure, it becomes a happy space of authentic expression of our true selves.

Suffice it to recall Lukas Dhont's movie *Girl* (2018), a Belgian film about a 15-year-old girl, born in the body of a boy, who dreams of becoming a ballerina.[5] Why did this film trigger such ferocious reactions in some powerful postmodern, postgender circles? The predominant LGBT+ doctrine encourages the rejection of biologically and/or socially given gender identities and advocates an individual's self-acquaintance and politicization of its identities: "You are free to define yourself as how you feel yourself! And everybody shall accept you as how you define yourself." This, exactly, is what happens in the film: the teenager protagonist is fully encouraged to adopt "the way she feels," her identity; she is encouraged to improve "point" in ballet (despite very strict and difficult classical ballet training standards); her doctor prescribes hormones; the ballet instructor gives her private lessons; the father continuously asks her about her problems – she is encouraged to elucidate her fantasies to him and to her psychologist. And we see things getting worse. Many LGBT+ activists attacked the film ferociously for its focus on the traumatic aspects of gender transition, for its depiction of the painful details of gender change, claiming that it functions as a pornographic horror show – although the ballerina on whose life the movie is based defended it staunchly, insisting that it portrays perfectly her troubles. In these critiques, we are obviously dealing with a conflict between the painful reality of gender transition and its official sanitized version, which puts all the blame on social pressure. As one of the trans people put it,[6] it is difficult to live if you hate your body.

It is crucial to note how, in all their effort to historicize gender identities and render visible their constructed nature, the LGBT+ ideologists accept the fact of gender identities, the way they operate in our everyday ideology. There is no effort in their work to deconstruct gender identities, to bring out their failed/incomplete nature; all they do is add that the gender binary does not cover the entire field or play a central role – i.e., that there are other identities that do not fit this binary vision.

Here is a happier version of the transgender transition: in yet another case of the happy marriage between big corporations and the most "progressive" sexual politics, the shaving products company Gillette was recently bombarded with praise for publishing an ad in which a transgender man is learning to shave. The ad shows Toronto-based artist Samson Bonkeabantu Brown while he is shaving

> with some coaching from his father. "I always knew I was different. I didn't know there was a term for the type of person that I was. I went into my transition just wanting to be happy. I'm glad I'm at the point where I'm able to shave," he says. "I'm at the point in my manhood where I'm actually happy. . . . I shot this ad for Gillette and wanted to include my father, who has been one

of my greatest supporters throughout my transition, encouraging me to be confident and live authentically as my best self."[7]

One has to listen carefully to the words used here: there is no social constructionism of gender mentioned here, you just discover your true self and then try to live authentically, reaching happiness by being faithful to it – if the term "essentialism" has any meaning, this is it. One should also note that, in both cases (*Girl* and the Gillette ad), we witness a weird patriarchal spin: although the transition was done in the opposite direction (man to woman in the film, woman to man in the ad), it is the father (a good one, this time) who benevolently watches over it. Not surprisingly, we get here a father who serves as the support of the subject's authentic life, of living true to its self – which was always the function of the Name-of-the-Father. Should we then not evoke here Lacan, who said that "any shelter in which may be established a viable, temperate relation of one sex to the other necessitates the intervention of that medium known as the paternal metaphor"?[8] So the father not only guarantees a viable relation of one sex to another, he also guarantees a soft and painless passage from one to another sex.

Many observers have noticed a tension in LGBT+ ideology between social constructivism and (some kind of biological) determinism: if an individual biologically identified/perceived as a man experiences himself in his psychic economy as a man, it is considered a social construct; but if an individual biologically identified/perceived as a man experiences herself as a woman, this is read as an urge, not a simple arbitrary construct but a deeper non-negotiable identity, which, if the individual demands it, has to be met by sex-changing surgery.[9] The solution is here quite simple: yes, psychic sexual identity is a choice, not a biological fact, but it is not a conscious choice that the subject can playfully repeat and transform. It is an unconscious choice, which precedes subjective constitution and which is, as such, formative of subjectivity, meaning that the change of this choice entails the radical transformation of the bearer of the choice.

26

Sherbsky Institute, APA

In the fall of 1913, Lenin wrote a couple of letters to Maxim Gorky[10] in which, deeply disturbed by Gorky's support of the humanist ideology of the "construction of God," he implies that Gorky succumbed to this deviation because of his bad nerves, and advises him to go to Switzerland and get there the best medical treatment. In one of the letters, after making it clear how he is shocked at Gorky's ideas – "Dear Alexei Maximovitch, what are you doing, then? Really, it is terrible, simply terrible! Why are you doing this? It is terribly painful. Yours, V.I." – Lenin adds a strange postscript: "P.S. Take care of yourself more seriously, really, so that you will be able to travel in winter without catching cold (in winter, it is dangerous)." Obviously, Lenin is worried that, apart from catching cold, Gorky will catch a much more serious ideological disease, as is clear from the subsequent letter (posted together with the previous one): "Perhaps I don't understand you well? Perhaps you were joking when you wrote 'for the moment'? Concerning the 'construction of God,' perhaps you didn't write that seriously? Good heavens, take care of yourself a little bit better. Yours, Lenin."

What should surprise us here is the way the root of Gorky's ideological deviation is located in a bodily condition (overexcited nerves) that needs medical treatment. One should note that this is not (yet) Stalinism: in Stalinism, the cause of illness is no longer "objective" but is brutally re-subjectivized – i.e., the accused is considered fully responsible for his crimes. Occasionally, however, the objectivizing approach returns with a vengeance in late Stalinism. From my youth, I remember reports on the notorious Sherbsky institute in Moscow (which, incidentally, continues to thrive in the post-Soviet era). In the Soviet years, the Institute was well known for categorizing dissidence as a form of mental illness characterized by illusions of grandeur, pathological obsession with ideas of justice, distrust in accepted social values, etc. They claimed to identify the neuronal disturbance that causes such pathology and, as expected, proposed drugs to cure it. Is this just a memory of the dark days of communism? Not quite – is exactly the same not happening today? A recently obtained official Chinese Communist Party recording characterizes Uyghurs who have been sent for political "re-education" as "infected by an ideological illness" (harboring "strong religious views" and "politically incorrect" ideas) – here are some passages worth quoting in detail:

> Members of the public who have been chosen for re-education have been infected by an ideological illness. They have been infected with religious extremism and violent terrorist ideology, and therefore they must seek treatment from a hospital as an inpatient. The religious extremist ideology is a type of poisonous medicine which confuses the mind of the people. Once they are poisoned by it, some turn into extremists who no longer value even their own lives. . . . If we do not eradicate religious extremism at its roots, the violent terrorist incidents will grow and spread all over like an incurable malignant tumor.
>
> . . .
>
> Although a certain number of people who have been indoctrinated with extremist ideology have not committed any crimes, they are already infected by the disease. There is always a risk that

the illness will manifest itself at any moment, which would cause serious harm to the public. That is why they must be admitted to a re-education hospital in time to treat and cleanse the virus from their brain and restore their normal mind. We must be clear that going into a re-education hospital for treatment is not a way of forcibly arresting people and locking them up for punishment, it is an act that is part of a comprehensive rescue mission to save them.

. . .

In order to provide treatment to people who are infected with ideological illnesses and to ensure the effectiveness of the treatment, the Autonomous Regional Party Committee decided to set up re-education camps in all regions, organizing special staff to teach state and provincial laws, regulations, the party's ethnic and religious policies, and various other guidelines. They mobilized the public to learn the common language [Mandarin Chinese], complete various technical training courses, and take part in cultural and sport activities, teaching them what is correct and incorrect . . . so they can clearly distinguish right from wrong . . . At the end of re-education, the infected members of the public return to a healthy ideological state of mind, which guarantees them the ability to live a beautiful happy life with their families.

. . .

Some people worry that once they have been through the re-education process, they will be classified as bad people, and that even after having worked hard to complete the re-education program they will be discriminated against and treated differently. In fact, this is an unnecessary concern. Just like people who have had an operation, and have taken medication before recovering from their illnesses, the public won't see them as someone who is ill.

. . .

However, we must be cautious about one fact: having gone through re-education and recovered from the ideological disease doesn't mean that one is permanently cured. We can only say that they are physically healthy, and there is no sign that the disease may return. After recovering from an illness, if one doesn't exercise to strengthen the body and the immune system against disease, it could return worse than before.[11]

Before we shrug these lines off as a typical expression of Chinese communist totalitarianism, we should remember that exactly the same logic is at work in the recent public statement of the American Psychological Association, which proclaimed "traditional masculinity" as toxic – again, "medicalizing" an ideological conflict by way of reducing the opponent to a product of medical illness. In the terms of Lacanian psychoanalysis, what we get here is a pure case of the "university discourse," a social link whose agent is a bearer of objective knowledge. This agent does not impose himself as a master giving orders and demanding obedience; he acts like a neutral expert establishing facts. Just think about what economy experts are telling us again and again: they present tough austerity measures, lower taxes for the rich, etc., as something required by economic reality, not as decisions that are based on some politico-ideological preferences. (This is why we should also dismiss the way some "experts" rejected Alexandria Octavio-Cortez's Green New Deal as senseless expenditure of financial resources that would ruin economy: if Ronald Reagan's immense investment in the new arms race in 1980s proves anything, it is precisely that spending resources in a "non-productive" way can boost the economy. Recall that the US drew themselves out of the Big Recession only in the course of World War II – and is the struggle against the threat of ecological catastrophes not our great war?) Here is a simple but superb case of the oppressive exercise of university discourse: when Margaret Thatcher learned of Mozart's scatology during a visit to the theater to see Peter Shaffer's *Amadeus*, producer Peter Hall relates:

> She was not pleased. In her best headmistress style, she gave me a severe wigging for putting on a play that depicted Mozart as a scatological imp with a love of four-letter words. It was inconceivable, she said, that a man who wrote such exquisite and elegant music could be so foul-mouthed. I said that Mozart's letters proved he was just that: he had an extraordinarily infantile sense of humour. "I don't think you heard what I said", replied the Prime Minister. "He couldn't have been like that." I offered (and sent) a copy of Mozart's letters to Number Ten the next day; I was even thanked by the appropriate Private Secretary. But it was useless: the Prime Minister said I was wrong, so wrong I was.[12]

Although Thatcher arguably wanted to say that, due to Mozart's spiritual greatness, the scatological aspect of his work should be ignored, it is important to note that she didn't say this – she rather presented this value judgment ("one should ignore it") as a statement of fact. The hidden truth of such a discourse is, of course, that the neutral expert knowledge is based on politico-ideological choices: economic measures advocated by experts are a form of brutal domination, in the same way that the "science" that treats dissidence as an illness relies on ruthless political domination, and the same holds for today's Chinese treatment of Uyghurs who resist Chinese domination – and for the APA categorization of "toxic masculinity" as a form of psychic illness. Here we are, then, today: when the task is to dismiss political or ideological opposition through brutal medicalization, Chinese totalitarianism and a politically correct stance can work well hand in hand. The APA statement is again worth quoting in detail – here are the exact words that somehow entered the public space without blushing out of shame: "Traits of so-called 'traditional masculinity,' like suppressing emotions & masking distress, often start early in life & have been linked to less willingness by boys & men to seek help, more risk-taking & aggression – possibly harming themselves & those with whom they interact."[13]

A careful reader cannot miss the mixture of ideology and neutral expertise: a strong ideological gesture of excluding phenomena considered unacceptable is presented as a neutral description of medical facts – i.e., under the guise of medical description, we are imposing new normativity, a new figure of the enemy. In the old days of heterosexual normativity, homosexuality was treated as an illness – remember the brutal treatment to which Alan Turing and many others were submitted. Now it is masculinity itself that is medicalized, turned into an illness to be fought; we should not be surprised if chemotherapies to cure toxic masculinity were soon to be available. In justifying this diagnosis, the APA refers to power, patriarchy, and oppression of women – but all this cannot obfuscate the ideological brutality of the operation. Let's not forget that we are dealing with the APA, the psychological wing of the medical establishment, which means that we are dealing with nothing less than a shift in the mainstream ideological hegemony.

The lesson of the reign of expert knowledge is that here are worse things than a Master: when we are caught in the cobweb of the expert knowledge that regulates our lives, only an authentic Master figure can save us. Recall the basic of today's permissive hedonism: we are free, solicited even, to fully enjoy our lives beyond imposed limitations, but the reality of this freedom is a new network of (politically correct) regulations that are in many respects much tighter than the old patriarchal regulations.

So what is going on? In an echo of the famous Gillette ad about making men less violent and better, we often heard the idea that the ad was not directed against men, just against the toxic excess of masculinity – in short, the ad just signals that we have to throw out the dirty water of brutal masculinity. However, the moment we take a closer look at the list of features supposed to characterize "toxic masculinity" – suppressing emotions and masking distress, unwillingness to seek help, propensity to take risks even if this involves the danger of harming ourselves – we ask what is so specifically "masculine" about this list? Does it not fit much more a simple act of courage in a difficult situation, where, to do the right thing, one has to suppress emotions, one cannot rely on any help but take the risk and act, even if this means exposing oneself to harm? I know many women – as a matter of fact, more women than men – who, in a difficult predicament, don't succumb to the pressure of their environment and act like this. To take the example known to everyone: when Antigone decided to bury Polyneices, did she not commit exactly an act that fits the basic features of "toxic masculinity"? She definitely suppressed her emotions and masked her distress; she was unwilling to seek help; she took a risk that involved great danger of harming herself. Insofar as we can define Antigone's act as in some sense "feminine," we should conceive of it as a moment in an antagonist couple that, more than a single feature or stance, defines a (historically conditioned) "femininity." In the case of Antigone, the couple is easy to define: it is the opposition between Antigone and her sister Ismene, who is much closer to the predominant figure of the feminine (caring, understanding, non-conflictual . . .).[14] Obviously, our age of politically correct conformism is the age of Ismene, and Antigone's stance poses a danger.

There is an old delicious Soviet joke about Radio Erevan: a listener asks "Is it true that Rabinovitch won a new car on the lottery?" The radio answers: "In principle yes, it's true, only it wasn't a new car but an old bicycle, and he didn't win it: it was stolen from him." Does exactly the same not hold for toxic masculinity? Let's ask Radio Erevan: "Is masculinity really toxic?" We can guess the answer: "In principle yes, it's true, only this toxic content is not specifically masculine at all, plus it stands for what is often the only reasonable and courageous way to act." What is replacing courage today? "Toxic masculinity" is left behind in the new politically correct atmosphere where one bad taste joke can ruin your career, but ruthless careerism is considered normal. A new universe of subtle corruption is thus emerging in which career opportunism and the lowest denouncing of colleagues presents itself as high moralism.

Let's take a brief detour. One of the few convincing arguments for the notion of toxic masculinity was offered by George Monbiot in the *Guardian*: "Why do so many men love Jordan Peterson and hate the Gillette ad? If they're truly strong they don't need to prove their virility." In short, if men are truly strong, why did so many of them react in such a panicky way to the APA's warning about toxic masculinity? Wouldn't an adequate reaction of a strong man be just to dismiss attacks on masculinity as a weakling's complaint? Incidentally, the same goes for the anti-immigrants' populist panic.

Signs abound that weakness is the key to the most brutal displays of toxic masculinity. Let's just mention the serial killings of women in Ciudad Juarez at the border with Texas: these are not just private pathologies, but a ritualized activity, part of the subculture of local gangs (first gang rape, then torture till death, which includes cutting off breast nipples with scissors, etc.). They target single young women working in new assembling factories – a clear case of macho reaction to the new class of independent working women. But what if such violent reactions point to the violent core of masculinity itself, which openly explodes when its reign is threatened? True, but one should for this reason not reject the type of strong person ready to take risks; one should rather desexualize it and, above all, look into what is replacing it.

Years ago, Alain Badiou warned about the dangers of the growing post-patriarchal nihilist order that presents itself as the domain of new freedoms. The disintegration of the shared ethical base of our lives is clearly signaled by the abolishment of universal military conscription in many developed countries: the very notion of being ready to risk one's life for a common cause appears increasingly pointless, if not directly ridiculous, so that armed forces as the body in which all citizens equally participate is gradually turning into a mercenary force. This disintegration affects the two sexes differently: men are gradually turning into perpetual adolescents, with no clear passage of initiation that would enable their entry into maturity (military service, acquiring a profession, even education no longer play this role). No wonder, then, that, in order to supplant this lack, post-paternal youth gangs proliferate, providing ersatz-initiation and social identity. In contrast to men, women are today more and more precociously mature, treated as small adults, expected to control their lives, to plan their career. In this new version of sexual difference, men are ludic adolescents, out-Laws, while women appear as hard, mature, serious, legal, and punitive. Women are today not called by the ruling ideology to be subordinated; they are called – solicited, expected – to be judges, administrators, ministers, CEOs, teachers, policewomen, soldiers. A paradigmatic scene occurring daily in our security institutions is that of a feminine teacher/judge/psychologist taking care of an immature asocial young male delinquent. A new feminine figure is thus arising: a cold competitive agent of power, seductive and manipulative, attesting to the paradox that "under the conditions of capitalism, [women] can do it better than men."[15] This, of course, in no way makes women suspicious as agents of capitalism; it merely signals that contemporary capitalism invented its own ideal image of woman, a figure that stands for cold administrative power with a human face.

To fight these new forms of subtle oppression, courageous individuals of both sexes who are ready to take risks are needed more than ever.

27

Welcome to the Brave New World of Consenticorns!

The alt-Right attributes the excesses of political correctness to the destructive influence of cultural Marxism, which tries to undermine the moral foundations of the Western way of life. But if we take a closer look at these "excesses," we can easily see that they are, rather, signs of the unbridled reign of what, decades ago, Fredric Jameson called cultural capitalism: a new stage of capitalism in which culture no longer functions as a domain of ideological superstructure elevated above economy, but becomes a key ingredient of the ever-expanding reproduction of capital.

One of the clearest imaginable examples of cultural capitalism is surely the commodification of our intimate life. This is a permanent feature of a capitalist society, but in recent decades it's reached a new level. Just think about how our search for sexual partners and for good sexual performance rely on dating agencies or websites, medical and psychological help, and so on.

House of Yes, a nightclub in Brooklyn, New York, adds a new twist to this game: the intricate problem of how to verify consent in sexual interplay is resolved by the presence of a hired controlling agent. The club is a hedonistic playground where "anything goes." *Time Out* voted it the second best thing to do in the world and *The Sun* described as "the wildest night club on the planet."[16]

In the House of Yes, customers can do anything from naked hot tubs to drag wrestling, but they have to adhere to a strict policy of consent. This consent is ultimately enforced by "consenticorns," the "consent guardians" who wear light-up unicorn horns. Their job is to observe interactions and look for signs that someone might feel unsafe. In most cases, making eye contact is enough to prevent trouble. Sometimes they'll engage more directly: "Hi. How are you guys doing? You good?" And if they spot a situation that seems really problematic, they dance up to the couple in question, maybe get right in between them, and gently but firmly reiterate the policies.

The ideal that motivates the House of Yes was formulated by the nightlife impresario Anya Sapozhnikova, who celebrated there her 32nd birthday with a massive party. In a short speech, she described the utopia the House of Yes was trying to will into being, a magical place where consenticorns would be obsolete: "Imagine a world where sexuality is celebrated. Pretend that equality and inclusivity are main-stream. Envision a place where people dance together instead of ripping each other apart."[17] Or, as Arwa Mahdawi put it in her comment for the *Guardian*: "House of Yes's success is an important reminder that the stricter we are about consent, the more fun everyone can have."[18]

I must confess that I don't want even to imagine such a place. Remember, we are talking about having (intimate, sexualized) fun, and the implication of Mahdawi's claim is that, in today's society, the consent required for pure fun can only be enforced through tight control – the stricter the control over us, the more fun everyone can have. Furthermore, the majority of us still prefer intimate sexual inter-play, while the House of Yes practices a certain form of sexual interplay (group orgy). So, letting an evil imagination run wild, will somebody propose also a consenticorn to observe and control a single couple's sexual interplay?

True, supporters of the House of Yes imagine a future state where consenticorns will no longer be needed, since individuals will leave behind their egotist aggression. However, if we have learned anything from psychoanalysis, it is that masochism and sadism, pleasure in pain in all its diverse forms, form an irreducible ingredient of our sexual lives, not just a secondary effect of social domination perturbing pure consensual joy. We would thus need consenticorns able to distinguish consensual sadomasochism from the exploitative one – an impossible task. And the imagined ideal state of a collective dance without consenticorns, far from presenting a happy utopia, would have been the ultimate suffocating nightmare: a zombie-like orgy of people deprived of their sexuality.

But there is an even greater complication: the lesson of psychoanalysis is that in exhibitionism, a third witness, his gaze on my sexual interplay, is a condition of my pleasure. So what if I need a consenticorn for full enjoyment? And what if I want to involve a consenticorn in the erotic interplay with my partner, either as a witness who scolds me or as another active participant? The basic point of psychoanalysis is that a controlling agent who exerts control and oppression can itself become a source of pleasure. In short, the entire vision of the House of Yes is based on the total ignorance of what we learned from Freud.

To conclude, the idea of consenticorns is problematic for two interconnected reasons. First, it offers to resolve the problem of nonconsensual sex by way of delegating responsibility to an external hired controller: I can remain the way I am; the consenticorn will take care of me if I go too far. And if I do behave properly, it is because I fear being caught by the controlling eye. Second, the idea of a consenticorn totally ignores the perverse implications of its practice, the unpredictable way the figure of the consenticorn may itself get eroticized. But, maybe, this is our perverse future. Maybe, we should learn to enjoy happy free sex with consenticorns.

28

Do Sexbots Have Rights?

In his *Summa Theologica*, Thomas Aquinas draws the conclusion that the blessed in the Kingdom of Heaven will see the punishments of the damned in order that their bliss be more delightful for them (and St. John Bosco draws the same conclusion in the opposite direction: the damned in Hell will also be able to see the joy of those in Heaven, which will add to their suffering). Aquinas, of course, takes care to avoid the obscene implication that good souls in Heaven can find pleasure in observing the terrible suffering of other souls: good Christians should feel pity when they see suffering – will the blessed in Heaven also feel pity for the torments of the damned? Aquinas's answer is no: not because they directly enjoy seeing suffering, but because they enjoy the exercise of divine justice. But what if enjoying divine justice is the rationalization, the moral cover-up, for sadistically enjoying a neighbor's eternal suffering? What makes Aquinas's formulation suspicious is the surplus enjoyment it introduces: as if the simple pleasure of living in the bliss of Heaven is not enough, and has to be supplemented by an additional surplus enjoyment of being allowed to take a look at another's suffering – only in this way, the blessed souls "may enjoy their beatitude more thoroughly." We can here easily imagine the appropriate scene in Heaven: when some blessed souls complain that the nectar served was not as tasty as the last time, and that blissful life up there is rather boring after all, angels serving them would snap back: "You don't like it here? So take a look at how life is down there, at the other end, and maybe you will learn how lucky you are to be here!" And the corresponding scene in Hell should also be imagined as totally different from St. John Bosco's vision: far away from the divine gaze and control, the damned souls enjoy an intense and pleasurable life in Hell – but from time to time, when the Devil's administrators learn that the blessed souls from Heaven are to be allowed briefly to observe life in Hell, they kindly implore the damned souls to stage a performance and pretend to suffer terribly in order to impress the idiots from Heaven. In short, the sight of the other's suffering is the *objet a*, the obscure cause of desire that sustains our own happiness (bliss in Heaven): if we take it away, our bliss appears in all its sterile stupidity. (Incidentally, does the same not hold for our daily portion of Third World horrors – wars, starvations, violence – on TV screens? We need it to sustain the happiness of our consumerist Heaven.) So, perhaps, this would be the way to read film director Ernst Lubitsch's title *Heaven Can Wait* – let's stay in Hell. Heaven can wait because the only true heaven is a moderate pleasant hell.

What Heaven alone lacks is surplus enjoyment, which can only be provided by looking at Hell. To make this point clear, let's take a case of the direct "critical" depiction of the oppressive atmosphere of an imagined conservative fundamentalist rule. The new TV version of Margaret Atwood's *The Handmaid's Tale* confronts us with the weird pleasure of fantasizing a world of brutal patriarchal domination – of course, nobody would openly admit a desire to live in such a nightmarish world, but this assurance that we really don't want it makes fantasizing about it, imagining all the details of this world, all the more pleasurable. Yes, we feel pain while experiencing this pleasure, but Lacan's name for this pleasure-in-pain is *jouissance*. The obverse of this ambiguity is the fundamental blindness of Atwood's tale for the limitations of our liberal permissive universe: the entire story is an exercise in what Fredric Jameson called "nostalgia for the present"; it is permeated by the sentimental admiration for our liberal permissive present ruined by the new Christian fundamentalist rule, and it never even approaches the question of what is wrong in this present so that it gave birth to the nightmarish Republic of Gilead. "Nostalgia for the present" falls into the trap of ideology because it is blind to the fact that this present permissive Paradise is boring, and (exactly like the blessed souls in Paradise) it needs to look into the Hell of religious fundamentalism to sustain itself.

It is for similar ideological reasons that the recent HBO miniseries *Chernobyl* became so popular. It deals with a catastrophic scenario that continues to pose a threat today, long after the fall of the USSR, but it treats it as something that belongs to the bygone era of Soviet communism – as if the Three Mile Island incident before and Fukushima after did not happen, and as if these other two incidents did not display the same attempts to cover up the magnitude of the threat by the state apparatuses, as in Chernobyl. The threat of a nuclear catastrophe is thus no longer part of *our* predicament; the blame for it falls on the inefficient Soviet bureaucracy, which cannot but make us feel good – it is again nostalgia for the present that fuels our perception of the catastrophe. To avoid a misunderstanding: yes, the clumsy reaction and attempts to cover up the catastrophe by the Soviet state are breathtaking, but so is the brutal efficiency of the Soviet endeavor to deal with it, calmly exposing thousands of rescue workers to high radiation, quite often with their full knowledge – something that in all probability also could not have happened in a similar incident in the West. But where the miniseries cheats is in its focus on the secret document that warned about the danger and from which the key pages went missing. The reality was much more complex and tragic: one should bear in mind that the catastrophe took place during a safety test – well aware of potential dangers, the authorities were performing safety tests all the time, and were quite obsessed by the safety measures. And it is here that things went terribly wrong: when those in charge of the test noticed that something was amiss, they performed a whole series of procedures in order to prevent a catastrophe, and we now know that these very procedures led to the explosion – to cut it short, if they had done nothing and just ignored the threat, there would have been no explosion. So the ultimate cause of the explosion was the inadequacy of the procedures to prevent it, not a general ignorance of the danger. Systemic failure and human error were here inextricably linked – and this type of danger is today more actual than ever.

This is ideology at its purest, ideology in the simple and brutal sense of legitimizing the existing order and obfuscating its antagonisms. In exactly the same way, liberal critics of Trump and the alt-Right never seriously ask how our liberal society could give birth to Trump. The same holds for the rise of Boris Johnson: instead of focusing on his clownish figure, one should rather explore the deep transformation of the entire political scene in the UK that has rendered the rise of such a figure possible.

Back to *The Handmaid's Tale*: the surplus enjoyment that comes from staging a performance and/or observing it is what bothers political correctness. Even when it talks about the suffering of the victim, it effectively targets the enjoyment of the perpetrator – which is why it cannot endure enjoyment even when there is no suffering victim, just the perpetrator performing virtual brutality. Let's take the latest example: politically correct moralism reached one of its peaks in the recent debate about the need to regulate the human–sexbots (sexual robots) relations. Here is a report on this weird phenomenon:

Last year a sex robot named Samantha was "molested" and seriously damaged at a tech industry festival; the incident spurred debate on the need to raise the issue of ethics in relation to machines.

While the developers of sexbots have claimed that their projects will do anything to indulge their customers' desires, it seems that they might start rejecting some persistent men. . . . [P]eople ignore the fact that they may seriously damage the machine, just because it cannot say "no" to their "advances." . . . [F]uture humanoid sex robots might be sophisticated enough to "enjoy a certain degree of consciousness" to consent to sexual intercourse, albeit, to their mind, conscious feelings were not necessary components of being able to give or withhold consent. . . . [I]n legal terms, introduction of the notion of consent into human–robot sexual relationships is vital in a way similar to sexual relations between humans and it will help prevent the creation of a "class of legally incorporated sex-slaves."[19]

Although these ideas are just a specific application of the proposal of the EU to impose the basic "rights" of AI entities, the domain of sexbots brings out in a clear way the implicit presuppositions that determine such thoughts. We are basically dealing with a laziness in thinking: by adopting such an "ethical" attitude, we comfortably avoid the complex web of underlying problems. We should avoid the trap of getting caught in the debate about the status of sexbots with AI: do they really possess some kind of autonomy or dignity and therefore deserve some rights? The answer to this question is, at least for the time being, obviously negative: our sexbots are just mechanical dolls with no inner life. The heart of the matter lies elsewhere. The first suspicion is that the proponents of such demands do not really care about AI machines (they are well aware that they cannot really experience pain and humiliation) but about aggressive humans: what they want is not to alleviate the suffering of the machines, but to squash the problematic aggressive desires, fantasies, and pleasures of us, humans.

This becomes clear the moment we include the topic of video games and virtual reality. If, instead of sexbots (actual plastic bodies whose (re)actions are regulated by AI), we imagine games in virtual reality (or, even more plastic, augmented reality) in which we can sexually torture and brutally exploit persons – although, in this case, it is clear that no actual entity is suffering – the proponents of the rights of AI machines would nonetheless in all probability insist on imposing some limitations on what we, humans, can do in virtual space. The argument that those who fantasize about such things are prone to do them in real life is very problematic: the relationship between imagining something and doing it in real life is much more complex in both directions. We often do horrible things while imagining that we are doing something noble, and vice versa, we often secretly daydream about doing things we would in no way be able to perform in real life. We enter thereby the old debate: if someone has brutal tendencies, is it better to allow him to play with them in virtual space or with machines, in the hope that, in this way, he will be satisfied enough and not do them in real life? We encounter here the structure of fetishist disavowal: while the offender brutally mistreats his sexbot, he knows very well that he is just playing with a mechanical plastic doll, but he nonetheless gets caught in his fiction and enjoys it for real (the simple proof: his orgasm, if he reaches it, is real, not fiction). The implication of this fetishist structure is not that the subject who participates in it is naively stupid, but, on the contrary, that even in our real sexual interaction with another living human being, fiction is already at work – i.e., I use my partner as an object through which I stage my fictions.

In reality, even a brutal sadist who mistreats an actual woman uses her to enact his fictions.

Another question: if a sexbot rejects our rough advances, does this not simply mean that it was programmed in this way? So why not reprogram it in a different way? Or, to go further, why not program it in such a way that it welcomes brutal mistreatment? (The catch is, of course: will we, the sadistic perpetrators, in this case still enjoy it? The sadist wants his victim to be terrified and ashamed.) Yet another question: what if an evil programmer makes the sexbots themselves sadists who enjoy brutally mistreating us, its partners? If we confer rights to AI sexbots and prohibit their brutal mistreating, this means that we treat them as minimally autonomous and responsible entities – so should we also treat them as minimally "guilty" if they mistreat us, or should we just blame their programmer?

But the basic mistake of the advocates of rights of AI entities is that they presuppose our, human, standards (and rights) as the highest norm. What if, with the explosive development of AI, new entities emerge with what we could conditionally call a "psychology" (series of attitudes or mind sets) which are incompatible with ours, but in some sense definitely "higher" than ours (measured by our standards, they can appear either more "evil" or more "good" than ours)? What right do *we* (humans) have to measure them with our ethical standards? So let's conclude this detour with a provocative thought: maybe, a true sign of the ethical and subjective autonomy of a sexbot would have been not that it rejects our advances, but that, even if it was programmed to reject our brutal treatment, it secretly starts to enjoy it? In this way, the sexbot would become a true subject of desire, divided and inconsistent as we humans are.

29

Nipples, Penis, Vulva . . . and Maybe Shit

This rather tasteless title refers to one of the (very doubtful) trends in the struggle against "sexism." First, (some) women demanded that we end the fetishization of their breasts and accept them as just another part of a woman's body. One of the results of this struggle for "free nipples" was that, in some big cities, groups of women organized protest walks where they were naked above the waist – the point was precisely to de-eroticize (we can even say: renormalize) breasts. We are now entering the next logical step in this direction – the goal now is to "demystify" the ultimate sexual object. After publishing a book of portraits of breasts and then of penises, photographer Laura Dodsworth has since taken pictures of 100 vulvas. Here is a report (from the *Guardian*) on the last volume in this trilogy:

It's this shame that photographer Laura Dodsworth is aiming to overcome with her latest project, *Womanhood*. In a book and accompanying film for Channel 4, she tells the stories of 100 women and gender non-conforming people through portraits of their vulvas. It's the third instalment in a series: in *Bare Reality* and *Manhood*, Dodsworth photographed and talked to people about their breasts and their penises, respectively (both stories featured in *Weekend* magazine). . . . "The vulva is often seen just as a site of sexual activity," she says. "But we talked about so many areas that aren't 'sexy' – periods, menopause, infertility, miscarriage, abortion, pregnancy, birth, cancer." In this sense, she saw herself as a "kind of midwife, helping women to birth their own stories."[20]

We read in the same *Guardian* report how Dodsworth's book and film "arrive at a time when the vulva appears to be having a cultural moment": in the near future, Lynn Enright's book *Vagina: A Re-education* will appear; Liv Strömquist's bestselling *Fruit of Knowledge* (subtitled *The Vulva vs. the Patriarchy* and with stabs at Freud) is dedicated to the vulva and menstruation; there is a new British musical *Vulvarine*; live events that aim to reclaim the body are increasingly popular – from body-positive life-drawing classes to "pussy-gazing workshops."

Further steps in this process are on the horizon: new campaigns target periods, "encouraging young people to shake off any shame about menstruation." So why not go to the end and "demystify" and defetishize defecation? Let's organize some shit-gazing workshops . . . Some of us remember the scene from Buñuel's *Fantom of Freedom* in which relations between eating and excreting are inverted: people sit at their toilets around the table, pleasantly talking, and, when they want to eat, they silently ask the housekeeper "Where is that place, you know?" So why not try this in real life (better to prohibit eating from public spaces, since our excessive food production is one of the main reasons for our ecological crisis)?

To avoid a misunderstanding, the point that these phenomena are making is obvious and well-taken: to get rid of the male fetishization of the vagina as the ultimate mysterious object of (masculine) desire, and to reclaim the vulva for women in all its complex reality outside sexist myths. (Although, at this level already, one cannot but note a weird detail: feminists are fighting the fetishization of the vagina, while, for Freud, "fetish," by definition, cannot refer to the vagina because it is precisely the last object the male subject sees before he sees the naked vagina – hair, legs. Fetish covers up the lack of penis in a woman, the lack the male subject discovers when he sees a vagina – so can a vagina be its own fetish?[21]) Maybe yes, in a dialectical reversal where the lack itself is fetishized into a proof that the other (male) sex has what a woman lacks (penis), so that castration is deprived of its universal symbolic status and affects only women.

So what is wrong with it? Let's return to Buñuel. There is series of Buñuel films that are built around the same central motif of the – to use the filmmaker's own words – "non-explainable impossibility of the fulfilment of a simple desire." In *L'Age d'Or*, the couple want to consummate their love, but they are again and again prevented by some stupid accident; in The *Criminal Life of Archibaldo de la Cruz*, the hero wants to accomplish a simple murder, but all his attempts fail; in *The Exterminating Angel*, after a party, a group of rich people cannot cross the threshold and leave the house; in *The Discreet Charm of the Bourgeoisie*, two couples want to dine together, but unexpected complications always prevent the accomplishment of this simple wish; and finally, in *That Obscure Object of Desire*, we have the paradox of a woman who, through a series of tricks, postpones again and again the final moment of reunion with her old lover. What is the common feature of these films? An ordinary, everyday act becomes impossible to accomplish as soon as it finds itself occupying the impossible place of *das Ding* and begins to embody the sublime object of desire. This object or act may be in itself extremely banal (a common dinner, passing the threshold after a party). It has only to occupy the sacred/

forbidden, empty place in the Other, and a whole series of impassable obstacles will build up around it; the object or act, in its very vulgarity, cannot be reached or accomplished.

We should recall here Jacques Lacan's definition of the sublime: "an object elevated to the level of the Thing," an ordinary thing or act through which, in a fragile shortcircuit, the impossible Real Thing transpires. That's why, in an intense erotic interplay, one wrong word, one vulgar gesture, suffices, and a violent desublimation occurs: we fall out of erotic tension into vulgar copulation. Imagine, in the thrall of erotic passion, that one takes a close look at the vagina of the beloved woman, trembling with the promise of anticipated pleasures – but then, something happens, and one, as it were, "loses contact," falls out of the erotic thrall, and the flesh in front of one's eyes appears in all its vulgar reality, with the stench of urine and sweat, etc. (And it is easy to imagine the same experience with a penis.) What happens here? For Lacan, it is the exact opposite that takes place in the described scene: the vagina ceases to be "an object elevated to the dignity of a Thing" and becomes part of ordinary reality. In this precise sense, sublimation is not the opposite of sexualization but its equivalent.

And that's why, in eroticism also, it is only a small step from the sublime to the ridiculous. The sexual act and the comical: it seems that these two notions exclude themselves radically – does not the sexual act stand for the moment of utmost intimate engagement, for the point toward which the participating subject can never assume the attitude of an ironic external observer? For that very reason, however, the sexual act cannot but appear at least minimally ridiculous to those who are not directly engaged in it – the comical effect arises out of the very discord between the intensity of the act and the indifferent calm of everyday life.

This brings us back to the ongoing attempts to "demystify" the vulva. To use the old (and otherwise very problematic) proverb, it seems that, in trying to get rid of the dirty water, they court the danger of also throwing out the baby. Their attack on the idea of the vagina as the fetishized object of male desire also threatens to undermine the basic structure of sublimation without which there is no eroticism – what remains is a flat world of ordinary reality in which all erotic tension is lost. They display their "defetishized" organs, which are just that – ordinary organs.

The moment we take into account the arbitrary nature of sublimation (any ordinary object can be elevated to the level of the impossible Thing), it becomes clear that sexual sublimation can be easily freed from patriarchal mystification. What we are getting instead of this new space of eroticism is a version of something that, long ago, Max Adorno and Theodor Horkheimer, the two masters of Frankfurt School Marxism, baptized "repressive desublimation": our sex organs are desublimated, and the result is not new freedom but a gray reality in which sex is totally repressed.

So what about the rejection of "objectivizing" one's sexual partner? If we try to imagine a "non-objectivizing" sexual love, the only thing that comes to mind is a love that would operate in conditions of the "veil of ignorance" – a scenario imagined by John Rawls to illustrate his notion of social justice. When you try to decide which model of society is most just, your judgment is only valid if you ignore the (or act as if you don't know which) place you occupy in the social hierarchy – in short, the model you advocate must be the one you would also choose even if you were at the bottom of the social scale. The problem with love is that it is, by definition, unjust: the choice of love object is not only extremely partial, based on how you "objectivize" the beloved, but also "irrational" in that it is non-transparent to the subject in love. If you know why you fell in love, it is, by definition, not love.

30

Cuarón's *Roma*:
The Trap of Goodness

My first viewing of Alfonso Cuarón's movie *Roma* left me with a bitter taste: yes, the majority of critics are right in celebrating it as an instant classic, but I couldn't get rid of the idea that this predominant perception is sustained by a terrifying, almost obscene, misreading, and that the movie is celebrated for all the wrong reasons.

Roma is read as a tribute to Cleo, a maid from the Colonia Roma neighborhood of Mexico City who works in the middle-class household of Sofia, her husband Antonio, their four young children, Sofia's mother Teresa, and another maid, Adela. It takes place in 1970, the time of large student protests and social unrest. As already in his earlier film *Y Tu Mamé También*, Cuarón maintains a distance between the two levels, the family troubles (Antonio leaving his family for a younger mistress, Cleo getting pregnant by a boyfriend who immediately abandons her), and this focus on an intimate family topic makes the oppressive presence of social struggles all the more palpable as the diffuse but omnipresent background. As Fredric Jameson would have put it, History as Real cannot be depicted directly but only as the elusive background that leaves its mark on depicted events.

So does *Roma* really just celebrate Cleo's simple goodness and selfless dedication to the family? Can she really be reduced to the ultimate love object of a spoiled upper-middle-class family, accepted (almost) as part of the family to be better exploited, physically and emotionally? The film's texture is full of subtle signs that indicate that the image of Cleo's goodness is itself a trap, the object of implicit critique, which denounces her dedication as the result of her ideological blindness. I don't have in mind here just the obvious dissonances in how the family members treat Cleo: immediately after professing their love for her and talking with her "like equals," they abruptly ask her to do some household chore or to serve them something. What struck me was, for example, the display of Sofia's indifferent brutality in her drunken attempt to park the family Ford Galaxie in the narrow garage area; how she repeatedly scratches the wall causing chunks of plaster to fall down. Although this brutality can be justified by her subjective despair (being abandoned by her husband), the lesson is that, because of her dominant position, she can afford to act like that (the servants will repair the wall), while Cleo, who finds herself in a much more dire situation, simply cannot afford such "authentic" outbursts – even when her whole world is falling apart, the work has to go on.

Cleo's true predicament first emerges in all its brutality in the hospital, after she delivers a stillborn baby girl; multiple attempts to resuscitate the infant fail, and the doctors give the body to Cleo for a few moments before taking it away. Many critics who saw in this scene the most traumatic moment of the film missed its ambiguity: as we learn later in the film (but can suspect now already), what truly traumatizes her is that she doesn't want a child, so a dead body in her hands is actually good news.

At the film's end, Sofia takes her family for a holiday to the beaches at Tuxpan, taking Cleo to help her cope with her loss (in reality, they want to use her there as a servant, even though she just went through a painful stillbirth). Sofia tells the children over dinner that she and their father are separated and that the trip is so their father can collect his belongings from their home in their absence. At the beach, the two middle children are almost carried off by the strong current, until Cleo wades into the ocean to save them from drowning even though she herself does not know how to swim. As Sofia and the children affirm their love for Cleo for such selfless devotion, Cleo breaks down from intense guilt, revealing that she had not wanted her baby. They return to their house, where the bookshelves have been removed and various bedrooms reassigned. Cleo prepares a load of washing, telling Adela she has much to tell her, as a plane flies overhead.

After Cleo saves the two boys, they all (Sofia, Cleo, and the boys) tightly embrace on the beach – a moment of false solidarity if there ever was one, a moment that simply confirms the way Cleo is caught in the trap that enslaves her. Am I dreaming here? Is my reading not too crazy? I think Cuarón provides a subtle hint in this direction at the level of the form. The entire scene of Cleo saving the children is shot in one long take, with the camera moving transversally, always focused on Cleo. When one watches this scene, one cannot avoid the feeling of strange dissonance between form and content: while the content is a pathetic gesture of Cleo who, soon after the traumatic stillbirth, risks her life for the children, the form totally ignores this dramatic context. There is no exchange of shots between Cleo entering the water and the children, no dramatic tension between the danger the children are in and her effort to save them, no point of view shot depicting what she sees. This strange inertia of the camera, its refusal to get involved in the drama, renders in a palpable way Cleo's disentanglement from the pathetic role of a faithful servant ready to sacrifice herself.

There is a further hint of emancipation in the very final moments of the film, when Cleo says to Adela: "I have much to tell you." Maybe, this means that Cleo is finally getting ready to step out of the trap of her "goodness," becoming aware that her selfless dedication to the family is the very embodiment of her servitude. In other words, Cleo's total withdrawal from political concerns, her dedication to selfless service, is the very form of her ideological identity, it is how she "lives" ideology. Maybe, telling Adela about her predicament is the beginning of Cleo's "class consciousness," the first step that will lead her to join the protesters on the street. A new figure of Cleo will arise in this way, a much colder and more ruthless one – a figure of Cleo delivered from ideological chains.

But maybe it will not. It is very difficult to get rid of the chains in which we not only feel good, but feel that we are doing something good. As T.S. Eliot put it in his *Murder in the Cathedral*, the greatest sin is to do the right thing for the wrong reason.

31

Happiness? No, Thanks!

If there is a figure that stands out as the hero of our time, it is Christopher Wylie, a gay Canadian vegan who, at the age of 24, came up with an idea that led to the foundation of Cambridge Analytica, a data analytics firm that went on to claim a major role in the Leave campaign for Britain's EU membership referendum; later, he became a key figure in digital operations during Donald Trump's election campaign, creating Steve Bannon's psychological warfare tool. Wylie's plan was to break into Facebook and harvest the Facebook profiles of millions of people in the United States, and to use their private and personal information to create sophisticated psychological and political profiles, and then target them with political ads designed to work on their particular psychological makeup. At a certain point, Wylie was genuinely freaked out: "It's insane. The company has created psychological profiles of 230 million Americans. And now they want to work with the Pentagon? It's like Nixon on steroids."[22]

What makes this story so fascinating is that it combines elements that we usually perceive as opposites. The alt-Right presents itself as a movement that addresses the concerns of ordinary white, hard-working, deeply religious people who stand for simple traditional values and abhor corrupt eccentrics like homosexuals and vegans; but they are also digital nerds – and now we learn that their electoral triumphs were masterminded and orchestrated precisely by such a nerd who stands for all they oppose. There is more than an anecdotal value in this fact: it clearly signals the vacuity of alt-Right populism, which has to rely on the latest technological advances to maintain its popular redneck appeal. Plus, it dispels the illusion that being a marginal computer nerd automatically stands for a "progressive" anti-system position. At a more basic level, a closer look at the context of Cambridge Analytica makes it clear how cold manipulation and the care for love and human welfare are two sides of the same coin. In "The New Military-Industrial Complex of Big Data Psy-Ops," which appeared in *The New York Review of Books*,[23] Tamsin Shaw explores "the part private companies play in developing and deploying government-funded behavioral technologies"; the exemplary case of these companies is, of course, Cambridge Analytica:

> Two young psychologists are central to the Cambridge Analytica story. One is Michal Kosinski, who devised an app with a Cambridge University colleague, David Stillwell, that measures personality traits by analyzing Facebook "likes." It was then used in collaboration with the World Well-Being Project, a group at the University of Pennsylvania's Positive Psychology Center that specializes in the use of big data to measure health and happiness in order to improve well-being. The other is Aleksandr Kogan, who also works in the field of positive psychology and has written papers on happiness, kindness, and love (according to his résumé, an early paper was called "Down the Rabbit Hole: A Unified Theory of Love"). He ran the Prosociality and Well-being Laboratory, under the auspices of Cambridge University's Well-Being Institute.

What should attract our attention here is the "bizarre intersection of research on topics like love and kindness with defense and intelligence interests": Why does such research draw so much interest from British and American intelligence agencies and defense contractors, with the ominous DARPA (the US government's Defense Advanced Research Projects Agency) always lurking in the background? The researcher who personifies this intersection is Martin Seligman: in 1998, he "founded the positive psychology movement, dedicated to the study of psychological traits and habits that foster authentic happiness and well-being, spawning an enormous industry of popular self-help books. At the same time, his work attracted interest and funding from the military as a central part of its soldier-resilience initiative."

This intersection takes us far beyond daily politics, to the domain of pure ethics: it is not externally imposed on the behavioral sciences by "bad" political manipulators, but is implied by their immanent orientation: "The aim of these programs is not simply to analyze our subjective states of mind but to discover means by which we can be 'nudged' in the direction of our true well-being as positive psychologists understand it, which includes attributes like resilience and optimism." The problem is, of course, that this "nudging" does not affect individuals in the sense of making them overcome their "irrationalities" perceived by scientific research:

[C]ontemporary behavioral sciences aims to exploit our irrationalities rather than overcome them. A science that is oriented toward the development of behavioral technologies is bound to view us narrowly as manipulable subjects rather than rational agents. If these technologies are becoming the core of America's military and intelligence cyber-operations, it looks as though we will have to work harder to keep these trends from affecting the everyday life of our democratic society.

After the eruption of the Cambridge Analytica scandal, all these events and tendencies were extensively covered by the liberal mass media, and the overall image emerging from it, combined with what we also know about links between the latest developments in bio-genetics (wiring the human brain, etc.), provides an ample – and terrifying – impression of new forms of social control that make good old twentieth-century "totalitarianism" look like a rather primitive and clumsy machine of control. Assange was right in his strangely ignored key book on Google:[24] to understand how our lives are regulated today, and how this regulation is experienced as our freedom, we have to focus on the shadowy relation between private corporations that control our commons and secret state agencies. We should be shocked not at China, but at ourselves, who accept the same regulation while believing that we retain our full freedom and the media just help us to realize our goals (while in China people are fully aware that they are regulated). The biggest achievement of the new cognitive military complex is that direct and obvious oppression is no longer necessary: individuals are much better controlled and "nudged" in the desired direction when they continue to experience themselves as free and autonomous agents of their own life.

But these are all well-known facts, and we have to take a step further. The predominant critique proceeds in the way of demystification: beneath the innocent-sounding research into happiness and welfare, it discerns a dark, hidden, gigantic complex of social control and manipulation exerted by the combined forces of private corporations and state agencies. But what is urgently needed is also the opposite move: instead of just asking what dark content is hidden beneath the form of scientific research into happiness, we should focus on the form itself. Is the topic of scientific research into human welfare and happiness (at least the way it is practiced today) really so innocent, or is it already in itself permeated by the stance of control and manipulation? What if the sciences are not just misused? What if they find here precisely their proper use? We should put in question the recent rise of a new discipline, "happiness studies." How is it that, in our era of spiritualized hedonism, when the goal of life is directly defined as happiness, anxiety and depression are exploding? It is the enigma of this self-sabotaging of happiness and pleasure that makes Freud's message more actual than ever.

As is often the case, Bhutan, a developing country, naively spelled out the absurd sociopolitical consequences of this notion of happiness: two decades ago, the kingdom of Bhutan decided to focus on Gross National Happiness (GNH) rather than Gross National Product (GNP); the idea was the brainchild of ex-king Jigme Singye Wangchuck, who sought to steer Bhutan into the modern world, while preserving its unique identity. With the pressures of globalization and materialism mounting, and the tiny country set for its first-ever elections, the immensely popular Oxford-educated new king, 27-year-old Jigme Khesar Namgyel Wangchuck, ordered a state agency to calculate how happy the kingdom's 670,000 people were. Officials said they had already conducted a survey of around 1,000 people and drawn up a list of parameters for being happy - similar to the development index that is tracked by the United Nations. The main concerns had been identified as psychological well-being, health, education, good governance, living standards, community vitality, and ecological diversity. This is cultural imperialism, if there ever was one.[25]

We should risk here taking a step further and inquire into the hidden side of the notion of happiness itself - when, exactly, can a people be said to be happy? In a country like Czechoslovakia in the late 1970s and 1980s, people were in a way effectively happy: three fundamental conditions of happiness were fulfilled. First, their material needs were basically satisfied – not too satisfied, since the excess of consumption can in itself generate unhappiness. It is good to experience a brief shortage of some goods on the market from time to time (no coffee for a couple of days, then no beef, then no TV sets): these brief periods of shortage functioned as exceptions that reminded people that they should be glad that the goods were generally available. If everything is available all the time, people take this as an evident fact of life and no longer appreciate their luck. Life thus went on in a regular and predictable way, without any great efforts or shocks, and one was allowed to withdraw into one's private niche. A second extremely important condition of happiness was that the Other (the Party) could be blamed for everything that went wrong, so that one did not feel really responsible. If there was a temporary shortage of some goods, even if stormy weather caused great damage, it was "their" guilt. And last, but not least, there was an Other Place (the consumerist West), about which one was allowed to dream, and even visit sometimes – this place was just at the right distance, not too far, not too close. This fragile balance was disturbed – by what? By desire, precisely. Desire was the force that compelled the people to move beyond – and to end up in a system in which the large majority is definitely less happy.[26]

Happiness is thus in itself (in its very concept, as Hegel would have put it) confused, indeterminate, inconsistent. Recall the proverbial answer of a German immigrant to the US who, when asked "Are you happy?" answered: "Yes, yes, I am very happy, *aber gluecklich bin ich nicht* . . . [but happy I am not – in German!]." It is a pagan category: for pagans, the goal of life is to live a happy life (the idea of living "happily ever after" is already a Christianized version of paganism), and religious experience and political activity themselves are considered the higher form of happiness (see Aristotle). No wonder the Dalai Lama himself is having such success recently, preaching around the world the gospel of happiness, and no wonder he is finding the greatest response in the US, this ultimate empire of the (pursuit of) happiness. Happiness relies on the subject's inability or unreadiness to fully confront the consequences of its desire: the price of happiness is that the subject remains stuck in the inconsistency of its desire. In our daily lives, we (pretend to) desire things that we do not really desire, so that, ultimately, the worst thing that can happen is for us to get what we "officially" desire. Happiness is thus inherently hypocritical: it is the happiness of dreaming about things we really do not want.

Years ago, I asked Agnes Heller (who was, in the 1950s and 1960s, the assistant of Georg Lukács in Budapest) why Lukács traveled so little to the West during this time; why did he remain most of the time at home in Budapest? Was it because, after participating in the Imre Nagy government during the 1956 anti-Soviet rebellion, the authorities didn't trust him enough to allow him such trips, or was it because he simply didn't want to travel? Her answer was: both. He really didn't want to travel, but he wasn't going to admit this to himself, so he repeatedly asked for permission to travel to the West and then felt a sense of relief when his demand was rejected. In short, when this happened Lukács was happy – happy because he was able to avoid the truth of his desire, happy because he was able to dismiss the prohibition (to travel) that was inherent to his desire as externally imposed. The function of psychoanalytic treatment is precisely to compel us to get rid of such games and to assume the truth of our desire – this is what Lacan aimed at by his claim that the only thing you can be guilty of is to compromise your desire.

Do we not encounter a similar gesture in much of Leftist politics? When a radical Leftist party just misses winning an election and taking power, one can often detect a hidden sigh of relief: thank god we lost, who knows what trouble we would have gotten into if we were to win.

In the UK, many Leftists privately admit that the near-victory of the Labour Party in the 2017 general election was the best thing that could have happened, much better than the insecurity of what might have happened if the Labour government had tried to implement its program. The same holds for the prospect of Bernie Sanders's eventual victory. What would have been his chances against the onslaught of big capital? The mother of all such gestures is the Soviet intervention in Czechoslovakia, which crushed the Prague Spring and its hope of democratic socialism. Let's imagine the situation in Czechoslovakia without the Soviet intervention: very soon, the "reformist" government would have had to confront the fact that there was no real possibility of democratic socialism at that historical moment, so it would have had to choose between reasserting party control – i.e., setting a clear limit to freedoms – and allowing Czechoslovakia to become one of the Western liberal democratic capitalist countries. In a way, the Soviet intervention saved the Prague Spring – it saved the Prague Spring as a dream, as a hope that, without the intervention, a new form of democratic socialism might have emerged. And did not something similar occur in Greece when the Syriza government organized the referendum against pressure from Brussels to accept austerity politics? Many internal sources confirm that the government was secretly hoping to lose the referendum, in which case it would have to step down and leave it to others to perform the dirty job of austerity. Since they won, this task fell to themselves, and the result was the self-destruction of the radical Left in Greece. Without any doubt, Syriza would have been much happier if it had lost the referendum.

Perhaps the greatest portrait of happiness in the domain of arts is found in Giacomo Rossini's great male portraits, the three from *The Barber of Seville* (Figaro's "Largo al factotum," Basilio's "Calumnia," and Bartolo's "Un dottor della mia sorte"), plus the father's wishful self-portrait of corruption in *La Cenerentola*, enact a mocked self-complaint, where one imagines oneself in a desired position, being bombarded by demands for a favor or service. The subject twice shifts his position: first, he assumes the roles of those who address him, enacting the overwhelming multitude of demands that bombard him; then, he feigns reaction to it, the state of deep satisfaction in being overwhelmed by demands one cannot fulfill. Let us take the father in *Cenerentola*: in a wonderful *basso buffo caricato* role, he imagines how, when one of his daughters is married to the Prince, people will turn to him, offering him bribes for a service at the court, and he will react to it first with cunning deliberation, then with fake despair at being bombarded with too many requests. The culminating moment of the archetypal Rossini aria is this unique moment of happiness, of the full assertion of the excess of Life that occurs when the subject is overwhelmed by demands, no longer being able to deal with them. At the highpoint of his "factotum" aria, Figaro exclaims: "What a crowd / of the people bombarding me with their demands / – have mercy, one after the other / *uno per volta, per carita!*" referring therewith to the Kantian experience of the Sublime, in which the subject is bombarded with an excess of the data that he is unable to comprehend. This, then, is happiness: not a peaceful state of satisfaction but the mockingly desperate rejection of demands on us.

So, back to our starting point: not only are we controlled and manipulated, "happy" people secretly and hypocritically demand even to be manipulated for their own good. Truth and happiness don't go together – truth hurts, it brings instability, it ruins the smooth flow of our daily lives. Therein resides the ethical lesson of reality structured like an unorientable space – the ultimate choice that we confront is: Do we want to be happily manipulated or do we dare to expose ourselves to the risks of authentic creativity, to the continuing anxieties that these risks engender? And it is crucial to see how this ethics relies on the lack of support in any figure of the "big Other." One would have thought that, if there is no big Other, no higher agency that provides a firm point of reference, the only consistent ethical choice is a hedonist pursuit of happiness – we only have this world, fragile and unreliable as it is, so grab all the luck you can. And it seems that any privileging of ethical duty has to evoke some transcendent point of reference that guarantees its urgency. However, on closer look, it soon becomes clear that happiness, even in its most terrestrial version, always has to rely on some figure of the big Other. Why? G.K. Chesterton turns around the standard (mis)perception according to which the ancient pagan attitude is that of the joyful assertion of life, while Christianity imposes a somber order of guilt and renunciation. It is, on the contrary, the pagan stance that is deeply melancholic: even if it preaches a pleasurable life, it is in the mode of "enjoy it while it lasts, because, at the end, there is always death and decay." The message of Christianity is, on the contrary, that of infinite joy beneath the deceptive surface of guilt and renunciation: "The outer ring of Christianity is a rigid guard of ethical abnegations and professional priests; but inside that inhuman guard you will find the old human life dancing like children, and drinking wine like men; for Christianity is the only frame for pagan freedom."[27]

Far from being the religion of sacrifice, of renunciation to earthly pleasures (in contrast to the pagan affirmation of the life of passions), Christianity offers a devious stratagem to indulge in our desires without having to pay the price for them, to enjoy life without the fear of decay and debilitating pain awaiting us at the end of the day. If we go to the end in this direction, it would even be possible to sustain the idea that therein resides the ultimate function of Christ's sacrifice: you can indulge in your desires and enjoy; I took the price for it upon myself!

Is the US an exception here? In its declaration of independence, the

US defines itself as the land of the "pursuit of happiness." What this stands for is not a direct promise of happiness – as a US citizen, I am guaranteed the freedom to pursue happiness, not happiness itself, and it depends on me whether I will achieve it or not. Does this not bring into play the dimension of desire? No, since authentic desire is never a desire for happiness. The very notion of a "desire for happiness" is an abomination, it amounts to something like "a desire for no-desire, a desire to compromise one's desire."

32

Assange Has Only Us to Help Him!

It finally happened – on April 11, 2019, Julian Assange was dragged from the Ecuadorian embassy and arrested. It was no surprise: many signs pointed in this direction. A week or two earlier, Wikileaks predicted the arrest, and the Ecuadorian foreign ministry replied with what we now know is a blatant lie (that there were no plans to cancel Assange's asylum), peppered with further lies (about Wikileaks publishing photos of the Ecuadorian president's private life – why would Assange be interested in doing this and thus jeopardize his asylum?). The recent arrest of Chelsea Manning (largely ignored by the media) was also an element in this game. Although pardoned by President Obama, she was rearrested and is now held in solitary confinement in order to force her to divulge information about her links with Wikileaks, as part of the prosecution that awaits Assange when (if) the US gets hold of him.

A further hint was given when the UK said it would not extradite Assange to a country where he could face the death penalty (instead of simply saying he would not be extradited to the US because of Wikileaks) – this practically confirmed the possibility of his extradition to the US. No to mention the long and slow well-orchestrated campaign of character assassination that reached the lowest level imaginable earlier in the year with the unverified rumors according to which Ecuadorians want to get rid of him because of his bad smell and dirty clothes. In the first stage of attacks on Assange, his ex-friends and collaborators went public with claims that Wikileaks began well but then got bogged down with Assange's political bias (his anti-Hillary obsession, his suspicious ties with Russia . . .). This was followed by more direct personal defamations: he is paranoiac and arrogant, obsessed by power and control. Then we reached the direct bodily level of smells and stains. The only thing that really smells bad in this saga are some mainstream feminists who refused any solidarity with Assange under the slogan "No help to rapists." A very suspicious accusation (to say the least) is evoked to justify complicity with the brutal US pressure on a helpless individual who is now charged with 18 new counts of treason and espionage – this is *also* one of the faces of today's feminism. And the list of shameless acts goes on: on May 19, 2019, the media reported that "Julian Assange's belongings from his time living in the Ecuadorian embassy in London will be handed over to US prosecutors on Monday, according to Wikileaks. Ecuadorian officials are travelling to London to allow US prosecutors to 'help themselves' to items including legal papers, medical records and electronic equipment, it was claimed."[28] Can one imagine a more obscene act of illegal seizure?

Assange a paranoiac? When you live permanently in an apartment that is bugged from above and below, victim of constant surveillance organized by secret services – who wouldn't be paranoid? Megalomaniac? When the (now ex-) head of CIA says your arrest is his priority, does not this imply that you are a "big" threat to some, at least? Behaving like the head of a spy organization? But Wikileaks *is* a spy organization, although one that serves the people, keeping them informed of what goes on behind the scenes.

Our big media focus on Assange's links with Russia and his "meddling" in the US elections – did he meet Manafort or not? etc. We are dealing here with dirty political games. But we should not get caught up in these debates that concern only a "secondary contradiction" – Wikileaks is much more than an element in the struggle between the US and Russia, and in the struggle between Trump and the US establishment (the "Russian link" in the 2016 presidential elections). The "principal contradiction" here is the struggle against new forms of digital control and regulation of our lives, against the coalition of state agencies (the NSA) and big corporations (Google, etc.), which increasingly exert an invisible control over our lives, a control we are as a rule not even aware of. This is what Wikileaks is really about, and all the debate about Assange's mistakes is aimed at obfuscating this key point.

So let's move to the big question: why now? I think one name explains it all: Cambridge Analytica – a name that stands for all that Assange is about, for what he fights against: disclosure of the link between large private corporations and government agencies. Remember what a big topic and obsession the Russian meddling in the US elections were – now we know it was not Russian hackers (with Assange) that nudged the people toward Trump, but our own data-processing agencies, which joined forces with political groups. This doesn't mean that Russia and their allies are innocent: they probably did try to influence the outcome in the same way that the US does in other countries (only in this case, it is called helping democracy . . .). But it means that the big bad wolf distorting our democracy is not in the Kremlin – and this is what Assange was claiming all the time.

But where, exactly, is this big bad wolf? To grasp the whole scope of this control and manipulation, one should move beyond the link between private corporations and political parties (as is the case with Cambridge Analytica), to the interpenetration of data-processing companies like Google and Facebook and state security agencies.

The biggest achievement of the new cognitive-military complex is that direct and obvious oppression is no longer necessary: individuals are much better controlled and "nudged" in the desired direction when they continue to experience themselves as free and autonomous agents of their own life. This is another key lesson of Wikileaks: our unfreedom is most dangerous when it is experienced as the very medium of our freedom – what can be more free that the incessant flow of communications that allows every individual to popularize his/her opinions and forms virtual communities at his/her own free will? Since in our societies permissiveness and free choice have been elevated to a supreme value, social control and domination can no longer appear as infringing on a subject's freedom: it has to appear as (and be sustained by) the very self-experience of individuals as free. What can be more free than our unconstrained surfing on the web? This is how "fascism that smells like democracy" operates today.

This is why it is absolutely imperative to keep the digital network out of the control of private capital and state power – i.e., to render it totally accessible to public debate.

Now we can see why Assange has to be silenced: after the Cambridge Analytica scandal exploded, all the effort of those in power went into reducing it to a particular "misuse" by some private corporations and political parties – but where is the state itself, the half-invisible apparatuses of the so-called "deep state"? No wonder the *Guardian*, which extensively reports on the Cambridge Analytica "scandal," published a disgusting attack on Assange, accusing him of being a megalomaniac and a fugitive from justice.[29] The lesson is clear: write as much as you want about Cambridge Analytica and Steve Bannon, just discreetly ignore what Assange was drawing our attention to – that the state apparatuses that are now expected to investigate the "scandal" are themselves part of the problem.

Assange characterized himself as the spy of and for the people: he is not spying on the people for those in power, he is spying on those in power for the people. This is why the only one who can really help him now are we, the people. Only our pressure and mobilization can alleviate his predicament. One often reads how the Soviet secret service not only punished its traitors, even if it took decades to do so, but also fought doggedly to free them when they were caught by the enemy. Assange has no state behind him, just us, the people – so let us do at least what the Soviet secret service was doing: let's fight for him no matter how long it takes!

Wikileaks was just the beginning, and our motto should be a Maoist one: Let a hundred Wikileaks blossom. The panic and fury with which those in power, those who control our digital commons, reacted to Assange is proof that such activity hits a raw nerve. There will be many blows below the belt in this fight – our side will be accused of playing into the enemy's hands (like the campaign against Assange for being in the service of Putin), but we should get used to it and learn to strike back with interest, ruthlessly playing one side against the other in order to bring them all down. Were Lenin and Trotsky also not accused of being paid by Germans and/or the Jewish bankers? As for the scare that such activity will disturb the functioning of our societies and thus threaten millions of lives: we should bear in mind that it is those in power who are ready to selectively shut down the digital grid to isolate and contain protests – when massive public dissatisfactions explode, the first move is always to disconnect the internet and cellphones. This means that "Assange" is the name for the struggle that is only just beginning, and that the furious reactions of those in power should not surprise us. In the middle of June 2019, the UK home secretary Sajid Javid signed a request for Julian Assange to be extradited to the US; on BBC Radio 4's *Today* program on June 13, he explained his act:

> [Assange] is rightly behind bars. There's an extradition request from the US that is before the courts tomorrow but yesterday I

signed the extradition order and certified it and that will be going in front of the courts tomorrow. . . . It is a decision ultimately for the courts, but there is a very important part of it for the home secretary and I want to see justice done at all times and we've got a legitimate extradition request, so I've signed it, but the final decision is now with the courts.[30]

This mumbled short passage is worth reading in detail: what immediately strikes the eye is how the claim that it is for the courts to decide is repeated three times (the order he signed "will be going in front of the courts tomorrow"; it is "a decision ultimately for the courts"; "the final decision is now with the courts"), and this very triple insistence indicates that something is amiss here. Javid's actual unspoken premise is that it is precisely *not* for the courts to decide: the decision is already taken ("yesterday"), the UK justice system has already decided to comply with the US wishes, and the courts are here just to confirm it retroactively ("tomorrow"). In other words, his claim that he wants "to see justice done at all times" means that, in this case, justice was already done before the trial even began – that's the only way to understand his statement that Assange "is rightly behind bars." This is also the only way to understand another weird and blatantly illegal act that took place three weeks before the US deadline to file its final extradition request for Assange: Ecuadorian officials went to London to allow US prosecutors to "help themselves" (!) to Assange's belongings. Neither Assange's lawyers nor the UN officials were granted permission to be present at the illegal seizure of his property, which was "requested by the authorities of the United States of America." "The material includes two of his manuscripts, as well as his legal papers, medical records, and electronic equipment. The seizure of his belongings violates laws that protect medical and legal confidentiality and press protections."[31]

Baltasar Garzón, one of Assange's lawyers, aptly characterized this seizure:

> It is incomprehensible that the country that afforded him protection is now taking advantage of its privileged position to turn over his belongings to the country that is persecuting him. These belongings will be seized without a court warrant, without protecting the rights of political refugees, without respecting the chain of custody. And this is made worse by the system of illicit recordings that went on at the embassy, and over which a complaint has already been filed. The systematic violation of Assange's rights is going beyond conceivable limits.[32]

The only way to understand the illegal nature of this shameless act is that it was done on purpose in such a brutal mode, without respect for legal niceties, since the illegal nature is in itself its key message to the critical public: "Don't mess with us; if you do it we will crush you mercilessly." So where now are all those wise commentators who advised Assange to surrender, since he would spend just a couple of weeks in prison, and who dismissed the idea that he would face extradition and life-long imprisonment in the US as nothing more than the result of his paranoiac megalomania? Where now are those despicable columnists who mused on how Assange "overstayed his stay in the Ecuadorian embassy" – really? What choice had he? Where should he have gone? Where now are all those "feminists" who claimed that a rapist like Assange is not worthy of our solidarity? The most disgusting stance is the claim that Assange should be extradited to Sweden, not to the US: as if the accusations against him that are evoked to justify his extradition to Sweden are not deeply contested – i.e., as if, again, as with Javid's claim, Assange's guilt is already proven.

Those who really care for the freedom of our public space should do (at least) two things now. First, Assange, Manning, and Snowden are authentic public heroes who should be celebrated like the Chinese dissident artist Ai Weiwei (who, to his honor, did participate in a public protest for Assange in Berlin). Second, we should not only wait for, but actively solicit the rise of new Assanges in Arab countries, in China, and in Russia. Our liberals often ask what would have happened to someone like Assange in an authoritarian country like one of those listed above. Now we know the answer: something close to what is happening to him right now.

Appendix

33

Is Avital Ronell Really Toxic?

Yes, it's really about power!

The main motif running through the critical reactions to my two short texts on the case against NYU feminist professor Avital Ronell is that I ignore (or don't understand) the game of power in academia: the power that professors, especially thesis advisers, exert over their students and assistants, the power to make or break their entire career and job prospects. Is this the case? Far from ignoring the exercise of power, I just think one should take a closer look at how it worked in this case.

Avital of course made a grave mistake in engaging in the eccentric friendship relationship she had with her accuser – a blunder, but not a crime, as someone sympathetic to her put it. What was wrong is not this relationship as such, but the fact that it took place between a student and his mentor, and, in the eyes of her critics, this is enough to pass the final judgment: Avital exerted brutal power to exploit and humiliate her student. For me, it is here that problems begin. Institutionally, she was his superior, exerting power over him. In the media, Avital is portrayed as an academic megastar with the power to provide tenured jobs and ruin or create careers. This is not the Avital I know. What I know is that she had many enemies at NYU (some even tried to enlist me against her), that an African student accused her of racism because in her class she interpreted a Hölderlin poem that mentions "beautiful brown ladies," etc. Yes, she can be "bitchy," as they say, but she can also be very engaged and helpful. To see this, one just has to read the letters from her to him and from him to her, insofar as they are available. The figure of Avital that emerges from them is somebody who is demanding, bullying, controlling, sharp witted, nuanced, perceptive – but at the same time caring and helping, and above all pretty insecure, almost desperately clinging to formal assurances while being aware they are not sincerely meant (in the style of "even if you don't mean it, just pretend . . ."). This is definitely not a controlling master sadistically enjoying her power. As for her accuser, one should just read whatever is available of his messages to her, especially from the time when he was complaining against her in his messages to others. "I don't know how I would have survived without you. You are the best, my joy, my miracle. Sending you infinite love, kisses and devotion, your – n." "Sweet Beloved, I was so happy to see you tonight, and spend time together. It was so magical and important, crucial on so many ways. Our shared intimacy was a glorious cadence to our time in Berlin. Thank you for these moments of togetherness and utter and pure love! . . . Infinitely, – n" "Thank you for your being my most precious blessing. Loving, your – n." "Dearest, I have not heard from you all through this oriental trip . . . Please drop me a line to let me know you are well, I have been worried about you . . . hugs, n." Plus, his mother invited Avital to his sister's wedding in Israel. Plus, we can read in the acknowledgments of his thesis: "I thank Avital's teaching, careful reading, sensitive support . . . and her unremitting listening to all my whims."

Are these the words and acts of a helpless student terrorized by a figure of power? As for Avital's eccentricity, I should add that rumors about it are common knowledge – I consider it simply impossible that someone who decided to choose her as his/her supervisor hadn't heard them. So I think the accuser's words and acts are much more the words and acts of a man who ruthlessly seized the opportunity and played the game as long as it appeared to advance his career, trying to squeeze out of it as much as possible (note how often his emails include a request to review and edit his writings!), and who then turned against his mentor when it became clear there was no tenured post waiting for him. It's part of the academic game in the US that those whom a professor supervises succeed – this success adds to the professor's reputation, and Avital certainly did help her accuser in getting his texts published, in receiving his PhD in record time, in obtaining three prestigious postdoc positions. So yes, the case of Avital and her accuser is a case of power, of a professor who engaged in an almost self-destructive relationship, and of her student who ruthlessly exploited the situation and ended up asserting *his* power over her.

The relationship between Avital and her accuser is a very atypical example of how power works in US academia. It is a complex eccentric case, far from the typical self-assured professor who ruthlessly exploits students sexually or professionally. I guess this is one of the reasons why it attracted such attention in the wider media: it offers as an exemplary case of the abuse of power in academia a fascinating eccentricity and thus obfuscates the widely spread "normal" abuse of power.

Two general concluding remarks on the Ronell case

There are two recurring motifs in the critical reactions to my texts on the Avital Ronell case. I think they are indicative of the mess we are in, so they deserve a brief comment.

First, the claim is that, if, in a case of sexual harassment, there is no material proof nor any third-party witnesses, meaning that it is one word against another, the victim is to be believed – an act is harassment if the victim claims it is harassment, independent of the perpetrator's intentions. There are, of course, good reasons to take this claim seriously: the victim is structurally in the position of weakness, and the ruling ideology imposes on us the prejudice not to take too seriously the complaints of "hysterical" women. However, there are also some good counter-reasons, not only the obvious one that the self-professed victims can also lie and manipulate. The paradox is that, in some sense, the most brutal case of victimhood is the one in which the victim is not even aware of being a victim, being so identified with his/her subordinate role. An extreme case – is a woman who herself looks forward to her cliterodectomy, since it will signal full entry into her community, not in some sense more victimized than a woman who resists it? No wonder we quite often get cases where a woman didn't see anything problematic in her relationship with a man while this relationship was going on, and only began to protest and proclaim after the fact (sometimes years later), when she gained feminist awareness.

The second and – for me, at least – saddest motif is the reference to a career that is evoked to render non-problematic the behavior (of the accuser, in this case). I don't know the accuser, I never met him, and I didn't read anything written by him except his publicly available emails. My point is: let's suppose all he says is true – he was disgusted and oppressed by Avital, etc. So why did he fully respond to her messages and sometimes even heighten their emotional tone? His repeated answer is with reference to his career, as if this goes by itself.

Is this justification by career really so self-evident? At this point, I am predictably accused of not understanding how power functions in US academia. Nothing could be less true: from the 1970s when, after graduating, I was unemployed for years (yes, for *not* being a Marxist), until recent times, when I am almost exiled from US academia and public media because of my "problematic" positions (critique of political correctness, etc.), I was able to observe how power works in all its guises. I don't expect people to be heroic; I just think that there are certain limits, both professional (betraying one's theoretical vocation – if one has it, that is to say) and private (writing passionate love emails to a person one finds disgusting, like the accuser did), that one should not violate.

I want to emphasize that I am making here a general observation based on my experiences in US academia. Around two decades ago, I was engaged in a (private, not public) conversation with a well-known gender theorist who claimed that Lacanians are ideologists of the ruling patriarchy (the role of the name-of-the-Father in Lacan, etc.), while gender theorists are marginal and subversive. I challenged him to name one Lacanian theorist who occupies a strong academic position, in contrast to many gender theorists who exert strong power in academia, and the only name I got was Drucilla Cornell. Surprised, I replied that I was a short time ago at a colloquium in New York where her paper was a strong Derridean critique of Lacan. I was even more surprised when the gender theorist snapped back: "She is a Lacanian, she just had to do it for her career." Two things bothered me. First, how my interlocutor assumed the power to decide who is a Lacanian even when the person concerned declared herself to be anti-Lacanian (and criticized Lacan consistently in her writings), just to make the point that Lacanians are powerful in academia (and, to avoid a misunderstanding, this reproach in no way concerns Cornell herself, who is simply an honest Derridean); second, how the reference to a career worked without raising any ethical doubts – "she had to do it for her career" was mentioned as the most obvious thing, causing no shame. (Furthermore, this argument throws a strange light on US academia: it implies that "mainstream patriarchal" Lacanians have to pretend to be "marginal" deconstructionists to boost their careers, even in the case of someone as powerful as Cornell.)

And, incidentally, in recent weeks, more than a dozen friends and "friends" warned me that, although they sympathize with my position, my career will suffer because of my messages about the case of Avital. May they burn in hell!

34

Jordan Peterson as a Symptom

. . . of What?

The art of lying with truth

The wide popularity of Jordan Peterson is proof that the liberal-conservative "silent majority" finally found its voice. His advantages over the previous anti-LGBT+ star Milo Yiannopoulos are obvious. Yiannopoulos was witty, fast-talking, full of jokes and sarcasm, and openly gay – he very much resembled, in many features, a representative of the culture he was attacking. Peterson is his opposite: he combines common sense and (the appearance of) cold scientific argumentation with bitter rage at the threat to the liberal basics of our societies – his stance is that of "Enough is enough! I cannot stand it anymore!"

It is easy to discern the cracks in Peterson's advocacy of cold facts against politically correct dogmas. His main image is that of a radical Leftist conspiracy: after the failure of communism as an economic system and there was no revolution in the developed West, Marxists decided to move to the domain of culture and morality, and thus "cultural Marxism" was born. Its goal is to undermine the moral backbone of our societies and thus set in motion the final breakdown of our freedoms. But this kind of easy criticism avoids the difficult question: how could such a weird "theory" have found such a wide echo? A more complex approach is needed.

Jacques Lacan wrote that, even if what a jealous husband claims about his wife (that she sleeps around with other men) is all true, his jealousy is still pathological: the pathological element is the husband's need for jealousy as the only way to retain his dignity, his identity even. Along the same lines, one could say that, even if most of the Nazi claims about the Jews were true (they exploit Germans, they seduce German girls . . .) – which they are not, of course – their anti-Semitism would still be (and was) a pathological phenomenon because it repressed the true reason why the Nazis needed anti-Semitism in order to sustain their ideological position. The Nazi vision of society is an organic Whole of harmonious collaboration, so an external intruder is needed to account for divisions and antagonisms.

The same holds for how, today, the anti-immigrant populists deal with the "problem" of refugees: they approach it in an atmosphere of fear, of the incoming struggle against the Islamization of Europe, and they get caught in a series of obvious absurdities. For them, refugees who flee terror are no different from the terrorist they are escaping from; they remain oblivious to the obvious fact that, while there are among the refugees also terrorists, rapists, criminals, etc., the large majority are desperate people looking for a better life. The cause of problems that are inherent in today's global capitalism is projected onto an external intruder. We find "fake news," which cannot be reduced to a simple inexactitude – if they (partially, at least) correctly render (some of) the facts, they are all the more dangerously "fake." Anti-immigrant racism and sexism are not dangerous because they lie; they are at their most dangerous when the Lie is presented in the form of a (partial) factual truth.

The alt-Right obsession with cultural Marxism signals its refusal to confront the fact that the phenomena they criticize as the effects of the cultural Marxist plot (moral degradation, sexual promiscuity, consumerist hedonism, etc.) are the outcome of the immanent dynamic of late capitalism itself. In *The Cultural Contradictions of Capitalism* (1976), Daniel Bell describes how the unbounded drive of modern capitalism undermines the moral foundations of the original Protestant ethic that ushered in capitalism itself. In a later afterword, Bell offers a bracing perspective on contemporary Western society, from the end of the Cold War to the rise and fall of postmodernism, revealing the crucial cultural fault lines we face as the twenty-first century approaches. The turn toward culture as a key component of capitalist reproduction, and, concomitant to it, the commodification of cultural life itself, enables the expanded reproduction of capital. (Just think about today's explosion of art biennales – Venice, Kassel; although they usually present themselves as a form of resistance toward global capitalism and its commodification of everything, they are in their mode of organization the ultimate form of art as a moment of capitalist self-reproduction.) The term "cultural Marxism" thus plays the same structural role as that of the "Jewish plot" in anti-Semitism: it projects (or, rather, transposes) the immanent antagonism of our socioeconomic life onto an external cause: what the conservative alt-Rightists deplore as the ethical disintegration of our lives (feminism, attacks on patriarchy, political correctness, etc.) must have an external cause: it cannot emerge out of the antagonisms and tensions of our own societies.

Before we blame some foreign intruder for the troubles of our liberal societies, we should always bear in mind that the true shock of the twentieth century was World War I – all the horrors that followed, from fascism to Stalinism, are rooted in it. This war was such a shock for two reasons. First, it exploded after more than half a century of continuous progress in Europe (no big wars, rise of living standard and human rights . . .). There was no foreign agent fomenting it, it was a pure product of the inherent tensions within Europe. Second, it was a shock, but not an unexpected one – for at least two decades prior to it the prospect of war was a kind of public obsession. The catch was that it was precisely this incessant talk that created the perception that it really couldn't happen – if we talk about it enough, it cannot take place. This is why, when it erupted, it was such a surprise.

Unfortunately, the liberal-Leftist reaction to anti-immigrant populism is often no better than the way it is treated by its opponents. Populism and political correctness (the liberal-Leftist PC) practice the two complementary forms of lying that follow the classic distinction between hysteria and obsessional neurosis: a hysteric tells the truth in the guise of a lie (what it says is literally not true, but the lie expresses in a false form an authentic complaint), while what an obsessional neurotic claims is literally true, but it is a truth that serves a lie. Populists and PC liberals resort to both strategies. First, they both resort to factual lies when they serve what populists perceive as the higher Truth of their Cause. Religious fundamentalists advocate "lying for Jesus" – say, in order to prevent the horrible crime of abortion, one is allowed to propagate false scientific "truths" about the lives of fetuses and the medical dangers of abortion; in order to support breast-feeding, one is allowed to present as a scientific fact that not breast-feeding causes breast cancer, etc. Common anti-immigrant populists shamelessly circulate nonverified stories about rapes and other crimes of the refugees in order to give credibility to their "insight" that refugees pose a threat to our way of life. All too often, PC liberals proceed in a similar way: they pass in silence over actual differences in the "ways of life" between refugees and Europeans, since mentioning them may be seen to promote Eurocentrism. Recall the case of Rotherham in the UK, where, in 2014, police discovered that more than a thousand poor young white girls were being systematically abused and raped by a gang of Pakistani youth – the data were ignored or downplayed in order not to trigger Islamophobia.

The opposite strategy – that of lying in the guise of truth – is also widely practiced on both poles. If anti-immigrant populists not only propagate factual lies but also cunningly use snippets of factual truth to give an aura of veracity to their racist lie, PC partisans also blend lying with truth. In their fight against racism and sexism, they mostly quote crucial facts, but they often give them an imprecise twist. The populist protest displaces onto the external enemy the authentic frustration and sense of loss, while the PC Left uses its true points (detecting sexism and racism in language, etc.) to reassert its moral superiority and thus prevent true social-economic change.

And this is why Peterson's outbursts are so efficient, although (or, perhaps, because) he ignores the inner antagonisms and inconsistencies of the liberal project itself: the tension between liberals who are ready to condone racist and sexist jokes on account of freedom of speech and PC regulators who want to censor them as an obstacle to the freedom and dignity of the victims of such jokes is immanent to the liberal project and has nothing to do with the authentic Left. Peterson addresses what many of us somehow feel goes wrong in the PC universe of obsessive regulation – the problem with him does not reside in his lies, but in the partial truths that sustains his lies. If the Left is not able to address these limitations in its own project, it is fighting a lost battle.

A reply to my critics

Just a couple of remarks in reply to numerous critiques of my comment on Jordan Peterson. I see two levels in his work. First, there is his liberal analysis and critique of PC, LGBT+, etc., with regard to how they pose a danger to our freedoms, and although there are things I disagree with in it, I also see in it some worthwhile observations. The difference with him is that, while critical of many stances and political practices of PC, identity politics, and LGBT+, I nonetheless see in them an often inadequate and distorted expression of very real and pressing problems. Claims about women's oppression cannot be dismissed by referring to *Fifty Shades of Grey*, the story of a woman who enjoys being dominated (as one of my critics claims), the suffering of transgender people is all too real, etc. The way racist and sexist oppression works in a developed liberal society is much more refined (but no less efficient) than in its direct brutal form, and the most dangerous mistake is to attribute women's inferior position to their free choice.

But what I find problematic is how Peterson interprets PC (and his other targets) as the extreme outgrowth of cultural Marxism (a block that comprises the Frankfurt School, "French" poststructuralist deconstructionism, identity politics, gender and queer theories, etc.). He seems to imply that cultural Marxism is the result of a deliberate shift in Marxist (or communist) strategy: after communism lost the economic battle with liberal capitalism (waiting in vain for the revolution to arrive in the developed Western world), its leaders decided to move the terrain to cultural struggles (sexuality, feminism, racism, religion . . .), systematically undermining the cultural foundations and values of our freedoms. In recent decades, this new approach proved unexpectedly efficient: today, our societies are caught in the self-destructive circle of guilt, unable to defend their positive legacy.

I see no necessary link between this line of thought and liberalism – the notion of "cultural Marxism" manipulated by some secret communist center and aiming to destroy Western freedoms is a pure alt-Right conspiracy theory (and the fact that it can be mobilized as part

of a liberal defense of our freedoms say something about the immanent weaknesses of the liberal project). First, there is no unified field
of cultural Marxism – some of today's representatives of the Frankfurt
School are among the most vicious denigrators of "French thought,"
many cultural Marxists are very critical of identity politics, etc. Second,
any positive reference to the Frankfurt School or "French thought"
was prohibited in socialist countries, where the authorities were much
more open toward Anglo-Saxon analytic thought (as I remember from
my own youth), so to claim that both classic Marxism and its "cultural"
version were somehow controlled by the same central agent has to rely
on the very suspicious notion of a hidden Master who secretly pulls the
strings. Finally, while I admit (and analyze in my books) the so-called
"totalitarian" excesses of political correctness and some transgender
orientations that bear witness to a weird will to legalize, prohibit, and
regulate, I see in this tendency no trace of a "radical Left" but, on the
contrary, a version of liberalism gone astray in its effort to protect and
guarantee freedom. Liberalism was always an inconsistent project
ridden with antagonisms and tensions.

If I were to engage in paranoiac speculations, I would be much more
inclined to say that the politically correct obsessive regulations (like the
obligatory naming of different sexual identities, with legal measures if
one violates them) are, rather, a Left-liberal plot to destroy any actual
radical Left movement – suffice it to recall the animosity against Bernie
Sanders among some LGBT+ and feminist circles (who have no problems with big corporate bosses supporting them). The "cultural" focus
of PC and MeToo is, to put it in a simplified way, a desperate attempt to
avoid confrontation with actual economic and political problems – i.e.,
to locate women's oppression and racism in its socioeconomic context – but the moment one mentions these problems, one is accused
of vulgar "class reductionism." Walter Benn Michaels and others have

written extensively on it, and, in Europe, Robert Pfaller has written books critical of the PC patronizing stance and has started a movement "Adults for Adults." Liberals will have to take note that there is a growing radical Left critique of PC, identity politics, and MeToo.

A concluding note on my debate with Peterson

I cannot but notice the irony of how Peterson and I, billed in the publicity for our debate as major opponents, are both marginalized by the official academic community. If I understand it correctly, I am supposed to defend, at this duel of the century, the Left-liberal line against neoconservatives. Really? Most of the attacks on me come precisely from Left liberals (Chomsky, the outcry against my critique of LGBT+ ideology), and I am sure that if the leading figures in this field were to be asked if I am fit to stand for them, they would turn in their grave, even if they are still alive. It is typical that many comments on the debate point out how Peterson's and my positions are really not so distinct – this is literally true in the sense that, from their standpoint, one cannot see the difference between the two of us, I am as suspicious as Peterson. So I see the task of this debate to at least clarify our difference.

Let me begin by a point on which Peterson and I seem to agree: problematizing happiness as the goal of our lives. What if, to have a chance of happiness, we should not posit it as our direct goal? What if happiness is necessarily a byproduct? Yes, a human life of freedom and dignity does not consist just in searching for happiness (no matter how much we spiritualize it) or in the effort to actualize one's inner potentials; we have to find some meaningful Cause beyond the mere struggle for pleasurable survival. (One should introduce here the distinction, elaborated by Kierkegaard, between genius and apostle: a genius expresses its inner creativity, while the apostle is a bearer of a transcendent message.) However, two qualifications should be added here.

First, since we live in a modern era, we cannot simply refer to an unquestionable authority to confer a mission or task on us. Modernity means that, yes, we should carry the burden, but the main burden is freedom itself; we are responsible for our burdens. Not only are we not allowed to make cheap excuses for not doing our duty; duty itself should not serve as an excuse (for example, if I know someone will be hurt if I do my duty, I should never say "Sorry, I have to do it, it's my duty"). So yes, we need a story that gives meaning to our life, but it remains our story: we are responsible for it, it emerges against the background of ultimate meaninglessness.

Second, yes, we should carry our burden, accept the suffering that goes with it. But a danger lurks here, that of a subtle reversal: don't fall in love with your suffering, never presume that your suffering is in itself proof of your ethical value or your authenticity. In psychoanalysis, the term for this is surplus enjoyment, enjoyment generated by pain itself: renunciation of pleasure can easily turn into pleasure of renuncia-tion itself. For example, white Left liberals love to denigrate their own cultural and blame "Eurocentrism" for our evils – but it is instantly clear how this self-denigration brings a profit of its own: through this renunciation of their particular roots, multicultural liberals reserve for themselves the universal position, graciously soliciting others to assert their particular identity. White multiculturalist liberals thus embody the lie of identity politics.

This brings me to my next critical point. What I sincerely don't get is Peterson's designation of the position he is most critical about, not as the usual "cultural Marxists," but as "postmodern neo-Marxists." Nobody calls himself or herself that, so it's a critical term – but does it hold? Peterson likes to give precise references, he mentions books, etc., so I would like to know his precise references here. I think I know what he has in mind – the politically correct multicultural, anti-Eurocentric, etc. mess. But where are Marxists among them? Peterson seems to oppose "postmodern Marxism" to the Western Judeo-Christian legacy. I find this opposition weird. First, postmodernism and Marxism are incompatible: the theory of postmodernism emerged as a critique of Marxism (in Lyotard and others). The ultimate postmodernists are today themselves conservatives. Once traditional authority loses its substantial power, it is not possible to return to it – all such returns are today a postmodern fake. Does Trump enact traditional values? No, his conservativism is a postmodern performance, a gigantic ego trip. In this sense of obscenely playing with "traditional values," of mixing references to them with open obscenities, Trump – not Obama – is the ultimate postmodern president. If we compare Donald Trump with Bernie Sanders, Trump is a postmodern politician at its purest, while Sanders is an old-fashioned moralist. Yes, when we make political decisions, we should think carefully about possible non-intended actual consequences that may turn out to be disastrous. But I would worry here about the Trump administration – it is Trump who is now waging radical changes in the economy, international politics, etc. The very term "postmodern Marxism" reminds me of the typical totalitarian procedure of combining two opposite trends into one figure of the enemy (like the "Judeo-Bolshevik plot" in fascism).

Second, can one imagine anything more "Western" than postmodernism or Marxism? But which Western tradition are we talking about? In Europe today, I think the greatest threat to what is worth saving in the European tradition are precisely the populist defenders of Europe like Salvini in Italy or le Pen in France. No wonder they are joining hands with Putin and Trump, whose shared goal is to ruin European unity. As for me, that's why I am unabashedly Eurocentric – it always strikes me how the very Leftist critique of Eurocentrism is formulated in terms that only have sense within the Western tradition.

Third, Peterson condemns historicist relativism, but a historical approach does not necessarily entail relativism. The easiest way to detect a historical break is when society accepts that something (which was hitherto a common practice) is simply not acceptable. There were times when slavery or torture were considered normal; now they are considered unacceptable (except in the US in the last decade or so). And I see MeToo or LGBT+ as part of this same progress – which, of course, does not imply that we should not ruthlessly criticize eventual weird turns of these two movements. And, in the same way, modernity means you cannot directly refer to the authority of a tradition – if you do it, it's a comedy, an ego trip (if not something much worse, as in fundamentalism).

Another often repeated motif of Peterson is the idea that, according to postmodern neo-Marxists, the capitalist West is characterized by "tyrannical patriarchy" – and Peterson triumphantly mocks this claim and enumerates cases of how hierarchy existed not only in non-Western societies but also in nature. Again, I sincerely don't know which "neo-Marxists" claim that patriarchy is the result of the capitalist West. Marx says the exact contrary: in one of the famous passages from *The Communist Manifesto*, he writes that capitalism tends to undermine all traditional patriarchal hierarchies. Furthermore, in "Authority and Family," an early classic of the Frankfurt School of Marxism (the origin of cultural Marxism), Max Horkheimer is far from just condemning the modern patriarchal family; he describes how the paternal role model can provide a youngster with a stable support to resist social pressure. As his colleague Adorno pointed out, totalitarian leaders like Hitler are not paternal figures. I am well aware of the obsession of postcolonial and feminist theorists with patriarchy, but I think this obsession is a reaction to their inability to confront the fact that the predominant type of subjectivity in the developed West today is a hedonist subject whose ultimate goal in life is to realize its potentials and, as they say, reinvent itself again and again by changing its fluid identity. What annoys me are theorists who present this type of subjectivity as something subversive of the capitalist patriarchal order. I think such fluid subjectivity is the main fork of subjectivity in today's capitalism.

Let me now briefly deal with what became known as the lobster topic. I am far from a simple social constructionist; I deeply appreciate evolutionary thought – of course we are (also) natural beings and the fact that our DNA overlaps around 98 percent with that of some apes means something: it sets some coordinates. Maybe I just focus on different authors here – my references are Stephen Jay Gould with his notion of ex-aptation as opposed to adaptation, or Terrence Deacon with his notion of incomplete nature. Nature is not a complete determinist order: it is in some sense ontologically incomplete, full of improvisations; it develops like French cuisine. Is the origin of many of its famous dishes or drinks not that, when they wanted to produce a standard piece of food or drink, something went wrong, but then they realized that this failure can be resold as success? They were making cheese in the usual way, but then the cheese got rotten and infected, smelt bad, and they found this monstrosity (measured by the usual standards) charming in its own way. They were making wine in the usual way when something went wrong with the fermentation, and so they began to produce champagne . . .

And the same goes for tradition – let me quote T.S. Eliot, this great conservative, who wrote that "what happens when a new work of art is created is something that happens simultaneously to all the works of art which preceded it. . . . [T]he past should be altered by the present as much as the present is directed by the past. And the poet who is aware of this will be aware of great difficulties and responsibilities." This holds not only for works of art but for the entire cultural tradition. Let's take the radical change enacted by Christianity – yes, I define myself as an atheist Christian. Does Christianity not break radically with the traditional order of hierarchy? It's not just that, in spite of all our natural and cultural differences, the same divine spark dwells in everyone, but this divine spark enables us to create the Holy Spirit, a community in which hierarchic family values are abolished. Democracy extends this logic to the political space: in spite of all differences in competence, the ultimate decision should stay with all of us – the wager of democracy is that we should not give all power to competent experts. It was communists in power who legitimized their rule by posing as (fake) experts. And something of the same order is implied by our judicial systems: a jury means that not only experts but also our peers should be the ultimate judges. I mention these well-known facts only to point out how far they are from any hierarchy grounded in competences. I am far from believing in ordinary people's wisdom: we often need a Master figure to push us out of our inertia and (I am not afraid to say this) force us to be free. Freedom and responsibility hurt, they require an effort. But the highest function of a Master is to awaken us to our freedom.

So what about grounding hierarchy in competence? Do men simply earn more because they are more competent? I think that social power and authority cannot be directly grounded in competence: in our human universe, power (in the sense of exerting authority) is effectively something much more mysterious, even "irrational." Kierkegaard put this nicely when he wrote that if a child says he will obey his father because his father is competent and good, this is an affront to his father's authority, and Kierkegaard applies the same to Christ himself: Christ was justified by the fact of being god's son, not by his capacities – every good student of theology can put it better than Christ. And what I simply claim is that there is no such authority in nature: lobsters have hierarchy, but the main guy among them has no authority; he rules by force, he does not exert power in the human sense. Again, the wager of democracy is that power and competence or expertise should be minimally kept apart – this is why already in Ancient Greece the popular vote was combined with a lottery. In principle, capitalism abolishes traditional hierarchies and introduces personal freedom and equality. But are financial and power inequalities really grounded in different competences? (Thomas Piketty, in his *Capital in the Twenty-First Century*, provided fair amount of data here.)

Another of Peterson's motifs is that, when an individual (or, presumably, a society) is in a crisis, one has to offer it a mythic narrative, a story that enables it to organize its confused experience as a meaningful Whole. However, problems lurk here – Hitler was one of the greatest storytellers of the twentieth century. In the 1920s, many Germans experienced their situation as a confused mess: they didn't understand what was happening to them, with military defeat, economic crisis, and what they perceived as moral decay. Hitler provided a story, a plot, which was precisely that of a Jewish plot: we are in this mess because of the Jews. And, incidentally, we should not forget here that, as Freud already pointed out, the paranoiac construct is also a perverted attempt at healing, a story by means of which we try to organize our universe. We are telling ourselves stories about ourselves in order to acquire a meaningful experience of her existence. However, this is not enough. One of the most stupid wisdoms is: "An enemy is someone whose story you have not heard." There is, however, a clear limit to this procedure: is one also ready to affirm that Hitler was an enemy because his story was not heard?

Furthermore, ideological stories always locate our experiences into a social field. From what I know about Peterson's clinical practice, I fully appreciate what he's doing, his focus on bringing his patients to assume responsibility, self-reliance, and purpose in life. But when he says, "Put your own house in order before you try to change the world," my reaction is: OK, but why the choice? What if, in trying to achieve the first, you discover that your house is in disorder because of what is wrong in your world? Let's take Peterson himself: isn't he so active publicly (and in this sense trying to change the world) precisely because he realized how the predominant liberal ideology prevents individuals from putting their house in order? This is evidently true if you live in Congo or North Korea, but also with the extension of digital control in our world, etc. In a communist society, those in power would love to see you focusing on putting your house in order – and leaving their power in the world undisturbed.

The ultimate big Story that guarantees meaning is, of course, religion. Is religion still the opium of the people? This formula of Marx needs to be seriously rethought today. Religion (at least a certain – fundamentalist – version of it) is still an opium of the people. It is true that radical Islam is an exemplary case of religion as the opium of the people: a false confrontation with capitalist modernity that allows Muslims to dwell in their ideological dream while their countries are ravaged by the effects of global capitalism – and exactly the same holds for Christian fundamentalism. Mike Pompeo recently said it is "possible" that President Trump was sent by God to save Israel from Iran: "I am confident that the Lord is at work here," he added. The danger of this stance is obvious: if you oppose US politics in the Middle East, you oppose the will of god. If and when God judges Pompeo, we can guess what his defense will be: "Forgive me, father, for I knew what I was doing!" – I knew I was acting on your will.

However, apart from "neutral" expertise (the evocation of experts to justify choices that are clearly ideological), there are two other main opiums of the people at work today: opium and the people. When we think of opium, our first association is with evil Mexican cartels. But those cartels will exist as long as there is a large demand for drugs in the US and other developed countries. Maybe here too it is the case that, before saving the world from drug traffickers, we should put our house in order. Remember the horror of the two Opium Wars fought (not only) by the British empire against China. Statistics show that, until 1820, China was the strongest economy in the world. From the late eighteenth century, the British were exporting enormous amounts of opium into China, turning millions of people there into addicts and causing great damage. The Chinese Emperor tried to prevent this, prohibiting the import of opium, and the British (together with some other Western forces), intervened militarily. The result was catastrophic: soon after, China's economy shrank by half. But what should interest us is the legitimization of this brutal military intervention: free trade is the basis of civilization, and Chinese prohibition of the import of opium is thus a barbarian threat to civilization. One cannot abstain from imagining a similar act today: Mexico and Colombia acting to defend their drug cartels and declaring war on the US for behaving in a noncivilized war by preventing free opium trade . . .

But is schematic egalitarianism also not ideological? Yes, but is Marxism really egalitarian? Marx mostly mentions "equality" only to make the point that it is an exclusively political notion, and that, as a political value, it is a distinctively bourgeois value. Far from being a value that can be used to thwart class oppression, Marx thinks the idea of equality is actually a vehicle for bourgeois class oppression, and something quite distinct from the communist goal of the abolition of classes. He even makes the standard argument that equal right "can consist only in the application of an equal standard; but unequal individuals (and they would not be different individuals if they were not unequal) are measurable only by an equal standard insofar as they are brought under an equal point of view, are taken from one definite side only."

So what about the balance between equality and hierarchy? Have we really moved too far in the direction of equality? Is there in today's US really too much equality? Does a simple overview of the situation not point in the opposite direction? We recently learned that South Africa is the world's most unequal country – 25 years of freedom have failed to bridge the divide.[1] Far from pushing us too far, the Left has been gradually losing its ground for decades. Its trademarks – universal healthcare, free education, etc. – are continuously being diminished. Look at Bernie Sanders's program: it is just a version of what was half a century ago in Europe the predominant social democracy, but it is today decried as a threat to the American way of life. Furthermore, I see no threat to free creativity in this program – on the contrary, I see free healthcare and education etc. as enabling me to focus my life on more important creative issues (where, of course, we are not at all equal, where differences do abound). Equality can also be creating the space for as many as possible individuals to develop their potential.

So, to conclude, let me just indicate how I see the fact (which bothered many Leftists) that the exchange between Peterson and me was relatively peaceful and polite. The reason is not just that there are definitely aspects of his work that I appreciate (above all his clinical work, but also his critique of political correctness, his claim that white supremacism is identity politics appropriated by the Right, etc.). The main reason was that the basic difference that separates us was evident, so there was no need to reassert it violently. And, ultimately, this difference concerns our view of the present constellation of humanity.

The way I see it, Peterson is much more of an optimist – he thinks that capitalism will be able to manage its problems; while I think that we are approaching a global emergency state and that only a radical change can give us a chance.

Notes

Introduction: From the Communist Standpoint

1 See https://www.theguardian.com/world/2019/apr/01/harry-pot ter-among-books-burned-by-priests-in-poland.

2 See https://www.thenewsminute.com/article/outlandish-claims-indian-science-congress-6-point-rebuttal-science-activist-94691.

3 https://edition.cnn.com/2019/01/16/health/new-diet-to-save-liv es-and-planet-health-study-intl/index.html.

4 There should be no taboos here. For example, the hypothesis that the stream of millions of refugees into Europe which climaxed recently was not spontaneous but masterminded with certain geopolitical aims is not to be dismissed as Islamophobic para-noia. Both the US and Russia are clearly interested in the weaken-ing of Europe and silently tolerate its Muslim reconquista, which also explains why the rich Arab countries (Saudi Arabia, Kuwait, Emirates . . .) receive no refugees, while amply financing the con-struction of mosques in Europe.

5 Jean-Pierre Dupuy, *Petite Metaphysique des tsunamis* (Paris: Seuil, 2005), p. 19.

The Global Mess

1 Karl Marx, *Capital*, Volume One. Available at: http://www.marx ists.org/archive/marx/works/1867-c1/ch01.htm.

2 Quoted from https://www.marxists.org/archive/marx/works/18 75/gotha/ch01.htm.

3 Quoted from https://www.marxists.org/archive/marx/works/download/pdf/Capital-Volume-III.pdf.

4 Quoted from http://crisiscritique.org/april2019/milner.pdf.

5 I rely here heavily on Maria Chehonadskih, "Soviet Epistemologies and the Materialist Ontology of Poor Life: Andrei Platonov, Alexander Bogdanov and Lev Vygotsky." Unpublished manuscript, from which all non-attributed quotes are taken.

6 Etienne Balibar "Towards a New Critique of Political Economy: From Generalized Surplus-Value to Total Subsumption," in *Capitalism: Concept, Idea, Image* (Kingston: CRMEP Books, 2019).

7 Balibar, "Towards a New Critique of Political Economy," p. 51.

8 Balibar, "Towards a New Critique of Political Economy," p. 53.

9 Balibar, "Towards a New Critique of Political Economy," p. 57.

10 See https://www.nytimes.com/2019/03/19/world/middleeast/ayelet-shaked-perfume-ad.html.

11 See https://www.theguardian.com/world/2019/mar/10/benjamin-netanyahu-says-israel-is-not-a-state-of-all-its-citizens.

12 It happened at the conference of the Union for Radical Economics at Amherst, Massachusetts, in September, 2018.

13 Ernesto Laclau, *On Populist Reason* (London: Verso, 2005), p. 90.

14 Quoted from https://www.theguardian.com/technology/2019/jan/20/shoshana-zuboff-age-of-surveillance-capitalism-google-facebook.

15 https://www.apnews.com/9d43f4b74260411797043ddd391c13d8.

16 See https://boingboing.net/2019/04/04/bald-eagles-are-taking-trash-f.html.

17 Quoted from https://www.popularmechanics.com/science/environment/a27035441/bald-eagles-are-stealing-trash-from-a-seattle-landfill-and-dropping-it-in-the-suburbs/.

18 Quoted from https://edition.cnn.com/2019/06/25/world/climate-apartheid-poverty-un-intl/index.html.

19 Quoted from https://www.theguardian.com/sustainable-business/2015/mar/18/fully-automated-luxury-communism-robots-employment.

20 Quoted from https://www.newyorker.com/news/our-columnists/

the-fifteen-year-old-climate-activist-who-is-demanding-a-new-kind-of-politics.

21 Quoted from https://www.politicsweb.co.za/opinion/ramaphosa-must-explain-comment-of-white-people-and.

22 G.W.F. Hegel, *Phenomenology of Spirit* (Oxford: Oxford University Press, 1977), p. 288.

23 F.W.J. Schelling, *Die Weltalter. Fragmente. In den Urfassungen von 1811 und 1813*, ed. Manfred Schroeter (Munich: Biederstein, 1946; reprint 1979), p. 13.

24 See https://www.theguardian.com/world/2019/may/29/myanmar-police-hunt-buddhist-bin-laden-over-suu-kyi-comments.

25 I rely here on Kate Aronoff, "The Plan to Block Out the Sun," *In These Times* (December 2018).

26 *In Search of Common Ground: Conversations with Erik H. Erikson and Huey P. Newton* (New York: Norton, 1973), p. 69.

27 https://www.ft.com/content/670039ec-98f3-11e9-9573-ee5cbb98ed36.

The West . . .

1 Quoted from https://eu.tennessean.com/story/opinion/columnists/2019/06/21/democratic-party-civil-war-donald-trump/1503516001/.

2 I owe this idea to Gabriel Gonzales-Molina.

3 Yuval Harari, *Homo Deus: A History of Tomorrow* (New York: Random House, 2016), p. 249.

4 Peter Sloterdijk, "Aufbruch der Leistungstraeger," Cicero (November 2009).

5 See https://americanaffairsjournal.org/2018/11/the-left-case-against-open-borders/.

6 Incidentally, the weirdest argument for open borders is: "Europe needs immigrant workers for its economy to continue to expand." *Which* Europe? Capitalist Europe: capitalism needs them for its expanded reproduction.

7 In what follows, I rely on a line of thought of Alenka Zupančič.

8 https://www.theguardian.com/commentisfree/2019/jan/25/fight-europe-wreckers-patriots-nationalist.
9 Alain Badiou, *I Know There Are So Many of You*, trans. Susan Spitzer (Cambridge: Polity, 2019), p. 61.

. . . And the Rest

1 Personal communication from my Swedish Letftist friends.
2 Ruth Klüger, *Still Alive: A Holocaust Girlhood Remembered* (New York: Feminist Press, 2001), p. 64.
3 See https://www.project-syndicate.org/commentary/poland-memory-law-amendment-by-slawomir-sierakowski-2018-08.
4 See https://www.theguardian.com/world/2019/may/26/jews-in-germany-warned-of-risks-of-wearing-kippah-cap-in-public.
5 http://www.nytimes.com/roomfordebate/2014/10/16/should-nations-recognize-a-palestinian-state/there-should-be-no-palestinian-state-23.
6 Todd MacGowan, *Emancipation After Hegel: Achieving a Contradictory Revolution* (New York: Columbia University Press, 2019), p. 194.
7 MacGowan, *Emancipation After Hegel*, p. 195.
8 Peter Sloterdijk, *In the World Interior of Capital*, trans. Wieland Hoban (Cambridge: Polity, 2013), p. 12.
9 Sloterdijk, *In the World Interior of Capital*, p. 46.
10 Sloterdijk, *In the World Interior of Capital*, p. 171.
11 Quoted from https://www.documentcloud.org/documents/5770516-The-Great-Replacement-New-Zealand-Shooter.html.
12 https://stalinsmoustache.org/2018/07/01/the-passing-of-domenico-losurdo/.
13 https://stalinsmoustache.org/2018/07/01/the-passing-of-domenico-losurdo/.
14 Quoted from https://www.marxists.org/archive/marx/works/1859/critique-pol-economy/preface.htm.
15 For this view, see, among others, *International Critical Thought*, Vol. 7, No, 1 (March 2017), especially the articles by Domenico

Losurdo, William Jefferies, Peggy Raphaelle, and Cantave Fuyet.

16 Quoted from https://www.theguardian.com/world/2019/apr/12/ millions-of-chinese-youth-volunteers-to-be-sent-to-villages-in-echo-of-mao-policy.

17 Julia Buxton, "Chavismo's Descent," *New Left Review*, 99 (2016).

Ideology

1 See https://www.theguardian.com/commentisfree/2018/dec/22/ rape-joke-metoo-movement-career-repercussions.

2 See https://www.bbc.com/news/world-europe-46428380.

3 Similarly, the Haiti Revolution turned into massacres of all white people precisely when the new black elite wanted to fortify its rule, also at the expense of the black majority.

4 See https://www.thecut.com/2018/10/tarana-burke-me-too-foun der-movement-has-lost-its-way.html.

5 I owe this reading to Engin Kurtay, Istanbul.

6 In a private conversation with me.

7 https://www.theguardian.com/world/2019/may/28/gillette-ad-shaving-transgender-son-samson-bonkeabantu-brown.

8 Jacques Lacan, *The Four Fundamental Concepts of Psychoanalysis* (New York: Norton, 1998), p. 276.

9 Along the same lines, kindergartens in Norway were told that, if a small boy is seen playing with girls, this orientation should be supported: he should be stimulated to play with dolls, etc., so that his eventual feminine psychic identity can articulate itself.

10 Available online at http://www.marxists.org/archive/lenin/works/ 1913/.

11 Quoted from https://www.rfa.org/english/news/uyghur/infected-08082018173807.html.

12 Quoted from https://en.wikipedia.org/wiki/Mozart_and_scatolo gy#cite_note-9.

13 See https://www.rt.com/usa/448410-apa-masculinity-bad-psych ology/.

14 The question to be raised here is, of course, which antagonism would be the masculine counterpart to the antagonism between Antigone and Ismene. One can argue that it is Oedipus versus Creon (on condition that we don't reduce Creon to the caricature of a brutal authoritarian and see in him the embodiment of a consistent and even necessary sociopolitical stance).

15 Alain Badiou, *The True Life*, trans. Susan Spitzer (Cambridge: Polity, 2017), p. 99

16 https://www.timeout.com/about/latest-news/the-50-best-things-to-do-in-the-world-right-now-a-polka-dot-paradise-in-tokyo-a-hedonistic-party-venue-in-new-york-and-an-insanely-cool-sau na-in-kiruna-top-the-list-111618; https://www.thesun.co.uk/ne ws/5333052/house-of-yes-new-york-inside-the-wildest-club-on-the-planet/.

17 See https://medium.com/s/powertrip/kavanaugh-consent-and-the-new-rules-of-nightlife-14fb8a5759f0.

18 See https://www.theguardian.com/commentisfree/2018/dec/22/metoo-movement-office-parties-decline-weinstein-moonves.

19 Quoted from https://sputniknews.com/science/201804101063394 315-sex-robots-reject-humans/.

20 Quoted from https://www.theguardian.com/lifeandstyle/2019/feb/09/me-and-my-vulva-100-women-reveal-all-photographs.

21 I owe this point to Robert Pfaller, Vienna.

22 See https://www.theguardian.com/news/2018/mar/17/data-war-whistleblower-christopher-wylie-facebook-nix-bannon-trump.

23 All quotes that follow are from https://www.nybooks.com/daily/2018/03/21/the-digital-military-industrial-complex/?utm_med ium=email&utm_campaign=NYR%20Wolves%20Orban%20Cam bridge%20Analytica&utm_content=NYR%20Wolves%20Orban% 20Cambridge%20Analytica+CID_54761ca178aa65ea5c4a4410b96 16c02&utm_source=Newsletter&utm_term=The%20New%20Mili tary-Industrial%20Complex%20of%20Big%20Data%20Psy-Ops.

24 See Julian Assange, *When Google Met WikiLeaks* (New York: OR Books, 2014).

25 See "Bhutan tries to measure happiness," *ABC News* (March 24, 2008).

26 I resume here the line of thought fully deployed in chapter 1 of Slavoj Žižek, *First as Tragedy, Then as Farce* (London: Verso Books, 2009).

27 G.K. Chesterton, *Orthodoxy* (San Francisco: Ignatius Press, 1995), p. 139.

28 Quoted from https://www.theguardian.com/media/2019/may/19/us-prosecutors-julian-assange-wikileaks-ecuadorian-embassy.

29 See the report on how the *Guardian* covered the Assange case at: https://www.blacklistednews.com/article/69548/the-guardians-vilification-of-julian.html.

30 https://www.theguardian.com/media/2019/jun/13/julian-assange-sajid-javid-signs-us-extradition-order.

31 https://defend.wikileaks.org/category/news/#post-2562.

32 https://elpais.com/elpais/2019/05/13/inenglish/1557735550_398996.html.

Appendix

1 See https://edition.cnn.com/2019/05/07/africa/south-africa-elections-inequality-intl/index.html.